TEÓFILO CABESTRERO

translated by Donald D. Walsh

FAITH:
CONVERSATIONS WITH
CONTEMPORARY THEOLOGIANS

Ladislaus Boros • Georges Casalis • Joseph Comblin
Enrique D. Dussel • Segundo Galilea • Giulio Girardi
José M. González Ruiz • Gustavo Gutiérrez • Hans Küng
Jürgen Moltmann • Karl Rahner • Joseph Ratzinger
Edward Schillebeeckx • Juan Luis Segundo • Jean-Marie Tillard

ORBIS BOOKS
Maryknoll, New York 10545

First published as *Conversaciones sobre la fe*, copyright © 1977 Ediciones Sígueme, Apdo. 332, Salamanca, Spain

English translation copyright © 1980 by Orbis Books, Maryknoll, NY 10545

Manufactured in the United States of America

Library of Congress Cataloging in Publication Data

Cabestrero, Teófilo.
   Faith, conversations with contemporary theologians.

   Translation of Conversaciones sobre la fe.
   Bibliography: p.
   Includes index.
   1. Theology—20th century—Miscellanea. I. Title.
BR96.C313   230'.2   80-14131
ISBN 0-88344-126-8 (pbk.)

Contents

Introduction

"On earth there are always some inspired men. An encounter with them is priceless." This saying of Plato's, which seems coined for days when clarification and search are a conscientious duty, defines this book, a faithful document of conversations over a period of three years with men inspired by Christianity.

I have sought out these men to hear from their lips, in simple, spontaneous words, their answers to the disquieting questions raised by the changes and the pluralism in which we Christians live and shall always live. In this time so cruel and fecund, so uncertain, so painfully pregnant with the future, where are the threats and the mortal risks for our faith, and where are the possibilities of purification and historic service? What is, in truth, the positive and what the negative in our current forms of believing, hoping, and living as Christians? Where are we being led by the roads of Christian existence that penetrate into the struggles of the world? Where and how shall we today seek God? Where do the signs of the Spirit sparkle? What possibilities are left to us to authenticate ourselves as the church of God and the gospel? Being faithful to life, how can we believe today in Jesus, the Christ, and celebrate and bear witness to his memory in a way that is credible to our contemporaries? How can we exist today with God for people, waging the human battle of the gospel? What is the scope of the just relations between faith and social struggle, faith and political commitment, faith and revolution, faith and class struggle, faith and violence? In a word, what should be the content today of the identity and relevance of Christian faith? In addition, the theologies that attempt their answers to these questions (political theology, theologies of hope and of the cross, of celebration, of liberation and of captivity), what light do they contribute and what ambiguities do they bring? Do they offer guarantees deserving of our confidence? About all this, and about several other things, I have conversed with "some inspired men."

I can testify that, for me, in fact, "an encounter with them is priceless." Each conversation has been a provoking experience, and they all add up to a time of reflection, confrontation, and questioning, of clarification and creation, of indescribable value. The duty of contributing to the recovery of the Christian identity—the greatest challenge today to the gospel and the world—and the hope of rendering a

1

service to those who seek, move me to publish these fifteen conversations exactly as they occurred.

To avoid misunderstandings, I should advise the reader that I have not tried to compose a mosaic of the different theological opinions that exist today in the church. I have not started from scratch, nor have I tried to reach all theological persuasions. I have started from my own uneasiness and doubts. I have started from my choices in favor of those tendencies and those theologians who persuade me, at the time of interpreting the gospel of Jesus, to live in his memory. This choice implies no scorn of anyone, for I did not intend to undertake a journalistic task of impersonal, objective investigation but a personal search to find the way (personal and communitarian, and also ecclesial) for my conscience.

I have talked with twenty-six Central European, Spanish, and Latin American theologians. Because of space limitations, not all the conversations appear here, and honesty forces me to say that several of those which do not appear are in no way inferior to the fifteen that are published. I must also say that I did not manage to talk with all the theologians I wanted to talk with: some were not accessible to me, others did not like the dialogue form (a German, an Austrian, two Frenchmen, four Spaniards: this is why among these fifteen interlocutors only one Spaniard appears).

I admit that it was my intention to contrast the three blocks of theological thought (Central European, Latin American, and Spanish) and I therefore decided to address to each one certain fixed questions about the half dozen matters that most concerned me; the adaptation to each person and to his work, and spontaneity, would make that decision flexible and would introduce variations, as happened in fact. Then, because some did not participate as planned, I cannot say that each group is representative; and, in view of the answers, I decided to leave the confrontation in the hands of the readers. That is why I have arranged these conversations alphabetically by interlocutor. The concurrences and approximations (which are greater than one might think) as well as the nuances and divergences are self-evident and reveal the common ground and the distances that exist among the stands taken by these fifteen men.

With the exception of González Ruiz, who chose to answer in writing, all the conversations were really conversations and I can testify to the spontaneity of the answers. I tried to adapt myself to the personality and work of each interlocutor, and I wanted especially to have him speak, express himself, declare himself on the proposed questions, in clear verbal synthesis. At times I acted as the devil's advocate. I raised objections, fears, doubts, and opinions that are not mine but that are real and quite common. At other times I presented my own doubts and argued from my convictions, reluctant to accept freely certain answers. I needed time to digest certain things. On the other hand, I do not generally make value judgments about what these men have told me.

Taped directly (with the exception noted) the conversations were first transcribed verbatim in the language of each interlocutor, who revised the text, correcting in his own hand occasional vague or inexact phrases and leaving unchanged his spontaneous replies. Then they were faithfully translated into Spanish. [The English translation was made from the Spanish version.—Ed.] All this work exceeded my personal capacity and my possibilities: I would not have had the conversations and this book would not have come into existence without the valuable help of numerous companions and friends who acted as liaisons, mediators, guides, transcribers, and translators. I cannot list their names here because they add up to more than twenty, but to all of them I am in debt and grateful; this book is in good part their book. But both I and the book are in debt even more to the fifteen famous theologians whose conversations are recorded here. To them and to all those who welcomed me and listened to me, my gratitude and the testimonial of these pages.

A Conversation with Ladislaus Boros

Ladislaus Boros was born October 2, 1927, in Budapest, Hungary. Entering the Jesuit order, he studied philosophy at Szeged, Hungary; Innsbruck, Austria; and Chieri, Italy. He took his doctorate at the University of Munich (1951–54). He studied theology at Enghien, Belgium; Chantilly, France; and Flintshire, Wales, and was ordained a priest in 1957. He did advanced literary study at Oxford and Paris, and in 1963 became professor of religion at the University of Innsbruck. His works, many of them translated into several languages, include Angels and Men; Meeting God in Man; The Mystery of Death; We Are. Future; Open Spirit; Living in Hope; You Can Always Begin Again; The Closeness of God; and Christian Prayer.

Ladislaus Boros interested me first, some fifteen years ago, by his contribution to the new theological concept of Christian eschatology. To speak of death, the last judgment, purgatory, hell, and heaven as he did at a time when preaching was silent about "these eternal truths" because it couldn't name them in the words of today would have sufficed to perpetuate the name of Boros.

Meeting God in Man, published in 1971, began to divulge to us his exquisite Christian sensibility and his scholarly theology. Since then about a dozen of his books have been published in English, as well as in Spanish.

Through his writings I admired his deep religious sense, his perception of the divine in the human and the human in the divine, his anthropological vision of theology, his scholarly reflection on the Christian mysteries that he puts within reach in simple words. A biographical note confirmed my intuition about his deep philosophical, theological, and literary formation,

4

as well as his experience of grief. I later learned, through some friends, that his health is very fragile.

After talking with Boros that whole afternoon, I admired his veracity. I annoyed him quite a bit, I put his availability to the test, and I saw that he lives what he writes. In his best pages on magnanimity, mercy, seeking, suffering, and friendship, I now see his friendly face.

It is Holy Saturday and the bells sound grave and solemn through all of Zurich. "Your colleagues advised me to look for you in the hospital." But Ladislaus Boros laughs without saying a word. It is true: in Paris, in Munich, and in Ratisbon, when I asked theologians who know him about Boros, many answered: "You'll find him in the hospital. Look for him in the Zurich Hospital." He's not in the hospital now, but I see the pharmacy in his room: bottles and boxes of medicine everywhere, on his work table, on the shelves, and in a few handy spaces in his enormous library. I also see fruit, and his furniture is white. From the first greeting downstairs, I was impressed by his jovial, fine, joyful face, radiant in friendship, like that of a healthy thirty-year-old, on the body of a sickly old man of seventy. I saw, as he climbed stairs and walked, that his body doesn't follow him, he pulls it along, that he walks with dragging arms and bent back. What tracks has sickness left in him? But Boros smiles and begs me to begin by telling him all at once all my questions. After concentrating on them silently, he thinks, gets up, offers me cognac and tobacco, walks around silently, lights a little cigar that looks mild, sips cognac, walks some more, opens the balcony window—and a gust of air breaks our silence with birdsong and a pealing of bells. It smells of wet fields. Boros sits down next to me in friendliness, picks up the microphone, and asks me to go back to the questions one by one.

To Testify That Heaven Exists

What demands do faithfulness and faith present to us today? Is faith in crisis?

It would be extremely unfortunate, in my opinion, to speak today of a crisis of faith. We are not really faced with a crisis. We are faced with growing troubles and these difficulties are the ones that we must see clearly. I think the whole problem comes down, in the end, to a question of attitude, of clearly facing the problems of our faith. For me what is most important, and certainly the most vital question about our faith, is sincerity, honesty, veracity. For me this means, above all, that what we are is at the level of what we say. That between our being and our saying there not be an abyss, as has frequently happened in the church. I often remember what Pope Leo XIII used to stress: "God has no need of our lies." It's necessary to be totally sincere with people. Neither God nor our faith has anything to lose by this. And if our church loses something, it's because it ought to lose it. We must not present ourselves before the world as sinless if we are not so.

You reflect about faith on the frontiers of culture and modern anthropology.
What problems and questions today are most disturbing to people with
regard to faith?

I shall answer you from my experience, and above all from my
experiences with young college students. The first thing that seems to
upset them is the question of the absence of God. In our talks together
there were frequent questions about God, but most of the time they
referred to the possibility of achieving an authentic experience of God
in today's world, where God does not appear. Theological answers to
this question must take seriously the difficulties of contemporary
people in their experience of the absence of God, and perhaps must
share this experience.

The second question that almost always appeared was the question
about Christ. And it is raised, although it seems strange, at the
universal level; that is, on the horizon of a single history of salvation
that must embrace, in advance and without exception, all of humanity. Stated thus, the question allows us to understand Christ as the
culminating point of the world and of humanization. An answer of
this kind would still be capable of saying something to the people of
today. Besides, the stimulating writings of Teilhard de Chardin are
particularly useful in this sense, as long as they are purified of that
certain mythological tone that they have for the ears of people of our
time.

Another upsetting question is usually that of the universality of
redemption. This question almost always comes up in our talks and, of
course, with a tone of special uneasiness. Contemporary people cannot bear the thought that anyone be excluded from the salvation
brought by Christ. The theological axiom "outside the church there is
no salvation" is constantly brought up as a reproach to the church. It
has always surprised me that this axiom should provoke such reactions. I myself have never found it oppressive—quite the contrary—
because if we think of this axiom "outside the church there is no
salvation" in the reverse, without departing from the most elementary
rules of logic we spontaneously get another reading, which is profoundly liberating: wherever salvation occurs, there is the church. To
say "where the church is, there is salvation" (*ubi ecclesia, ibi salus*) is
equivalent to saying "where there is salvation, there is the church"
(*ubi salus, ibi ecclesia*). In this sense, this doctrine is a liberating
affirmation. Is it not liberating to think that the church is already
present, even though in elementary or hidden form, wherever people
devote themselves, out of sincerity of heart, to good, to truth, or to
justice, or try to excel, or devote themselves to the service of others, or
commit themselves completely to a cause? Where this occurs, salvation occurs, and the church is present.

Today there is the disquieting possibility of an up-to-date Christian anthropology. Today's intellectuals expect of us an answer that will interpret human beings just as they experience themselves in fact in their own existence, which takes in much more than the "rational animal" of an abstract metaphysics. A Christian anthropology must be outlined in the terrain that includes the original unity of nature and grace and that does not confine what we call Christian grace to a different sphere, beyond concrete experience. An anthropology, therefore, that does not simply relegate to moral theology and pious literature themes like friendship, love, virtue, as well as the experience of the absurd and of death.

My experience tells me that today there is also a great deal of uneasiness and interest in references to the bodily dimension of the human being. To this question were related other problems in almost all my talks with students. What was sought was an honest theological clarification, in the first place, about how our bodies develop through evolution; then, what is their relation with what we usually call "body and soul"; and finally, what possibility is there for that absolute transformation that we call "resurrection and glorification"? If we look for an answer to these questions in our scholastic theology, we soon lose hope.

Dr. Boros, you have taken part in many meetings of theologians and thinkers in search of a new concept and formulation of eschatology. And you have thought and written a good deal about this. The first book of yours that I read, in fact, was on this subject, and we have copies of your The Mystery of Death *and your theological meditations on death, the last judgment, purgatory, and resurrection. In what state today is the theology of eschatology?*

In current conversations about faith, many questioners make pronouncements about what would belong thematically to dogmatic eschatology. Today, nevertheless, we lack an adequate interpretation of the isolated affirmations of theology in relation to the doctrine of last things. On questions of eschatology Christian thought in recent times has undergone a revolutionary change of perspective. New forms of thought have appeared and new hypotheses have been formulated that involve a break with previous conceptions. Especially with regard to death and heaven, people today would like to hear things that have to do with the full realization of the human being. I believe that among those devoted to pastoral work it is a deceptive myth to think that people today avoid questions about death; the truth is just the opposite. Death disturbs them deeply, but they would like to think of it in accord with their fundamental tendency toward security and the affirmation of life. They would like to hear from theologians how the harsh reality of death can be integrated into a fundamental affirmation of life. Death as the origin of a deeper life. To establish philosophically and theologically this truth so genuinely Christian and to make it kerygmatically visible is a grave urgency of our time, a duty of Christian thought and preaching that cannot be postponed.

I also think that we are asked, equally, for a radical interpretation of the terrestrial realm from the point of view of the celestial. It is a disquieting sign to note that a considerable number of priests today no longer preach about heaven. Unfortunately, in my talks I have had repeatedly to regret that the most deficient treatises in our theology are precisely those devoted to talk about heaven. If one wants to read something existentially lively about heaven, I think the best answer is to pick up the Marxist Ernst Bloch's *Das Prinzip Hoffnung* (The Hope Principle). There one can find a surprisingly exact analysis of what comes out in our aspirations on encountering an absolute future. Moreover, this is a cause of embarrassment to Catholic theologians and philosophers. Perhaps our most urgent task is to testify that heaven exists, a heaven not only thought about and hoped for in the abstract but felt every day, every hour, in the depths of our experiences. Finally, I should like to allude to another problem: the hope and the postulate of an individual eternal life are not hypotheses but attitudes into which humanity, in the present and in the future, must be constantly and carefully introduced. A theology of hope cannot be elaborated simply with the schematic affirmations of our dogmatic scholar upon the theological virtue of hope.

How shall we open new, attractive, persuasive perspectives for Christians of today upon experiences as concrete and fundamental, and as forgotten now, as confession and prayer?

People today, rightly or wrongly, abhor the attitude that we might describe as withdrawal from life and daily contacts to be alone with God. Nevertheless, I believe that if we explain to them that confession exists precisely to be able to free our friends, those we love, from the weight of our sins, today's person is capable of understanding in a new way the meaning of confession. Human existence, as we all know, is essentially living together. If I lead a sinful, egotistical existence, my sins affect the whole community, to which I am essentially tied. When I repent of my sins and confess them to the representative of the church community, I am really freeing my friends from the ballast of my wretchedness. Why confess? Simply so that people, in their reconciliation with God, may bring a breath of purification to the world, to the beings that they love, to their own being. It is sad to observe how many Christians who go to confession regularly think only of themselves. Confession is for them an act of egotism. If confession is not in some way a service to others, it is at bottom not even confession, nor does it bring any increase in the presence of salvation in the world. People today understand perfectly this way of thinking, and in my opinion it is a genuinely Christian way of thinking.

As to prayer, people today find it almost impossible to pray. When they shrink from praying, I would say that they are not trying to shrink from God but from themselves in their superficiality, from the hollowness of their own souls. We must make these people understand that waiting in the presence of God, simply being silent in his presence—that is prayer. It is even the deepest thing that one torn apart inside can do in the presence of God. Suffering under the inward incapacity to pray is already prayer. To elaborate a broader theology about prayer in accordance with today's urgencies and expectancies is perhaps the most urgent task in this hour of salvation, and it might also be the most shining testimony of a living theology.

Only Those Who Suffer the Cross Speak Liberating Words

What would be the most suitable task of theology today? What does it mean to be theological today? In other words, how can answers be worked out for the problems that are posed to faith today?

The question is extremely opportune and I was anticipating it. The people with whom I have happened to work, especially today's intellectuals, expect theologians to have the boldness to speak about the mysteries of the faith. Let their immediate and absorbing urgency not be politics; let them remain faithful to their most inescapable task: to speak about the mysteries of the faith. The first thing demanded of theologians, of course, is exactness, painstaking preparation, personal effort in the development of their own thought. Fragmentary thoughts made up on a train trip, disjointed words hastily noted down are no good at all. Each formulation must be in its place; after each affirmation there must be present that care with which thinkers are to meet the needs and aspirations of their listeners. I know theologians who spend a good forty hours in preparing a meditation or a talk of a single hour. It may perhaps not be noticed in the style, but it is noticed in the perfection and transparency of their thought, in the loftiness and fluidity of their language.

Another thing that the contemporary person expects of those who speak about God is simply that they feel sincerely bound to the truth and that they carry it out dynamically. On another occasion I have sketched the figure of the theologian of today with this brief formula: the person who, on a basis of faith, understands our today and works for our tomorrow. Theologians like that must think, in my judgment, from the situation. They must introduce into theology an existential dissatisfaction. They must be "progressive" in the best sense of the word and, at the same time, very critical and very conscious that, in our tortuous world, what at first glance seems most simple and expressive can be a mask for evil. Their qualities must be, in my opinion, serenity of spirit, an honest expression, sincerity in the face of mystery. All these theologians must unite with a special insecurity that makes them more attractive. They must give up easy solutions, superficial explanations. They must joyfully unite theological thought with prayer, with deep communion with God. They must reject prejudice, not think in accordance with preestablished schemata, not admit in advance that anything is impossible or worn out, avoiding the dogmatism of academic opinions or of established authors. Another very important thing: not to make a facile division of the world of thought into friendly and unfriendly. What is fruitful is to be able to experience the joy of true thought in contact with reality. The intellectual effort of theologians must be charismatic, must respond to an inner need. Their thought, therefore, must take place within the thick forest of human worries, of human responsibilities and even despairs. A thought that perhaps may not find an answer for many questions but that will accept this condition honestly.

Such theologians will be persuaded that a theology that does not in any way praise God, or that does not help a soul to rise, or does not bring to the world some growth in friendship or love, is basically a false theology. With their *thoughts* those theologians must try to do their friends some good. A strange and difficult responsibility can be conjectured behind their words. They must clearly think that their thought brings them to judgment, that their salvation hangs on what they think and on what they say to others. They probably want to trace, in the exercise of what we would call their professional need, the grace of God, the grace for our time. In them there is typically a peculiar mobility of perception, a fundamental openness to the new and the unknown. For them theology is a mental effort to make life more beautiful and more luminous, to help their friends to overcome the sin of existential weakness. Thinking is for them a humble service to being, a welcoming and protecting of everything worthy of welcome and protection. They have experienced in themselves the suffering and poverty of human existence and therefore they try to think from those experiences. This they seek and this is important to them, not their own success or their own prestige. They have an innate aversion, if we can so express it, to any cheap apologetics, to any heated dispute. They care nothing about winning over others simply for the pride of having won. They never forget that only people who have experienced the profound misery of our existence, which is to say, the cross, can speak words of liberation. I think these are the theologians of the future.

What do you think about all the criticism that is spreading today within the church itself?

The sincerity with which I would like to answer this question forces me to reflect a little, above all, on this basic question: whether Christ originally wanted the church to exist, or not. I know that this is a very difficult question. As I interpret the gospel, and I think it is a true interpretation, what our Lord wanted first and most directly was to bring about the kingdom of God, that is, to create a situation in which God reigns over us. And I ask myself: what is it that reigns over us today? A tree that I encounter on my walk is more real than God. That tree "reigns" over me at the moment when it forces me to go around it if I want to continue my walk, whereas God does not reign over me. Over me reign representations, ideas that have come to me from other people. Over me reign other people, and God only to the extent that he reaches me through them. This situation in the world is the one that Christ wanted to abolish, but he couldn't manage it. He left it dependent on the free acceptance of people, for there is no way of leading people to salvation except through their free will. This decision had a kind of negative result, and then Christ found a forced solution. This forced solution is what we call "church." The church is not the kingdom of God; it exists to lead us to the kingdom of God whose coming Christ placed at the end of time. And I think in this church is surely announced the kingdom of God. Through the church comes the kingdom and it is closer every day. But this bridge to the kingdom, which we call "church," is and remains always a road and a forced solution.

But I would also like to view this question from another angle: how many mysteries are there in our faith? I think there is one single mystery: the mystery of God. God has communicated to us of this unique mystery what is necessary for salvation. It contains within itself, certainly, many more mysteries, since it is infinite, but of this infinite mystery God has given us only fragments. I consequently judge that the official church has a mission to interpret for us and to bring us close to only those mysteries that God in his goodness has given us. The mission doesn't even have the right to announce a systematics of all truths but only to inform us about those truths that bring us close to salvation. When it announces such truths to us it must speak to us reliably. All the rest is to be excessively proud and not to act in the spirit of Christ. I therefore think that any criticism of the church that criticizes it for its ideology—whatever the ideology—is justified. Besides, I must confess that I have no sympathy at all for critics who criticize only for the sake of criticizing. If I criticize the church as it exists in the present, my criticism will be constructive if it points to a better future. I mean that there is a criticism of the church that is not justified because it is not beneficial, but if the criticism looks to the future, if it tries to bring the church out of its deficiencies and make possible a better future for it, to help it to be simply a bridge between Christ and his definitive kingdom, then criticism is a good and beneficial thing.

Jesus Was Not a Leader—Jesus Is the Christ

Many people today see Jesus as a human leader, as an admirable man, and they are not concerned whether he is God. Some theologian has said that "from the theology of the death of God we have passed on to the theology of Jesus-Superman." Do you believe that we are facing the danger of disfiguring Jesus Christ and of weakening faith in him?

There are tendencies that would like to convert Jesus into a Führer, yes. Well, I wouldn't have anything to say against the fact in itself. Paul said that as long as there is talk about Jesus, we are agreed about something. I wish there were more talk about Jesus. But I'm against those movements in this sense: to the degree that they approach the problem from a purely psychological point of view. Possibly there are people who need a leader, but the fact is that Jesus was not a leader; he never appeared as a great man, nor did he try to dazzle. I might here refer to my book on the temptations of Jesus, where I consider, for example, how he chose poverty, simplicity, helplessness. The people expected him to appear forcefully and spectacularly, descending from heaven. All the expectations of grandeur Jesus rejected, and for profound reasons. His intention was not to introduce an exterior kingdom but to influence us from within, from bases perhaps still hidden, but alive and palpitating within us. What mattered to him was to bring to reality in us that inward *metanoia* through which the kingdom of God actually comes.

I do not wish to defend hereby an exaggerated inwardness, but I do wish to stress the fact that Christ certainly preached an inner kingdom. Therefore, to try to say of Jesus that he was a great man, that he had the personality of a leader, etc., may be true in some sense, but it is forgetting what is decisive in our faith. Jesus does not need to appear as a leader to be important for us. And his resurrection, however it is explained, is an essential part of our faith in him. As St. Paul said: "If Christ was not resurrected, our faith is in vain." Consequently, Jesus is important to us as a man, but what is decisive for our faith is that he is the *kyrios*, that is, "Jesus Christ." These two expressions, Jesus and Christ, are decisive for us, and I am convinced that without the union of those two names our faith would be impossible; it would not be faith. There would remain, perhaps, a psychological movement, from time to time an enthusiasm for the man Jesus, but if this Jesus were not at the same time, for us, the Christ, for whom would we be living? For me "Jesus Christ" is what is important, and in the union or separation of those two names our faith remains steady or sinks. With this I have obviously not exhausted the question of the relation between the Jesus of the gospels and the Christ of the resurrection, but my intention was only to show my position on this problem. I believe that in speaking of the Lord we should always say "Jesus Christ."

No Road Leads to God apart from Fellow Humans

In your books we see that you are extraordinarily profound about the Christian faith in its personal and interpersonal aspects. But I'd like to know what you think about social, political, and revolutionary commitment from the point of view of faith. Does it seem to you, Dr. Boros, that this commitment is an essential dimension of faith?

You speak of "revolution" in a sense that perhaps not all of us accept. That's why I'm going to begin my answer with some thoughts about Christian revolution. "Christian revolution" is the attitude of Jesus Christ himself, an attitude of inner transformation of the human being. This transformation must take place above all within the human being and in the sense of the Beatitudes: to be poor, to be meek, to suffer persecution for justice, etc. All this is good, and to the extent to which a person is prepared to accept it for self, one's transformation and liberation begin. And this is the first and unconditional presupposition for a Christian revolution. Of course, we must highlight a second movement: this transformation or inner *metanoia* of a human being cannot occur turned in upon itself. In the discourse on the last judgment Christ speaks of this: one is blessed because of feeding others, offering them drink, sheltering them, visiting them in jail, etc. For me the most important thing in this discourse is that Christ did not mention God at all, only fellow humans. Blessed are you who have done this, because you have known me and have served me in my smallest friends. Then comes the surprise, the "perplexity," I would say, of this person; whether it is just or unjust: "Lord, when did we do this?" We ought to understand this clearly: in our world, in our church, no road leads to God apart from one's fellow humans. I wrote a book about this with which I continue to be totally identified: *Meeting God in Man*. (I don't mean by this that contemplative vocations, like other vocations that don't have much to do directly with others, have no value. Such vocations make sense precisely to the extent that they are a service to humanity.)

From these simple reflections I should like to answer your question about whether people, insofar as they are Christian, have the right and perhaps the duty to encourage revolution. I am going to answer in a totally affirmative sense on the basis of these two considerations. People have not only the right but also the obligation to oppose everything that is the cause of suffering in others, let's say in my mother, my brother or, in general, my fellow human beings. And this is, at the same time, the most urgent duty of Christians. In this I would go to the extreme of stating that it is perhaps the only road by which Christians can open a path to their inner propensity to the break with themselves and with the world. But at the same time I must insist that the first revolution consists in our poorness of spirit, in our meekness, and in all the rest that the Beatitudes demand of us. To sum up, how a revolution is produced is not, in my judgment, a theological question but a question that directly concerns the conscience of Christians. If from the sincere demands of their Christian conscience they decide to make a revolution, they ought to make one, they will feel forced to make one. But this should be done with a well-purified and well-examined conscience. If it happens that way, I am in complete agreement.

And violence? When establishment-violence is in force, musn't we choose between the violence-of-the-revolution and establishment-violence? To what does our faith force us in the face of this alternative?

A very difficult question, which I hear above all as a challenge to myself. I am a man who never in his life has approved of what you call "violence." I understand that violence moves people to rise up against injustice. I understand it perfectly, and I even approve of it. But I find myself incapable of carrying it out, not because of cowardice but because of something that I find in the spirit of Christ, which is that he never judged anybody, never wished harm to anybody. I understand, on the one hand, that injustice must be overcome, and that there are occasions when it can be overcome only with violence. I accept this, but I would say that I don't hold it as a Christian, that is, that it does not respond to the spirit of our Lord Jesus Christ, although as a man I understand it perfectly. So you have put me in a blind alley. On the one hand, I must affirm absolutely as a man the use of violence and armed uprising, and at the same time, as a Christian, I must warn against it, because I think it does not respond to the spirit of Christ, it does not respond to the way he lived and frequently expressed himself. Understand me. I come from a country that was very harshly put to the test, Hungary. In 1956 there was an uprising there that I, as a Hungarian, completely approve of, but at the same time, I think that uprising was not, as I understand it, a Christian uprising. There is a difference between what is purely human and national and what is Christian. How to understand that difference, or how to resolve this aporia I don't know—at least, it's not clear to me. But don't mistake me: I do not here preach cowardly compromises with a given situation of oppression, or approval of the unacceptable. I wonder only about the method and I understand clearly that with only the method of meekness one does not always achieve what is needed. The others will trample on us at will, and this is not good either. So what can we do? I really don't know. As a human being, my feelings are on the side of those who rebel to avoid an injustice, even though eventually they may have to use guns and bombs. On the other hand, I know from my faith that I must not use gun or bomb.

Christian Positiveness of the Negative

I see in your books, Dr. Boros, that you locate faith and hope in the depth of this great paradox: in human weakness and impotence, freely accepted by believing people, faith and hope affirm the strength of God's presence; where people stop asserting themselves, God begins to assert himself in humanity. But don't you think that some may accuse us of reducing the person to passivity, to resignation, and that in this way we diminish and destroy the person?

I shall answer this schematically. I am a man who recognizes and loves the positive values of life. For others and for ourselves, we are *euangelion*, that is, good news. We are not always this, but we certainly ought to be it. The good news for me consists in a call to the positive values of life. If I have concerned myself, by preference, with suffering, misery, etc., it has been above all through my reluctance to admit that these things must be interpreted as negative in our lives. Therefore, if I have tried to study weakness and impotence it's because I have proposed (rightly or wrongly—let's not go into that now) to investigate those processes of existence in which people frequently despair because they feel as though they are in a blind alley. I have tried precisely to give to these processes a positive meaning, and for many theologians even too positive a meaning. I am in favor of what my friend Teilhard de Chardin called *le goût du bonheur.* And I am opposed to those who preach, as Christians, sadness, melancholy. Against this sadness I have constantly struggled, and I would like to struggle even more. Furthermore, this would perhaps be the moment to pass on to determine which are the positive aspects of life, but this is difficult. We speak easily of our misfortunes; to speak of our happiness there is scarcely any language. We shall have to create it.

It seems to me that in all your reflecting "sapientially" on the painful processes of human existence, you have been formidably positive and very evangelical. I agree and I congratulate you and I thank you for having concerned yourself in this way. I believe that a great many of your readers are grateful to you for this. In my question I was only trying to echo the tendency of people in today's societies to reject what is weakness, poverty, simplicity, their tendency to cling to effectiveness, force, dominance, power. A tendency, of course. Antievangelical and inhuman, it leads us to a schizophrenic competitiveness and to the unfair domination of some over others.

But any mature person who seriously faces life necessarily runs into moments when he or she is obliged to say: I'm licked, or, things can't go on this way. It's at just such moments that the person expects an answer from us. And I ask myself sincerely: can a person who has never felt alone or in despair, hungry or forsaken, stand facing others as if they were friends, and understand their solitude, their despair, their helplessness, their emptiness of God? I think it is completely impossible. The person would perhaps try to be kind to them, give them good advice, but the words would really sound hollow. That's why, at the beginning of this interview, I said that theologians of the future must have experienced despair in their own flesh as a basis for a true friendship with others. This would be my answer, and I hope that it would not be understood as a negative response. On the contrary, I think it is the most positive response we can and must give from our faith. It is too easy to want to change life from the outside, as at times happens, and it is sometimes our task to do this. But when our strength fails us, then we have nothing left but the help of our God by means of Jesus Christ.

I agree. Let me jump to another matter: do you believe that today we run the danger of reducing faith to ideologies?

I believe that I earlier hinted a certain answer to this question. We must affirm that faith must never be reduced to an ideology, never. Our God has revealed very little to us. He has certainly revealed it *all*, but I insist, all and only that which concerns our salvation. We cannot, then, convert our faith into an ideology, that is, into a universal doctrine valid for everything, so that we can say: this doctrine will help you in whatever you undertake. Our faith is always with us, but what we achieve in this life we must achieve with our reason. This runs the risk that we may do many things badly, but God helps us in our errors.

Some theologians assure us that we're already living in a "post-Christian time," while others think that we still live in a "pre-Christian time." What do you think?

I don't understand those words. I don't know what "pre-Christianity" means, or "post-Christianity." For me they are empty expressions. Scientists who are specialists in the matter tell us that a zoological specimen of average size has before it fifty million years of possible existence. Of these years we have lived at most three million. Therefore humanity is still at the dawn of its biological capacity and of its vital development. According to this, we may suppose that Christians within a few million years will think of us and say to one another: those primitive Christians did such and such; they were still naive; but they sacrificed themselves for their faith. And this is never pre-

Christian or post-Christian. We are living now until the end of time in the time of the church which, as I said, is a bridge toward the kingdom of God. How we can bring this to concrete reality in our lives, that is, in what forms and expressions, with what concepts or mentalities, is less important. What is important is that we are bearers and mediators of the spirit of Christ to help ourselves and others to overcome very concrete difficulties. And in this sense there is neither pre-Christianity nor post-Christianity, or whatever it wants to call itself; there is only a living from Christ with the hope of leading the world to its consummation.

We Are Threatened by the Atheism of Insincerity

What forms of atheism will Christians of our time and the future have to face?

I believe the only form of atheism that really threatens us is the "atheism of insincerity." Against the other forms of atheism we do not have to struggle, for it is very possible that an atheist is subconsciously a true believer, even when expressly denying God. We must believe in this if we believe that our Lord Jesus Christ has saved all people, absolutely all. All people now have the salvation of God-become-human, if they try to live sincerely as human beings regardless of the consequences. If they sincerely think they must reject the God that we have preached to them, they must do so; they not only can but they must do so. And they are not our enemies because of that. Our true enemies, if we can talk like that after Christ taught us to love our enemies, are the insincere ones, those who do not remain firm in the truth. These would be, in my opinion, "enemies." The others are perhaps anonymous Christians, as Karl Rahner called them. Besides, we must never call them that in their presence, for it would annoy them enormously and they might take it as a personal offense, and I think justly so. So, then, in my judgment, the most fearful form of atheism is the inner insincerity of a person.

Have we reached the time of "silence about God"? Shall we have to be silent and stop naming God for having talked too much about him and having misrepresented him with our words? Some people assert that today we must talk of God with silence, give silent testimony to him. What is your opinion: will God reveal himself better through our silence than through our words?

I agree that we have frequently talked too much about God, that is, we have involved him in everything, mixed him into everything. And this is not right. Let's say that God is a distinguished person who frequently, as happens in human social life, acts without becoming involved in the affair. This on the one hand. I also think that one can explain many aspects of the reality of the world without believing in

God. And this is not for me the denial of God but the acceptance of his preeminence and his goodness through which he does not become involved in everything. On the other hand, to the question of whether we should still talk of God, I would answer Yes. But not in such a way that we involve God in everything but in a way that we speak of his mystery, that is, of what he has revealed, referring it to the real questions of our lives, those questions in which God comes out to meet us, in which he really forces us to run into him. These questions assault us when we are forced to confess that we can go no further, that nobody can give us an answer, not even ourselves. Such questions exist, and we must answer those questions, and in the answer the word "God" must be pronounced. In this I do not agree with Bishop Robinson when he states that for some decades the word "God" should not be pronounced. I understand his request perfectly, but I have my reservations. Let us admit it: we are so forgetful. . . . What would happen to God if we, who have received the charge of announcing him to the others, did not announce him? And it isn't true either that people today don't want to hear about God. The truth is the opposite. They want to hear about God, but not with insincere language, and they don't want to address him with deceptive words. And in this they are quite right.

You Can Be True Only through Love

The greatest difficulty today in announcing the word of the gospel is to manage to talk of God to people in a veracious and credible way. What can we do to talk this way today to people about God?

Speak to them in truth and in love. These two things are fused in one: you can be true only from love. This is the Pauline definition of veracity. Paul says that we must be true in love. And this means for me, as for *veracity*, that we must tell people today what God has commanded (that is, announce his mystery and not our systems), but only what he has really commanded. I mean that we must not and cannot preach to people what is from our own harvest. We do not know how God thinks about many things that he has not revealed to us. We must abide by only what he has revealed to us, which is relatively little. We must limit ourselves to that, we must feel ourselves obligated to that. So, then, to say *all* that God has revealed to us, but *only* that. And that "only" means—and I speak here as a man who comes from an East European country—that there are many occasions when we should not substitute the gospel for politics, that we should not preach on matters such as the pill, birth control, and many other things that belong to various fields of science and culture but not to the gospel of salvation. It may surprise you that I say this, but it is a requirement of our sincerity and evangelical "veracity." And what

God has revealed to us we must say *in love*. Veracity is not a weapon with which we burst upon others. There are moments when a truth does not help others, and then love is the norm that dictates to us what we must say at those moments. As is clear, I here defend an attitude that I believe to be that of our Lord Jesus Christ, namely, the duty and the courage to be truthful, but in love.

And what is the criterion of truthfulness?

You place me before the true question. What is the criterion of my sincerity in faith? What must I say to other people? I believe that the only criterion of the truth that we proclaim, and that we must proclaim in love, is martyrdom. Announce, proclaim, hold fast to what you think you can affirm with the sacrifice of your own life. Nothing more than that. And when you proclaim it that way, in you there erupts spontaneously a theology of testimony. This is your theology, the one you must proclaim. This theology may not have everything, but nobody, no priest, no Christian, is obliged to tell everything or to present with the same urgency all that may perhaps be urgent on a general level. Say only what you can defend with the sacrifice of your own life. "Sacrifice of life" means to me not simply death but perhaps merely being assigned to the most humble service to one's fellows or being able to face failure, etc., etc. Our God demands no more of us, but also no less.

Finally, what would be the tone and style of the evangelization that we need today?

The gospel was proclaimed for all times, but, of course, in the language of *that* time. And life develops, evolves. Our task is to find the language in which the gospel can be understood by people of our time, and in this language we must understand it and proclaim it. I think that people today, and also Christians today, understand themselves more and more as investigative persons. Especially since Vatican Council II has had the daring to discuss, to explore new terrain, to force to a crisis the conceptual display of their understanding of faith. Narrowness of spirit, lack of comprehension, and inability to discuss are no longer the distinctive signs of the Catholic. The desire for understanding springs up in today's Christians not in an urge for novelty but in what is, in my opinion, the virtue of an alert and vigilant spirit. There are no grounds for considering our generation stupid. That virtue of an alert and vigilant spirit consists of a fundamental sincerity, in an attitude of openness toward all truth, wherever it comes from, left or right, and in a resolute search for justice. And here is the strange part: parallel to this, in the spirit of the humanity of today there is occurring a growth of God, a purification of his image. Today's Christian cannot endure a familiar, manageable God that you can carry around with indifference. You can thank atheists for the fact that, with their often disagreeable objections, they have forced the Christian to be sincere. This ceaseless struggle with mystery produces in the souls of today's Christians a deep humility—humility which is, to be exact, modesty and love of reality. Also our current proclamation of faith is controlled by this attitude of realism, of submission to reality. Faith remains intact. Many formulations and systems perish. It is precisely true faith that frees us from the temptation to attribute to human values and systems what belongs only to the Absolute. And so our faith is always a service to the person of each time. Our faith is neither dogmatic nor propagandistic. Its strength is concentrated more and more energetically in the sphere of personal or, if you prefer, existential testimony.

We have been talking for three hours. Boros has stood up several times, has walked around silently, and has lit, one after the other, quite a few little cigars. From time to time he himself shut off the mike and thought, or turned the tape back and listened to himself, cutting, erasing, correcting. Seeing him like that, silent for long stretches, absorbed, very concentrated, laboriously seeking and constructing his answers, I feared I was taking advantage of him and I told him that I was robbing him of time and strength, but he answered warmly: "Don't you worry, my friend. I have lots of time for you." When we stopped I begged his pardon, but he said: "Oh, no! I'm grateful to you. You force me to make my thinking precise and I thank you for this." Before this man who has devoted the afternoon to me until we reached hours that in Switzerland are late for supper, I find myself exhausted and joyful, and at the same time lost. I am joyfully exhausted by the magnanimity radiated over me by this "friend" with his attentive availability and his unselfishness. I savor in his manner the essence of what I have so often admired in his writings, and this indescribable savor liberates me. But I am literally "lost" because I did not expect to spend so many hours here and I have lost my contacts in Zurich (the few people I know cannot readjust their schedules to my delay and I now do not know where they are); I find myself in an unknown quarter of a strange city, far from the street where I live, whose name, number, and telephone I did not write down and I do not remember. This little anecdote allows me to testify to the magnanimity of Boros, who went out of his way to help me out of this situation that was embarrassing to me more for him than for myself. He called a taxi and came with me in search of the street and the house of my companions. He will not abandon me until he leaves me safely in the house. And so, on his jovial and friendly face, now unforgettable, is vividly engraved this thought that I learned in a book of his: before me, a troublesome fellow man, this man had no defenses.

A Conversation with Georges Casalis

Georges Casalis was born on January 4, 1917, in Paris. He studied theology in Paris and Basel, receiving his doctorate in theology in Strasbourg in 1970. He is a member of the French Reformed Church and professor of the Protestant Theology Faculty in Paris. He is a specialist in themes related to political theology. We cite among his works Prédication, acte politique *(Preaching, a Political Act), as well as his collaboration in several anthologies:* Situation de la théologie, théologie de la situation *(The Situation of Theology, The Theology of the Situation);* Théologie de la révolution et révolution de la théologie *(The Theology of Revolution and the Revolution of Theology);* Réflexions sur le ministère prophétique de l'église *(Reflections on the Prophetic Ministry of the Church).*

I knew little about Georges Casalis before talking with him. I first found out that a Spanish publisher was translating his Prédication, acte politique. *I then learned that the state censor pushed a red button. I learned further that Casalis is a good theologian, an excellent person, and a man very committed socially and politically in France and with respect to the human situation throughout the world. Since talking with him, I can testify to those three things.*

The war tempered him for opposition and critical struggle. "Decidedly, I have been, I am, and I shall be a partisan." He has been, is, and will be a militant in the resistance for liberty. "I am normally in the opposition. It has been my lot to play this role in most of the institutions with which I have had anything to do. Whether they are capitalist, socialist, Catholic, or Protestant institutions, my cooperation is always critical. I'm always on the alert." Lucidity is his obsession. "My wife sometimes makes fun of me for

21

*the frequency with which I use the word 'lucid.' From the time of my studies
I have believed that lucidity is the first Christian virtue."*

*He hides from no one his socialist militance. "This does not mean, in
any way, that I shut my eyes to the errors and crimes of regimes that claim
to be socialist. I denounced Stalinism, the invasion of Czechoslovakia, the
psychiatric treatments. . . . But I do and will say that a dictatorial regime
of torture is all the more horrible when its representatives claim to maintain
the regime in defense of Christian civilization." His lucidity. . . .*

*With this introduction, my readers already know much more about him
than I did when I met him in Paris on the recommendation of his great friend
José M. González Ruiz.*

*Along the corridors of the School of Theology of the French Reformed
Church, I ran into several young students and one of them led me to
Professor Casalis. He was waiting for me. He had the time set aside. We
entered a spacious library. At a corner of the large table surrounded by
chairs as if for a faculty meeting, the large window nearby gives me enough
light to see, above the green velveteen of an ancient jacket, the noble face of
Casalis haloed by silvery gray hair somewhat rumpled. I saw as I went in
that he limps. Only his friendly kindliness frees me from the feeling that I
am facing an illustrious figure in an illustrious frame of numerous collec-
tions of leather-bound books. Casalis speaks to me in a quite fluent Spanish
that, nevertheless, at times curbs his nimble speech. When he lacks a word,
he speaks to me with his expressive eyes.*

Faith Appears Useless

What major dangers for faith do you see today in our world?

I think there are two grave dangers. The first is that we live in a
materialistic world. The occidental world, the oriental world, and also
the Third World revolve around materialistic values. There is practically an equation between happiness and riches. The ideal proposed
to people of our time is always "to have more": more money, more
desires, a car, a television set, etc., etc. I believe the gravest danger is
that we have replaced "being" by "possessing." And especially in the
occidental world, which is a rich world. And in all classes. It's an ideal
that plays an important role among the poor. Because what is really the
hope of the poor? To become rich. I believe this is the greatest challenge to faith, because faith proposes something completely different:
to live in solidarity with others, to live for others and not for an ideal of
possession and wealth. I understand perfectly that the poor should
want to have more; but having more does not necessarily mean—just
the opposite—"being" more. And the problem is that churches
throughout the world have in practice accepted this materialistic
ideal. I don't believe that "materialism" is anything native to the East,
to the socialist countries. It is, above all, a myth of the western

countries, countries that in history were once Christian. Now it does seem to me that the tragedy of socialism is that it has not succeeded in proposing a different ideal to humanity. In the Soviet Union, which I know a little, the same as in East Germany and Romania, the ideal is always to attain the same material level as the United States. And it's very evident that this materialistic ideal is an ideal that is killing the world through pollution, through the exhaustion of material resources, and that the result of this materialistic development on the human psychological plane is that people lose the sense of life. This atmosphere of boredom is like a poison that flows through all humanity and prevents people from giving any sense to life. We live in tension between desire and resignation. I believe that all this is a great danger, a deep danger for the faith.

The second danger I see is in the close association that exists between religion and power. I must say that for me "religion" is the opposite of faith. Religion appears to me to be a sanctification of power. In practice the masters of the world take advantage of religion and in practice they are the allies of the leaders of the churches. So, for the poor and for many people of the world today, religion has totally lost its credibility. And then faith appears as a useless luxury and as an arm of the established order and as a means of integration.

Do you consider those two dangers also operative in socialist countries?

I believe that those dangers are also a threat to faith in the socialist countries that I know. I think of Eastern Europe. It's clear that there exists an ideology of material comfort that practically kills the free thought of people. Because we all, in Eastern Europe also, are more or less prisoners in the world of objects, in the words of a contemporary French philosopher. I believe that, in the socialist countries of Europe, ideology, as an organizing and directing force of society, is dead. It's a sad, tragic experience that we can observe in those countries; there is no hopeful ideological search; there is no doctrinal reflection to give a new definition of socialism; there is a certain way of living in a very definite line of continuity. And the distance and the distrust that exist, for example, between the established powers of those countries and the institutional churches is for fear that the churches may represent a force of political opposition. But that doesn't create a dialogue: in fact there exists no conflicting, redeeming vitality at the root of the question of faith or atheism. It's terrible, for example, to realize that it's impossible in the countries of Eastern Europe to start a dialogue between Christians and Marxists. They tell you that you can organize a dialogue in practice, but it's not a dialogue centered on the basic, essential questions. I believe the terrible thing is that the rich world of the West and the East lives on the surface of things. And the ultimate questions of human life are not raised.

A Possibility for Purifying the Faith

Do you have hopes about other parts of the world? Do you see the search for–or the reality of–another kind of socialism open to faith, or for a faith that will lead to a different society?

There is a search throughout the world that may perhaps be more hopeful in the countries of the Third World. I think especially of Latin America, which I have visited several times. There is a search for faith in relation to the revolutionary struggle to achieve the liberation of the people. And clearly many lay persons and priests who struggle in solidarity with the poor give a new definition, a new image, of faith. For them faith represents a dynamics that allows them to struggle with a new strength. It may be possible to say that in Cuba there is a kind of discovery of what a living faith might represent for the building of a new socialism. I'm not saying that Cuban society is a perfect socialist society; I'm saying that there is a serious search. I believe there is, in the consciousness of Fidel himself, a kind of intuition of what faith might represent. The remark of Fidel in Chile when—some time ago—he said that revolutionary Christians and socialists are strategic allies is a very important remark, because, I believe, it's the first time that a socialist leader has made a remark of that kind. Fidel didn't say that Christians were tactical allies in a limited struggle at one time and at one place: he said that they were allies because the ultimate goals of revolutionary Christians and authentic socialists were the same. And that is very important. It means that there is a kind of possibility of purification of faith in the revolutionary struggle and perhaps a possibility of a positive and critical contribution by faith toward the construction of socialism. I believe that the presence of faith, of a living faith, of an authentic faith in a socialist development would prevent the bureaucratization or the dogmatization of socialism.

I Admire Progressive Christians

Do you see any positive aspects in the evolution of faith from the past to today, in the forms in which today we tend to live it? Do you see positive aspects or do you believe that faith is in total crisis? Is everything negative or are there new values?

I am always happily surprised to find Christians who refuse to accept the traditional forms of Christianity and who severely criticize ecclesiastical institutions from various points of view, seeking at the same time a deepening of faith. I believe, then, that there are two very positive things: a clearer and clearer consciousness of the difference, perhaps of the opposition, between faith and religion. That is to say that faith can in no way serve as security for life. Faith does not mean a sacralization of life, of fecundity, for example, or of success. Faith always means to give your life to serve others. Faith is always a risk. And I should like to say that I find many Christians in many walks of life who think that way and who live that way. I feel a great admiration for many Christians who discover the authentic dimensions of the gospel and the faith of our society.

The second thing, which is practically the same, is that today there are many Christians who make a radical criticism of ecclesiastical institutions and who say: let us seek new forms of communitarian life. Because they think—and so do I—that Christian life cannot be lived in isolation, that it is necessary to have a community, to live in a community, but not in just any community. Many Christians refuse to live in a community in which they are treated as minors. I believe there is today a profound search in the direction of an adult Christianity where it can be said: "I have a responsibility for the definition of faith, for the definition and organization of Christian life for a new time." It is important to have theologians in the community, but these theologians are not going to decide for the community; they are going to be animators or servants of the community who have competence in the explanation of Holy Scripture and perhaps—why not?—in the celebration of the Eucharist, but at a level where there is no possibility of authoritarianism over the laity. I believe that is what is most important. I live in a normal community of the Reformed churches of France and that is important there. I am a layman in that community as a teacher of theology, because we have a very good pastor who is my friend, but after the preaching, for example, on Sunday, we will have the Eucharist one time, and the following Sunday a discussion on the preaching, that is, immediately after the preaching there is a dialogue in the community, in which, from time to time, the preaching is subjected to criticism. I believe that is very important. Then the people go off to their work, to their family life, and they live their Christian responsibility with adult independence. For me this is a new characteristic of the Christianity of our time and I believe that is important progress. I have profound hope for the future.

The Gospel Has a Future in This World

Facing that future in which you have so much hope, what do you believe should be, and what will be, the proper tasks of faith in the human world?

I cannot answer with much precision. But I would like to say the following. I believe that faith constitutes a specific identity in believers: I am a Christian and I have a specificity, a decisive contribution to the life of the world. If Christians have, on the one hand, very solid roots in the gospel and, on the other, they live in solidarity with other persons, I believe a spark will always fly between those two poles: the

Christian roots and the human commitment. For me this is the simplest explanation: to say that faith is a special form of human identity. And there are other forms of human identity; there are communists, there are leftists, there are atheists, there are—I don't know—capitalists also. I think the most important thing is to be conscious of one's own identity. My identity is in my humanity, a relation with Jesus of Nazareth. And that cannot be denied, cannot be proved, and I cannot escape from it: it is a fact. I am very happy in this relationship, without much of a problem: it is a fact. The word of Jesus of Nazareth is a word that always questions me, helps me, motivates me, and makes me live this way. I have never thought that faith means a separation between me and those who do not believe. On the contrary, it is a factor of unity, because I think that the gospel is so broad that it can understand and make understood those who do not believe, and it brings respect also to those who do not believe— precisely as nonbelievers.

But if what you are asking me is what is the future of the churches, I could not answer you precisely.

That's another question: the relation between faith and churches in the future.

I have a deep conviction that the gospel has a future in this world of ours. I don't know how, but I have a deep conviction about the future of Christ. I have visited many countries of the world, and I state that authentic faith cannot die, cannot disappear. Churches may disappear, but not faith.

Put the Great Institutions of the Church in Perspective

Don't you see as essential to the survival of faith in this world a visible communitarian dimension, an institutional dimension?

Yes, indeed. But what does that dimension consist of? For me the answer is very simple, perhaps too Protestant, but I cannot change. I will say that it's a very essential thing for faith to have a place to share the word and the sacrament. A place in which I can understand, receive, and also share the word, which means for me the gospel of loving your enemy, for example, or whether there is a contradiction between believing and struggling, or what is the practical meaning of all the phrases in Scripture about the danger of money. Because I don't have any fixed solution, I don't have any prescription. I always have to have a fresh understanding of the particularity of the gospel in each situation and in each time. And I also believe that receiving the sacrament of the Eucharist is essential to my life, if the Eucharist means not an evasion of history but a meal of communion with the Lord and the people of God.

I believe it will always be necessary to have some meeting places. I don't know if that means that we have need of cathedrals or basilicas, etc. It can be in a kitchen, in a farmhouse; it can be any place in the common life of people. I don't believe a very large organization is needed. I don't believe it is necessary to have paid functionaries for a religion, a cult. Our Reformed church, which is a very scattered minority in our country, is now making an important study on the distinction between church service and salary. That is to say, in various churches of the world, for example in the great Baptist church of the Soviet Union, the church ministers are never paid. They have a "profane" profession, if you can call it that (I make no distinction between what we might call the sacred and the profane); they have a human profession and in their free time they place themselves at the service of the church. I believe this is important, that there always will be people available for gospel service in the Christian community or through the Christian community.

We have to view the great ecclesiastical institutions in proper perspective, understanding that they are great factories, great organizations, with much power, with too many problems of administration and with an awesome jurisdiction. I am in complete agreement with Cardinal Suenens when he said at Vatican Council II: "There is a trinity of the devil: triumphalism, clericalism, and juridicism." And I believe we have to free Christians from this diabolical trinity. But the first condition is that we be free, because I believe that all those dangers have their roots in our hearts.

The Gospel Is Not Neutral

What is your opinion about the correct and essential relations between faith and politics?

Well, I have a very clear opinion on this point. I think that political commitment comes from the very act of being born. Aristotle said that man is a political animal; that is, a person lives in a whole community; to be a human is to live in society, to be a member of a society; it is to be politically commited, of necessity. There is no neutrality. There is no possibility of escape from this commitment. We are, by the very act of being born, politically committed beings. I once said that our first political act is our birth. Because it's not the same to be born in a country of the Third World as to be born in a rich country of Western Europe. There are immediate differences: biological, economic, cultural, political, etc. And I think that when we try to become politically neutral, we accept the fact that others will rule over us and our fellow beings. In practice, neutrality is a commitment to the side of the established order. And then I believe that the only possible alternatives presented to us are between an ingenuous acceptance of that apparent neutrality, which is in practice a surrender of responsibility as human beings, and a decision to take on the responsibility and look at political commitment as a calling of humanity, of any human being.

When this person, who is a political animal, becomes a Christian, it is obvious that faith means something to his or her political commitment because faith touches not only our spiritual dimension but our whole human life. And then to believe means also to live one's basic political commitment in relation to the word of Jesus of Nazareth. That means that faith cannot become apolitical and that the gospel is not neutral with respect to politics. If we read the Scriptures with eyes somewhat opened, we see some lines that define not a policy but some decisive options for a political life, for political commitment. Sometime ago I was with a Marxist friend at a meeting in Germany. We talked about these problems and he suddenly said: "If I accepted that sentence, 'Love your brother as you love yourself,' it would be enough to turn me against any kind of oppression." I believe it is very important to realize that love does not have only an interpersonal dimension: love has to have a social, collective dimension, and the social and collective dimension of love is justice. I believe that the central word of the Old Testament, which is an eminently political work, is justice: that any person can be authentic, not alienated, free, fraternal, with recognized rights. And I believe that, as Christians, we have to try to bring about in society the greatest predominance of justice; that is, we have to turn against many things in this world, against many structures, against many powers that are inhuman.

Each One of Us Reads the Gospel from Where We Are

But a political reading of the gospel (according to what you say, any reading of the gospel is in some way political) places us today before a multiplicity of opposing interpretations, because each one finds in Scripture the arguments he or she needs to justify a stand: the rightists, that all authority comes from God, and that violence is condemned by Christ (although they make use of violence as soon as it suits them); the leftists, that justice ought to be established, etc. How can we achieve today an authentically evangelical rereading of the gospels that will respect and take on the word of God over and for our historical conditions?

We have to do that rereading, yes. But I don't believe the gospel says black and white at the same time. It's a matter of interpretation. As a competent theologian, I must say that one can get from Scripture no justification of any established order. For me it's clear—and I would be happy to discuss this theme—that the gospel tends toward liberation from injustice. We must see how this can be carried out. Here I want to say two things. First, one cannot understand the gospel

GEORGES CASALIS   29

today without an analysis of our time, of our world, of our society. Because the values by which the gospel is read and was written are no longer the values of our time. And then there is a tension, a reciprocal appeal, between Holy Scripture and its reading in our time. The French evangelical philosopher Paul Ricoeur says that everything is always decided in a complete reciprocity between the reading of our world and the reading of the Bible. And that seems to me very important. And so I shall have to establish a dialogue between our time, the statistics of industrial growth, of salaries, of the relation between the various classes of society, and the gospel word that calls upon us to live the faith like a search for a better society for everybody. I believe also that the Bible is a measure and critique for every established order, starting concretely from the lot of the poor; I shan't ask myself if the rich countries have a superior standard of living but how they live in relation with their poor and also with outsiders.

In the second place, I would like to say that each person in practice has the opinions that correspond to his or her social and political praxis. It is quite normal for those who place themselves on the side of oppressive power to seek in the gospel the justification of their position. So there is a kind of condition that must always be observed for a reading of the Bible: on which side of the frontier of the class struggle is the Bible reader? If I am on the side of the oppressors, I shall give a conservative and authoritarian reading of the Bible. If I put myself on the side of the oppressed, I shall give a reading in the direction of liberation. This cannot be denied. And let us keep in mind the good discoveries that Karl Marx made in his analysis of ideology when he said that the dominant ideas are always the ideas of the dominant class. This poses very serious questions to Christian praxis and to the reading of the Bible. I think we have to make, in a profound way, a criticism of traditional religion or what is usually called "traditional faith," which is frequently a simple ideological decoration of the established order. Only if we are disposed to separate ideology from faith can we make a theological criticism of ideologies. Faith, theology, ecclesiastical life must be purified of ideological elements, in order to receive a new credibility, a new dose of authority to be able to make a critique of society.

I deduce from all that has been said that you are in close agreement with the theology of liberation as an interpretation of the praxis of faith?

In complete agreement. I believe it is a very important and decisive contribution of the theologians of Latin America to the ecumenical life of today. I have made long trips across Latin America especially to listen to the theologians of liberation and to learn from them with a view to my reading of the Bible and also my activities in the French society of today.

Revolutionaries Are Those Who Take Up Their Crosses and Give Their Lives

At times the political commitment of the believer in situations of injustice becomes a revolutionary commitment. Could you point out some specific contributions made by faith to the revolutionary struggle?

Yes, several things. I should like to say something, but I have a certain uneasiness and doubt in saying it because I shouldn't want to offer any possibility of evasion to Christians who refuse to take on their revolutionary commitment. But if we accept as a human and Christian necessity a revolutionary commitment, I am ready to say this: I think that for revolutionary action one danger is always pride, the *hybris* of which the New Testament speaks, the Promethean conviction of thinking people that they can free themselves with their own forces. I believe that no revolution, no revolutionary action can be achieved without deep humility. Authentic revolutionaries are the ones always ready to take up their cross and give their lives, and not those who try to achieve a success that will mean a profit for themselves. From this point of view the figure of Che Guevara is decisive for all Latin America, because in practice he did what Christ did, in accordance with what the apostle Paul says in the second chapter of the Letter to the Philippians, for he refused to keep his place as a rich man, his privileges as a minister, his family, etc., and he chose the fate of a man who lives in exile and who meets death in a foreign country, the death of a guerrilla fighter, with the betrayal of his friends and with the cruelty of political power. It is clear that the meaning of the figure of Che Guevara is very decisive because he is the revolutionary who truly left everything to live, struggle, and die for the freedom of others.

Another thing I wanted to say is that each revolution remains as something imperfect, that revolution is always a human and relative fact that can never achieve an absolute state. This means, for the Christian faith, that at any revolutionary moment or in any revolutionary state, it can always go forward in the direction of a better state of justice, of freedom for humanity. It also means that the revolution can never end but must make constant progress and that each form of establishment to the extent of its bureaucracy or dogmatism or totalitarianism is a negation of the revolution. We must maintain a critical attitude within a positive solidarity, for the critical function, if it is not exercised in the positive solidarity of the common struggle, is a destructive criticism, and the function of faith must be a function of positive criticism within a participation in revolution.

To Take to Violence to Destroy Violence

And the problem of violence?

It is something central, decisive. But it would be completely false to say that violence begins with revolutionary violence. Violence is, in the first place, the violence of unjust organizations that each day kill more people than can be killed by revolution in its reaction. I believe, in fact, that the gospel is opposed to violence. The question is—and it's a very difficult question—to know if at times it isn't necessary to take to violence to destroy violence. We unfortunately have some concrete experiences here. I'm thinking of the Algerians who took to guns and bombs against the French after having tried for years to win their rights. The order of violence established over a whole people was so strong that the only possibility of destroying this order was to take to violence and begin terrorism. I have a friend who was then in Algiers and he had many conversations with the leaders of the National Liberation Front. A few weeks ago he was telling me that in 1954 he saw the desperation of those nationalists because they had no other solution than violence to win their rights against the French forces. I believe that when we are in situations of violence and counterviolence, the nonviolence of the gospel forces us to be on the side of those who are struggling for freedom. At times we have to make a very difficult choice: to choose violence that frees against violence that oppresses.

Do Harvey Cox's "feast" and Jürgen Moltmann's "play" have anything to do with this?

That's my question to Cox and Moltmann. Whether the feast is a feast of evasion, whether it's a new form of alienation and of opium for the people. If the feast means that in the midst of the struggle I salute the day of liberation as a promise, I think that then the feast plays a positive role in the struggle. But if there is an abyss between feast and struggle, the feast is meaningless; it's a commitment to the side of the oppressors.

It has grown late. We go out together into the sharp cold air of the Parisian streets. As I say goodbye to this man with a generous and friendly look, his figure seems enormous to me, his famous limp and his noble head—the wind rumples his white hair—as if weighed down with struggles. "I'm on a black list in the police files in the United States and, consequently, in those of other countries. Resistance to the rearming of Germany, my often stormy collaboration with communist friends, Vietnam, Algiers, Latin America, frequent declarations of solidarity are placing me every day further on the wrong side of the barricade. But the rejection of Stalinism, the protest against the invasion of Czechoslovakia, the denouncement of the psychiatric cures used against opponents of the socialist totalitarian regimes won me expulsion from the Christian Conference for Peace and, in practice, exclusion from Eastern Europe. In no way do I glory in this. That's the way it is and that's the way it will be as long as I live, for I'm convinced that the progress of civilization, in which I firmly believe, will always leave intolerable side effects and it will always be necessary, for the future of humanity, to risk the eminently positive gesture that is an unconditional no." His own words make his figure of a tired struggler seem to me tireless. *"I always keep alive in my mind the plea of our youngest son who in May of 1968 said to me: 'Have you all fought against Nazism to allow this society to survive? You've only half done your job.'"* The lights of the streets of Paris do not seem to me festive; because the words of Georges Casalis force me to see the shadows, the necessary struggle: *"Under all skies and in all regimes, the struggles for humankind are the first task of those who live inspired by the Bible."*

A Conversation with
Joseph (José) Comblin

Comblin, born on March 22, 1923, in Brussels, was ordained a priest in 1947. He earned a doctorate in theology at the University of Louvain in 1950. He worked in Brussels parishes until 1958, when he left for Campinhas in the state of São Paulo, Brazil, as seminary teacher and adviser to Catholic Action. From 1962 to 1964 he was professor of theology in the Catholic University of Santiago de Chile; from 1965 to 1972, professor in the regional seminary in Recife, Brazil. In 1972 he was expelled from Brazil. Currently he is professor at the Catholic University of Chile in Talca and at the Catholic University of Louvain. Among his works are Jesus of Nazareth: Meditations on His Humanity; The Meaning of Mission; Sent from the Father: Meditations on the Fourth Gospel.*

I ran into Comblin on one of his trips to Louvain, where he teaches classes regularly in spite of having also lived in Latin America for twenty years. His European origin does not prevent him from being among the best Latin American theologians and pastoralists. He is a fine connoisseur of the political ideologies and forces that enter into the cruel game of the dependence of the countries of that whole subcontinent and into its liberation problems and ferments, a challenging and explosive terrain in which the church has to live by accounting for its hope.

Comblin is listed as "undesirable" in the gigantic archives of the Brazilian police, who expelled him in 1972 after fourteen years of residence in Campinhas, São Paulo, and Recife. When he was expelled he was a collaborator of Helder Camara's. He then took up residence in Chile, although it may be said that he resides in all of Latin America. There the timid Belgian professor who was Joseph Comblin has come to be, simply and affectionately, "José."

In a room at the Latin American School in Louvain I am facing a rather short man with long sideburns, with confident look and smile but extremely nervous when he talks to me. His nerves activate his whole body (head, eyes, legs, and hands) while he searches for and pronounces his words that are born with difficult labor. His undisguised timidity prevents me from sensing that I am facing a resolute and revolutionary man. But his answers to my questions make me see that to be timid is not to be frightened.

Faith Must Awaken a World of Utopias

José, when some are fearful for faith, frightened by what others claim (also for faith), I'm interested to know what are, in your view—which is not only European but also Latin American—the real dangers to faith today.

The gravest danger in the long run would be a reaction of anguish or panic at the disturbances and problems that have arisen after Vatican Council II—anguish and panic that lead Christians to pose problems of faith in individual terms, that is, as a solution to individual doubts, to individual questions, trying to solve them by means of introspection, of humanity reflecting about itself, of the search for what is specifically Christian, starting from individual reflection and with a view to individualistic security. And then faith would end outside the evolution of world culture. It would lead to a new privatization, it would create distances between secular searchings and Christian concerns.

That's why I think that the greatest problem in today's faith is the problem of knowing how, despite the dangers, to approach and confront the fundamental problems of today's world. Not to be afraid of the problem of the end of a civilization, of values, of a style. Today there exists a general "response" to the capitalist and bourgeois style of life predominant in the civilization in which we have lived up to now. The future of Christianity does not lie in the defense of the bourgeois and capitalist style of life that predominates in the western world but in the midst of the various kinds of search for new civilizations, of new styles of life and new ways of living, being carried out by the most restless spirits in today's world, especially in the Third World, but also in the most sensitive minorities in the Old World, whether North American or European.

"Novelty," according to what you say, would be the proper place for faith, the future that is gestating.

Yes. Faith is the basis of hope, and therefore it has to be a permanent source of renewal and hope. The center of faith is the conviction that

God comes to the world by means of Jesus Christ to liberate humanity, that is, not the knowledge of an abstract God, a philosophical God, a conceptual God, but an active revelation of God. God comes among people in spite of all exterior "stability," in spite of all the "short-term knowledge" that assures us that nothing changes and that everything always comes out the same. There is a promise in Holy Scripture, in divine revelation, and faith consists in accepting that promise: *promise of renovation*, promise of a new world, promise of a liberation of humanity. Therefore, faith consists in formulating that hope again, in proposing in the midst of the world that confidence that must constitute one of the major forces in the service of the discovery, in the concrete circumstances of life, of that new person who is the object of everyone's aspirations.

And, in the face of that new world that is coming, what are the proper functions of faith?

A faith that is open to hope will be a source of "utopias," of projects, of new tendencies, of experiences of personal and communitarian life, of new experiences beyond the structures of the one-dimensional society in which we live—new forms of community to develop people's new energies, which a production-oriented and purely industrial society have left to one side; the affective, emotive, poetic, artistic energies, the energies of communitarian life; everything that hasn't developed in the world of labor, in the world of material development, and which is an object of aspiration now on the part of the dominated cultures and also of western youth. In the midst of that fermentation, faith should arouse, more than the other ideologies, a world of utopias, ideas, experiences—many destined, without doubt, to fail, but in the midst of a fermentation of new experience will appear a new figure of Christianity for the people of tomorrow.

Open-minded Bishops: A Minority

To develop that creative function of faith supposes freedom of movement to seek and experiment, and even—as you say—to fail. It demands confidence, courage, audacity. And a notable pluralism. Do you think that the church is ready to take advantage of that climate? Do you believe that the hierarchy is aware of the importance of that creative function of faith, to the point of taking on its possibilities and its risks?

In fact, at the present time several tendencies are seen in the hierarchy. Some of them are anguished men, worried, who believe they can save themselves from anguish by keeping as much as possible the past, the structures and the spirit of the past. But there are also others, bishops and those responsible for religious institutions, who have adopted an attitude of confidence with respect to the future (of confidence in the force of the Spirit) and who do not allow themselves to be upset by the vacillations, by the experiments that fail at times, by the confusion of ideas; they do not allow themselves to be upset and they have faith in the strength of prophetic inspiration, of spiritual inspiration; and in any case they do not believe that the structures of the past can be resurrected; they know that today's risks must be accepted.

What percentage of the hierarchy do you see as open-minded like that?

I believe the proportion of the hierarchy open to the future is more or less equal to the proportion in the clergy or among the laity. Dom Hélder Câmara would say there is always fifteen percent open to the future, without worry, without anguish.

But everywhere a great distrust is spreading with regard to the hierarchy. I don't know if the other eighty-five percent close off the paths; or if there is a contagious mirage, but what is certain is that between the progressive groups and the institution and its hierarchy the distances are increasing. How do you see this problem?

I believe it is very serious on the level of relations between the minorities and the mass of people. The great mass will not let itself be moved; it is quite worried by the risks; and there exists a very great temptation for the minority oriented toward the future to break away from the majority, with the danger of isolation. At times we can have the impression of carrying out a purer, more authentic action by breaking relations with the great masses that do not move, but there is danger of no longer being able to act for lack of contact with the masses and of imagining forms of action that in reality no longer reach the people who would have to be moved. The same is true in society at large as in the church: every form of action looks to the transformation of everyone, of the great masses. To cut off relations is not the safest and most effective method of achieving this goal.

Faith That Acts

In various sectors of the church, and perhaps most strongly in Latin America, for obvious reasons, Christian reflection sees more and more social and political commitment as a requirement of faith. Some people are enthusiastic about this as something tremendously new, and others are frightened by it as a catastrophic novelty. What would you say to both groups?

In the first place, I would insist that the political dimension of faith is not a "novelty" but has been the most constant in the history of the church, and especially in the Roman Catholic church. If Protestantism has privatized itself since the time of the Reformation, individualized itself, in the Catholic church the opposite has always happened: much importance has been given to the political aspect. But it has happened that that political aspect has been reduced to the preservation of ancient Christendom, that is, the alliance of the church and power. And here is the big problem: the political dimension of the gospel, does it demand acting with power or does it, precisely, demand not acting with power? Does it call for entering into alliances with power or, rather, to act outside of power and like a force that, if it does not always oppose, in any case is always distinguished from and separate from the powers? The great concern and the tendencies of the new forms of theology (in Latin America it is called "theology of libera-tion," elsewhere "political theology") is exactly that of making a distinction between a pastoral approach based on an alliance with the powers (economic, cultural) and a prophetic action, in the line of the political mission of the poor of Israel within their nation.

Jesus, his example, is the light that distinguishes between those two lines, showing that (objectively) one is more evangelical than the other, isn't he? Which of the two seems to you more in conformity with the nature of faith according to the gospels, according to the life and the message of Jesus?

It seems to me that the attitude of Jesus is quite clear. Two facts appear simultaneously: in the first place, Jesus Christ refused any form of power; he declined to be the "Messiah" in the Jewish sense: that is, he did not accept a political power as an instrument of his divine mission, of his own mission; he refused to place power at the service of his mission; he wanted to do without power. But at the same time his message is addressed to society entire and complete. He does not look to the transformation of pure inwardness but of human society and all social relations; he looks to the formation of a true Israel, that is, of a new people, renovated in all its dimensions, but not through the force of power but through the force of martyrdom, of the word, of prophetic signs, of signs directed by God, by supernatural forces, by his miracles, by his preaching, by his Passion. That is, by the strength of God that manifests itself in the weakness of humanity, as St. Paul says. Christ's mission has political reach, but not by means of power.

In the current tendency toward social and political commitment, do you see a danger of reducing faith to ideology, of "utilizing" faith?

That danger has always existed and still exists. It's the danger of reducing faith to a Machiavellian game, to a game for the conquest of power. This is found among the prelates of the Middle Ages, within Christianity; it is found in some popes, like Julius II, or Alexander VI; it is found among Christian princes and it is probably found today in all Christian movements that aspire in a certain way either to the conquest of power or to the carrying out of political tasks. That is, this danger is not new, it is of all times. And at bottom it consists of confusing the cause of God with the cause of a power, of a movement, of a party candidate, or of a person or group that wants to promote itself and confuses its self-promotion with the promotion of the kingdom of God. This danger exists naturally, and therefore Christian existence amid the transformation of society will always be existence "in danger," but this is what happens in all the dimensions of life and in all the dimensions of Christian existence.

I ask you for a distinction, José: do you see any essential difference between those who get involved in the revolution from faith, in the name of Christ, and those who enroll in it through an ideology? Do you see specific differences?

I would say there is a specific difference between a person who gets involved in the good of his brothers and sisters simply from psychological motivation, desire for improvement, resentment, class hatred, antagonistic reaction of a social group, personal or group hostility, or other purely psychological factors, and another person who gets involved for the good of others with a true spirit of sacrifice, going beyond one's own aspirations, one's own egotism. In this one we shall recognize the true Christian. Such a person will not be recognized simply by virtue of invoking the name of God or the name of Jesus Christ. Christ said: "It is not the person who says, 'Lord, Lord,' who is saved but rather the one who does the will of my Father." Therefore, what Christians specifically need is to *do*; to do and not to talk. To say "Lord, Lord" is not essential for Christians. All people can invoke pretty names; the problem is to *do*. And the true disciple, according to the criteria of Jesus Christ, is the one with a faith that acts. As St. James says: "Faith is known by its works."

As long as, in doing them, it is faith that acts and not motives that supplant it, of course. It's a question of doing, of functioning, that will not detract from faith but will heighten it and make it manifest.
    Certainly.

The Risks of Violence

Some people wonder if it is licit and Christian to choose violence, even if it is inevitable in the revolutionary commitment out of faith. What do you think of that statement of the problem of violence? How would you state it?

This problem is often stated this way, but I don't believe it is well stated. Because there is no real choice for violence and there is nobody, except in the case of psychological abnormality, nobody that chooses violence. I would state the problem by distinguishing between two categories of people: people who are willing to seek social reforms and transformations, even at the risk of provoking violence, and other people who are not willing to urge transformations and reforms if there is a risk of violence. The problem then, as we face the risk of possible violence, is whether or not to accept the risk. No one is going to want violence, and if reforms and transformations can be achieved without violence, that is everyone's preference. The problem is whether, in the face of the risks, one retreats and does not act, or whether one is impelled to act even at the risk of violence. There you have two kinds of people. And I believe that in the whole Christian tradition there has always been a feeling that the danger of violence does not justify inaction.

Do you include in that "risk of provoking violence" being also a protagonist of violence, even physical violence?
This problem was raised in early Christian times, when the matter came up about whether or not Christians could be soldiers in the Roman Empire. And some said that in no way could a Christian be a soldier, bear arms. But on the other hand, especially after the Christianization of the empire and the pacts with Constantine and Theodosius, Christians were also soldiers. Today all churches, in practice, except for Jehovah's Witnesses and a few others, allow their members to be soldiers. Some churches accept this to the point where there are priests who are military advisers or chaplains. And of course it is much more dubious if support of possible violence reaches the point of giving an unofficial mission to a priest within an army; but even so, they accept it. The ecclesiastical hierarchy accepts it. That is, it accepts the risk that Christians may use violence. And we are not trying, by this, to justify the excesses that occurred during the two world wars, when there were even bishops that went so far as to sanctify war. Instead of taking the attitude of being resigned to violence because there's no other way out, they sanctified it directly as if it were a kind of crusade, something undertaken in the name of God. Now there is nothing that allows us to justify this.

Today there is a risk of anachronism, and we may be so inconsistent as to condemn the old sanctification of violence and consecrate a new sanctification of violence. Just as others inconsistently condemn the new violence (we mean, of course, violence "of the leftists") and do not condemn the old violence ("of the rightists"), the violence of the establishment, but instead support and even bless it. In these inconsistencies there is an ideological opportunism. And it is also ambiguous to condemn violence no matter which side it's on. One ought to analyze the causes carefully, and blame, even more than the effects, the causes of the spiral of violence. Moreover, don't you think that, as a Christian ideal, active nonviolence and demonstrations on conscientious grounds bring to the transformation of the world something more evangelical and efficacious than violence? Won't it always be a requirement of faith for us to struggle to reduce as much as possible the risks of violence in any social and political commitment, and above all to overcome the basic violence that engenders acts of violence?

In today's world there are certainly many impatient people who would embrace forms of violence that are without justification, without hope, without reason, thinking hastily that the time has come to provoke an act of violence, without having gone through all the peaceful means. Facing this, of course the Christian world has an enormous experience that it can place at the service of humanity and political movements. An experience of self-control, of ascetic self-discipline. It has resources, in short, to show people ways that are more rational, more thoughtful, more attentive to the complexity of problems, to the complexity of the necessary strategies. In this sense Christians, like Buddhists and Hindus, have reserves of struggle against aggressiveness that they can place at the service of humanity and precipitant people.

And also—I would insist—reserves of nonviolent struggle against the violence of injustice established and exercised by people who are completely different from impatient revolutionaries, but no less violent. And right there I make my point, when I speak of "reducing the risks of violence" and "overcoming the violence that engenders acts of violence." The peace of the love of justice is what the Christian offers in the face of violence.

The Third World, Faith, and Freedom

Thinking of your vision and your experience in Latin America, I'm going to ask you two complementary questions. First: what can and should Christian faith bring to the struggle for the freedom of the Third World, and specifically Latin America?

Experience teaches us that revolutions—which are not only to replace one power by another, one dominant class by another dominant class but, rather, to seek a world more just, more unfettered, in which social relations are determined not in terms of domination but of fraternity—have always sprung up in the Christian world. Because, in fact, it takes a very great hope to be convinced that it's worthwhile to work in the service of a world more human, transformed; it takes confidence in the latent energies of humanity; it takes confidence in the presence of a new principle, a principle of renovation, a spirit superior to the one that is in human "flesh." That is what the Christian can give: the possibility of hoping against all hope, against all the illusions of perception; if the world of perception seems to us inert, untransformable, faith brings us a hope capable of overcoming appearances. And this is what faith can give us, although up to now it is, rather, certain "Christian heresies" that often provide this hope, socialist heresies or the Marxist heresy rather than the Christians in the great churches.

Here's my second question: what can the Third World, and Latin America within it, out of its awakening and its struggle, give to Christian faith and to the faith of the other countries, of our western churches?

In the western world, most Christians have become so integrated into capitalist industrial society that they have adapted their hope to that society. They no longer hope for anything except the comfort that society can give them; their aspirations don't go beyond that material comfort and an increase in material comfort. In such a cramped life plan, the scope of faith is reduced and faith itself is progressively devitalized. What the peoples of the Third World, and of Latin America in particular, being Christian, can give is precisely a new dimension of hope capable of making Christian hope specific in utopias and actions that tend toward the formation of a new society beyond the mere production of material goods or material comfort, new ideals of collective life, of civilization, of human activities. The nations of the Third World, at least in their most active minorities, at present reject the lifestyle of western civilization and want to promote another lifestyle. They feel more deeply the deficiencies of the western style because they perceive more deeply the unjust and oppressive parts of this style. Therefore, there is probably in them more sensitivity to the desire for and the tendencies toward a new society, whereas the westerners resign themselves and adapt themselves with great ease to the society that capitalism offers them.

To Reevangelize Is to Awaken Hope

In some churches we have an urgent need to reevangelize the baptized, in order that faith be purified and mature evangelically. Will you give us your vision of this phenomenon, of this great problem, and perhaps some clue to how we can move toward the true faith without unnecessary anguish?

I believe that the Christians most faithful to the church are the ones who make up the last remains of the ancient rural Christendom, the ancient rural society. And the unrest they feel nowadays comes from the fact that they belong, in great part, to a culture, a civilization that is outmoded; they are noticing that the world is changing, that youth is changing, that ideas are changing, that there is an evolution that at the same time endangers their Christianity, because their Christianity had been adapted to an ancient civilization. They find it easy to believe that the world is hostile to their faith. But there is no hostility toward their faith; it's that culture is changing, the world is changing and naturally the Christians that have a Christianity adapted to a rural world feel themselves progressively rejected by world progress. What must be done?

At bottom it's the problem (perhaps a little less serious) of an African when he comes to Europe; this African feels that his whole tribal culture is now valueless, outmoded. He feels that all his values, the values of his morality and of his traditional social life no longer function. He feels that his pagan religion is not accepted, and so he feels himself rejected and he doesn't know what to do: he either locks himself into the values of his past or he feels in himself very strong tensions when he enters a new culture. Nevertheless, it is impossible to remain blindly glued to the past, because evolution is inevitable. That ancient rural society, that ancient parochial Christianity will be able to last as folklore. It is condemned to disappear, just as the ancient villages, so pretty, so idealized, are condemned to disappear. The villages may be reborn later as tourist attractions, but they disappear as traditional rural communities, and with them disappears a form of traditional Christianity. It is psychologically painful for a farmer to see that his village is disappearing, that it is dying, and that the young people are going off to the city. So also for the Christians of an old Christianity it is painful to notice that the young are moving toward other types of society, other forms of life. But there is precisely where Christian hope lies: "We have here no permanent society," as the Epistle to the Hebrews says. We cannot build here a permanent, definitive church but have to live as pilgrims, to live as people who wander, who can abandon their homes, the homes that they have built and that have belonged to their families for centuries. They can abandon those homes and walk toward other homes in the midst of the desert.

Don't you think that in order to obtain from the faithful that mobility, with peace and hope, we have to begin by changing considerably our psychology, customs, ideas, and styles in the announcement of the faith, in the pastoral ministry, in the testimony of religious life?

Of course, the clergy and witnesses of the gospel should be the first to inculcate hope and confidence. In a people in transition it is not fitting that they be the builders of anguish, of panic, but rather, those who can, under difficult circumstances, renew hope, confidence. We must show that the dangers are not so terrible. We must achieve, in essence, what Moses was doing in the midst of the people of Israel in the desert: to drive away the ghosts, the fears of the people who are walking through the desert and to show them the light that comes from the new land that is at the end of the road.

Even in his final greeting he appears timid, absorbed, slow, this curious, unfaltering renovator who is Joseph Comblin, or simply José, a "dangerous" man according to the Brazilian police, who shipped him to Belgium. But this European can now see Europe only as a way-stop before returning to his real country, which is that shifting and suffering land in the world that seeks to be new and free in Latin America.

A Conversation with
Enrique D. Dussel

Enrique Dussel was born in 1934, in Mendoza, Argentina. He earned a master-in-philosophy degree at the National University of Cuyo, in Mendoza, and a master-in-theology degree at the Catholic Institute in Paris. A Ph.D. at the University of Madrid and a doctorate in history at the Sorbonne followed. He also studied at the universities of Mainz and Münster in Germany. A layman, married, he has taught at the National University of Cuyo, the Latin American Pastoral Institute in Bogotá, at CIDOC in Cuernavaca, Mexico, at the Mexican American Cultural Center in San Antonio, Texas, at Lumen Vitae in Brussels, etc. He is president of the Commission on Studies of Church History in Latin America. Among his works are History and the Theology of Liberation *and* Ethics and the Theology of Liberation.

The conversation with Enrique D. Dussel was a unique experience in this whole series of interviews. From his first reply I felt myself swept away by a flow of rapid, measured, dense sentences. His mental agility and his aggressive dialectic spurred me on and forced me to react by improvising questions. I was asking, but I knew it was he who was leading the conversation.

When I shut off the tape recorder it seemed to me that I had managed to get an interview different from all the others, with astounding answers, but around this conviction were whirling certain suspicions.

I still do not know whether his discourse was dominated by the skill of his phrasing and the magic of his words, or by a critical daring half brilliant and half naïve, or by the depth of thought, or by the power of synthesis and

43

interdisciplinary relationships, or by a highly creative capacity. There is surely a little of all that. And in any case there is lightning and hailstones in the storm of his speech. His talk carried truths along like boulders, and from time to time it offered a disembodied vision of things.

In a simple room in the residence hall, Enrique and I face each other with the tape recorder open on the bed. With his thin frame, his sharp face and black goatee, with his flashing glance behind his glasses and his talk, brilliant, agile, incisive, and dialectical, I see in the man a sharpshooter of words. He speaks with ease and dialectical fluency from an astounding culture and interdisciplinary capacity. If he chooses, he is capable of creating a rhythm of challenging suspense and of daring, to lead his listeners to approach positions, theses, doctrines, whole philosophies that he has examined, attacked, destroyed, or reconstructed. I do not know whether he will in a simple conversation venture into this as I have seen him do before a vast audience. But I know intuitively the exciting risk of plunging into conversation with this man. I go in frankly, with the basic questions that I address to everyone. We shall see.

They Have Deified European Culture

For you, what are today the real dangers that threaten faith?

I think the greatest danger for faith is not being able to have it, and not "losing one's faith," as is frequently said. I even go so far as to think that it is very exceptional to lose one's faith. For example: I don't believe that Judas lost his faith but that it is quite possible that he never had any. So I insist on saying that the most serious question is not the "loss of faith" but situations in which faith is impossible. What is called "loss of faith" comes to be the disorganization of a certain system in which one thought one had faith, when there was only a "catechism knowledge" but not a true faith. And so one hasn't lost faith but, on the contrary, by disassembling the structure of what one thought faith was, one is in just the right situation to be able to have faith. Thus, in situations in which it is usual to confess that one is losing faith, one would have to probe into that experience of loss that is produced when the Christian faces a new situation to which habitual structures or doctrine cannot respond. This probing of established structures or doctrines is the result of the confrontation with a new situation that requires following an unaccustomed path to discover the "other," who is beyond doctrine and in whom one must believe.

Paradoxically, then, I believe that the greatest peril is to be in a situation where faith is impossible. And here is the gravest question: I believe that a great deal of European thought has, as it were, supernaturalized, deified, its own European situation—a "Christendom" that continues to be in some way valid—as unique and universal. It has then included the other "worlds" of the periphery (Latin America, the Arab world, black Africa, Asia) as constituent parts of what is already "known," and for that very reason, as conceptualized entities. As soon as I conceptualize the "other," I can no longer "believe" in the person because I make of that one a thing and I do not respect the person as someone who is beyond the doctrine that I know or possess. That is the gravest peril: to totalize oneself in a *knowing* that claims to be faith, with the consequent impossibility of believing in the poor person (the "other") who is beyond the system of organized doctrine. The loss of sanctification of the organized whole, the realization that what was thought to be universal and definitive was a historical moment, that loss of the security of the doctrine that seemed to be loss of faith is, precisely, the condition of possibility for beginning to believe. In this I see the gravest danger for faith: not having had faith.

We Need the Death of That God

Is it on that line that are located the current tensions and that stubborn struggle between what they call "defense of tradition" or "preservation of faith" and the new statements and efforts of renovation?

It's really a question of something more than renovation. One would above all have to consider what "tradition" is. I think that the identical permanence of a certain traditionalism is confused with true tradition. Tradition would be the perennial opening to the other, the belief in the voice of the poor. Tradition is to be able always to turn to what is new in history, where the spirit is revealed. In the confusion of "fixed traditionalism" with true tradition it has been possible to deify modern European culture, which has been made to pass as the only "tradition"—to such a degree that when one goes against the totality it seems that one is taking an antitraditional posture. And it's not so. On the contrary: to be "traditional" is to desanctify all that. The phrase of Nietzsche's—which was Hegel's and goes back even farther—"God is dead," and which according to Hegel is "the Good Friday of reason," can be interpreted two ways: it can be said that it is the negation of the Christian God; but this Nietzsche and Marx could not say because they did not know him. What Marx denies is Hegel's "god," the totality of European reason. And that is what Zarathustra announces, shouting: "God is dead." This poetic, inspired assertion of Nietzsche, which shows that his hands are covered "with the blood of god," is the effective assertion that Europe begins not to believe in its own divinity; that is, at bottom it is beginning to turn atheist about itself: Europe is no longer "god." The condition of the possibility of faith is the death of that "god." We Latin Americans were born within that deification, as colonies and as if reified within that "totality." To be able to be born as "others" and be respected as "others," we need the death of that god who, of course, is written lower-case.

But the One Who Is Dead Is the Poor Person

If in fact god is dead, there are groups in power who prop up the corpse.

Of course they preserve the corpse. That's why I frequently use the beautiful gospel words: "Let the dead bury the dead, but you follow me." In fact there are those who believe they can save the "God of Israel" by staying with the theistic affirmation of European totality, which is Christendom in which Christianity is confused with a culture. In not accepting the death of that god, they also do not accept the death of a system in which they've murdered the poor person, who was the Indian, the African sold into slavery, the Asian oppressed in the opium war. The poor person is the epiphany of God the creator. When the poor person of the Third World is murdered, God disappears. In not accepting the death of the European god, one does not accept the revelation of God the creator.

That's why in Europe the problem of the death of God is a theoretical, theological question, while in Latin America, in Asia and Africa, and equally for the future universality that is approaching—and in it European theology is reduced to a moment surpassed—the death of God is a problem of justice, at the international as well as at the personal level. God will reveal himself when the "other," liberated, can speak. His word is the historical and concrete "content" of the revelation of God. For God to reveal himself again, for him to rise from his apparent death, it is necessary to resurrect the real corpse, which is the colonial brother or sister. That is, the one who is dead is not God (now taking the phrase in another sense); the one who is dead is the Indian, the African, the Asian. When justice is done them, God will reveal himself. From that we deduce that for these peoples the problem of the death of God is a problem of liberating praxis, and, of course, this demands a new theology. But I think it is, moreover, the theology of the Old and New Testaments; it is a withdrawal from a theology supported, in the end, by the *ego cogito*. All European theology is an "I think what is given." And "what is given" is the European "totality," which is confused with the natural and the divine; it is a tautology. That tautological tautology has concealed the original sin of modernism, which is the control of the metropolis over the periphery. And in not accepting this politico-economic sin, its whole theology is floating in the air.

The Mediation of the Poor

You have announced (and denounced) a series of matters that we shall come back to. Speaking of the confusion of tradition with "traditionalism" you have suggested to me the problem of the formulation of faith that plays an important role today: some people confuse tradition with the traditionalism

that is a defense of a specific formulation of faith based on a concrete
culture. You have touched on that matter; say more about it.

In saying "formulation of faith" one would have to see if it is a
formulation of what people think is faith or of the real faith as an
attitude that allows God to be revealed. Faith is an "attitude" (*virtus*,
said Thomas) by assent, *ex voluntate*. It is an assent of reason toward
something that the will loves first of all; *ex voluntate* here means the
ethical, therefore the level of praxis. This means that there is assent to
something but starting from a previous practical commitment. That is,
that faith, with regard to its concrete historical content, as an "attitude," cannot be formulated, because it is precisely the situation that
cannot be formularized that is concretely described. Well now, if I
refer to *"what* I believe," I should just consider *"whom* I believe."
Whom I believe is God, the eschatological God who is not exhausted in
the historical. But that eschatological God always reveals himself—
and the question is a real one—in his historical economy; he always
talks through the mouth of the poor. Besides, he reveals to us—and
this would be the *constitutive* revelation—the interpretive rules of the
voice of the poor. This voice is the historical content of revelation. The
rules are forever, and they are very simple. I would almost say that
they are like operative-interpretive categories. These have been revealed to us pedagogically from the time of the prophets, and through
Jesus in a definitive way. Besides, Jesus makes *real* the rule that he
reveals; that is, on a metaphysical plane Jesus carries out by means
of Christian grace the salvation that he reveals. Revelation
gives us interpretive rules that are directed toward reason. These
rules must be accepted, assented to, because God reveals them
to me and because I believe in him. Now, they are going to
allow me to interpret the "content" of the *voice of the poor*, which
is the concrete way that those rules are used at every historical
moment.

So what does the "formulation" of faith mean? It's a complicated
matter. If by this I'm saying that I'm going to explicate or conceptualize those interpretive rules, yes. But what are those interpretive
rules? For example, Jesus says: "The law and the prophets." The law is
the organized whole. The law is the *flesh (basar, sarx);* the prophet, on
the other hand, announces what is coming, the *Spirit*. These two
categories are fulfilled in me, says Jesus in the transfiguration. He
reveals himself as the only category or rule from which there spread
out the other rules that are the essence of our faith. But these have
become unnecessarily complicated in history. And thus the historical
contents of Latin-Byzantine Christianity have somehow come to constitute the very rule of faith. That is, the revealed rules have become
unified with a historical content. One can, then, formulate faith, for
example the social doctrine of the church, which is like a rule, an
ecclesial doctrine with respect to the political. But in truth it was no

more than the use of certain rules with a very concrete European content, invalid for other spheres.

So again, what does it mean to formulate faith? I would say: it would be essentially to discern explicitly which are those revealed rules or categories, knowing that they do not include abstractly the anticipated content of history, because it is one rule of faith to be able to listen to that content. And this is a kind of methodical position of subjectivity, which always questions the organized system and which knows how to listen to the voice of the poor, which is the voice of Jesus. And so between the poor and Jesus there is not a "mystical" relation; it is a theological and real unity. God is beyond any historical situation; he speaks by means of the poor because he is beyond the organized system, out in the storm. And for that reason the appeal of the poor ("I have rights that you do not contemplate in your legal system") is the appeal of Jesus. To cast my lot with these poor people and to give them a juridical system, for example, in which they have rights, is precisely to make history advance toward the Parousia. Besides, it is an act of "atheism" with respect to the organized legal order: it is a confession of faith in divine otherness; it is to recognize a historical content in the word of God. To do this always is tradition. But what is paradoxical, then, is that this demands never accepting the same content, because the content gradually changes in history. That's why in my *Ethics* I say that there is paradox in the situation of an authentic virtue that consists of habitually doing the nonhabitual. Faith, hope, charity, Christian prudence, compassionate justice, all the really Christian liberating virtues, are virtues that make us disposed to do the nonhabitual. And to the extent to which we are disposed to do the habitual (the same thing) we have shut ourselves up in the mystification of virtue, which is always a vice. This would, of course, be a new ethic, an ethic of "creation," because it means to rush toward the new and to know how to cope with "the new." The real new is the poor person who is "beyond" the system.

Isn't there, for certain mentalities, a restatement of the formulation of the faith, of the creeds, a placing of orthodoxy in orthopraxy?

Yes, of course. One begins thus adequately to describe the creed; what I have said is exactly the creed; the creed gives us the rules. For example: when it says "and he died under Pontius Pilate" this is a rule; it is not only a historical event: it says that every just person dies under the empire and that the arms of the empire are the ones charged with murdering the person.

To Believe Is to Love the Poor and to Die to Free Them

This gives to the formula of faith a committed dynamism and frees it from being reduced to a conceptual formulation by means of which we are

*content to repeat the "formula." One thus understands better that "one
cannot believe with impunity."*

Yes. And in fact that is what was always said. And I return to
Thomas. If he says that faith is an assent *ex voluntate*, he means that it
is through love that one can believe; but if I always do "the same
thing," that is, "the old thing," then I no longer have "assent" but, as
he says very well in *Quaestiones Disputatae*, I have either *intellectus*
(that is, intuition), or science through demonstration, or memory, but
I am no longer open to "the new." Faith is open to the new because it is
assent. One may say: of course, what happens is that faith opens to
God, who is a mystery. But can one believe in God alone, without
mediation of the poor? Here, precisely, we are going to face the
question raised by a Bloch or a Moltmann. That is, when in eschatology a God is proposed to us as Parousia, but it is forgotten that hope is
staked very concretely in historical commitments, then in whom does
one believe, or whom does one believe? We can believe in the system
by believing that we believe in God. The only guarantee of believing
in God is to believe in his word by mediation of the poor. And "by
mediation of the poor" means to believe in the voice of the poor at a
crossroad inevitably historical, economic, political, cultural, real.
Now, what's remarkable is that in almost all the eschatological thinking of European theology one has forgotten the relation between the
hardened plan of the present system and the need for a historical
future liberation plan. The liberation plan is revealed to me by the
poor. I don't impose it. I learn it from them because they, from the
wind and the rain, tell me where they need a house to live in; because
if I make them a house like my house and to my measurements, the
only thing I'm doing is controlling them and putting them into my
controlling plan.

So there is a historical liberation plan, future but historical, the sign
of the eschatological plan of the kingdom; both are future, both question the current plan, which is the "idol." If between the current plan
and the eschatological, the liberation plan does not intervene,
the eschatological kingdom "goes up in smoke." Why? Because if I
love and believe in the eschatological plan and at the same time love
and believe in the prevailing, concrete, historical plan, without questioning it from a future historical plan, at bottom I affirm it as the
status quo. All the eschatology of Moltmann (and also of Bloch, in part)
leaps over the concrete "other" and forces the status quo. And so what
is really eschatological is denied, because one doesn't discover the
concrete sign that one should propose so that the nonbeliever may
believe in the future, for in fact one loves the present and does
nothing. One believes the eschatological future, but—I would
say—on a cloud. Only by doing something for that future does one
mean something by faith, hope, and charity. Charity is love for the
other as "other." It's not only the *mutual fraternal* love of those who are

involved in an *all*. Friendly love is not the same as charity. Charity, if it were friendly love (I love him, he loves me; "we" constitute a whole), would be mistaken. Charity is properly a "first loving" as St. John said. God loves us first by creating us. I love first the poor person if I love him or her as such. This is love for the other one as "other." What is remarkable is that by loving the poor person I am in "friendship" with God. Loving the poor person as a poor person and hoping for his or her historical liberation, that is how I can believe in the person's word. To love the poor as "other" and to hope for their liberation. What they have revealed to me as the concrete and historical content of Christian faith (to the extent that Christian faith is the rule of interpretation, and what they reveal to me comes from a horizon that is beyond my possibility of understanding, because it is their world and not mine), what they have given me in their voice in a way that can be understood only inadequately, I shall understand adequately only by casting my lot *in fact* with them.

At the end of the liberating process I shall understand their word, I shall comprehend it better, I shall interpret their word completely. To understand and interpret completely the word of God one must already be in the kingdom. And I approach the poor only by casting my lot on their concrete, practical liberation. That's why there is a theology that is like a tautology, we might almost say that it is an ideology, and that it does not consider what is beyond its horizon because it does not know how to listen to the voice of the poor, of the poor European but also the poor colonial, expressed as extreme poverty, in which an oligarchy is included, but essentially the oppressed classes, over there in Africa, in Asia, and in Latin America.

There are passages in St. John very close to all this.

I am trying to approach St. John. But more than that, I believe that in this all the evangelists coincide absolutely. The Synoptics say this in the parables, for example, the one about the Samaritan. John says it in a much more explicit, theological way. But Paul also says it. The clearest formulation of this is his conceptualization of the "face to face" *(prosopos pros prosopon)*, when he speaks to us of love and hope, and of the fact that faith is going to disappear, because in the "face to face" faith disappears; its meaning is fulfilled. But that "face to face," this category, is also in John, and in the Synoptics, because it is the great experience of Jesus and of Hebrew thought in general, from the beginning, from Abraham and Moses. So in this all are at one.

The Idol against Faith, Faith against the Idol

What tasks do you consider most urgent to announce faith authentically, to awaken it and promote it?

For me the most urgent and most important thing is how to make faith possible. We must go back to the prophets and to Jesus; they show us their explicit methodology. They were theologians, although we have "devalued" them. To make faith possible we must begin by overturning the idol. Like Moses, we must destroy the golden calf. The first thing we must do is preach the atheism of money and the bourgeois design for living. It has always surprised me to see on the dollar the phrase "In God We Trust": that god is the dollar itself. As long as the plan of a bourgeois world is the basis of existence, faith is impossible. The idol must be overturned. We must say that the system, such as it is, is not paradise, is not the kingdom. Here sin is in control. The sin of domination, which is the only sin, because all sins are summed up in the death of Abel: Cain killed Abel, and to kill Abel is to remain alone and to "systematize" sin. It is Adam's temptation: "You will be like gods." The one who kills a brother is "god," for that one is left alone, adoring self and not God: it is an act of idolatry, of self-adoration. This means that to be able to adore the one creator, God, to prostrate oneself and to wait for his word and to believe it—to have faith—one must begin by overthrowing the idol. What is needed is preaching—denunciation facing and opposing the system that is sin. It is clear that it is sin, for example, if one can read theologically the economic statistics and the political and cultural structures. One must be a disbeliever of that god and denounce the sin of idolatry so that the God in whom we must believe can be revealed in the face of the poor. Because what happens is that the poor endure the system and are the only ones who are not unjust, because they have not committed domination but suffer under it, like Job.

To make faith possible is to begin by prophetic criticism of idolatry, which is the system. And afterward to show how it is the poor who give historical content to the revelation of God. To cast our lot with them is what makes the word of God comprehensible. The discipleship of Jesus must appear in the face of the poor. That's why Jerusalem kills the prophets. That's why the idol is going to kill the prophets, the beast of the Apocalypse is going to kill the just. The *martyr* is a *witness* of Jesus and of the poor and gives testimony of a future order: in struggling against the idol that is the system, the martyr is seen to be a witness of the future—not only of the ultimate, eschatological plan, but also of the next liberation plan. That's why it becomes dangerous for the system. And the system, in the "logic of totality," has to kill that person. But at the same time, in the "logic of the other," is discovered the meaning of the person's death. All this happens in Jesus. I believe that theology has not yet raised the question of why Jesus had to die tortured and speared by soldiers of the empire. It is always the solders of the empire who kill the just person, the soldiers of every empire. That's why—I insist—it was from faith that Jesus died "under Pontius Pilate." This Pontius Pilate is not in the creed simply as a small historical datum but as the "structure" of the cause of the death of the just person: Pilate is the idol; Jesus dies under the claws of the idol.

The Political Force of Prophecy Is the Critical Function of Faith

According to what you say, evangelization always has enormous political consequences.

I distinguish carefully between party politics, which goes as far as the assumption of power, and the political function of prophecy, which is always out in the open with the poor. Even at the moment of criticizing "totality," the politician who is going to assume power always acts in function of a liberation plan that makes provision for a new political "whole" that the politician is going to have the responsibility of organizing. On the other hand, the prophet, and the church in its prophetic function, criticizes the idol not with the intention of assuming power but with the foresight that in time it is going to have to criticize also the new "whole" that is being organized, because the church is always on the side of the poor. "My kingdom is not of this world": it will never have arms or political systems or coercive legality or repression, because its function is to cast everything again toward the eschatological. The political function of prophecy is precisely criticism of the divinity of the moment. And this is always political even though it utters the most innocent criticism. In denying the divinity of Caesar, in declaring that the empire is an idol and in saying that they did not adore the god Caesar, the Christians were transformed into subversives of the empire and went to the circuses to die as martyrs. Today Christians are dying in Brazil, are tortured in Argentina and in other countries of Latin America; they die tortured like Jesus on the cross. Those Christians went to the circus accused as "atheists" and the atheism that they professed and preached was the denial of the god-idol, totality, the empire, the system; they did not believe in the Roman gods, they were subversives, and they were witnesses of the future, not only of the eschatological but of the historical ultimate "step forward." Their prophetic gesture had a political function; they were not, however, politicians.

What is specific and peculiar to Christian faith in the sociopolitical and revolutionary commitment? Its critical function?

Yes. Total criticism. I would say that Christian faith is the most critical principle that can be imagined. In that I see a sign of divine clairvoyance. Whereas any critical system is worn out by the criticism of what it has before it—Marx, for example, wears himself out in the criticism of the bourgeoisie or the capitalist system—the critical function of faith is not worn out in any possible system, and precisely for that reason it is a guarantee of the eschatological. The church is an institution whose function is prophetic, and the prophetic is the critical function that reveals the discrete parts of every "whole"; it removes the cloak of sanctity covering "everything," and casts it into the future. This function is perceived down through the whole history of the church. The sin of the church begins when it turns inward and sanctifies itself as "divine institution," as "totality."

Do you think, then, that for a revolutionary commitment to be an option inspired by Christian faith, it must unite two conditions: historical concreteness and, at the same time, the transcendence that gives it the capacity for total criticism?

Of course. And at the same time this is extremely useful politically. If it's true that at the moment of the overthrow of organized "totality" there is need for an enormous enthusiasm (and that's why certain political doctrines with a religious aura inspire people to throw themselves into the struggle against "totality"—which may at times demand even the sacrifice of one's life), nevertheless, at the moment when the "totality" has been overcome, the plan in the mind of the political liberator can be transformed into a fierce new totalitarian "totalization." On the other hand, those who are capable of a profound enthusiasm based on eschatological faith cannot only stake their lives on the overthrow of organized "totality," but faith will allow a sane realism in relativizing the plan that they have in their political grasp. This means that there are also safeguards against turning the new system into a totalitarian entity. It is clear that the commitment of a Christian to the taking of power is a possible option: it is not a commitment of the church as church, but it is the possible choice of any Christian, who would thus have in the political area even greater possibility of effectiveness for the better.

No Escape from Ambiguity

But this commitment is extremely difficult to achieve without loss of faith. In the present outlook for the political and revolutionary dynamism of faith in Latin America, do you see ambiguities or falsifications of faith springing up, or situations in which faith is "used" or subverted into ideology?

Yes. Some have deified the "whole" in which they find themselves tranquilly satisfied because they enjoy it. They have identified the church with "western Christian civilization"; they are getting along well in so-called Christendom, and they say, "All is going well, why change?" Here there is an ambiguity, with falsification and utilization of faith, which has become ideologized. Yet others, seeing that they have to overcome this and make a new order, deify the future plan.

That's why certain Christians, of the old Catholic Action, even with great faith—I would say, rather, with a great, practically absolute, religious attitude—deify the next plan, and then practically lose eschatological faith. They keep this faith only in the plan made mystically feasible and, for example, they adopt Marxism or other positions. That is, they absolutize now the future historical plan. It's another ambiguity. There are still others who do not support the current situation but neither can they see clearly how to commit themselves politically and they propose a faith in God that is somewhat angelic eschatologically. They speak of love but not concretely. They speak of a love for fellow humans in the abstract and of the kingdom of heaven in the abstract—I would say "after Moltmann"—and then, criticizing the ambiguity of the political commitment of other Christians, at bottom they come to coincide with the first mentioned and with their ambiguity, because they affirm and reinforce the status quo.

All this means that there is no escape, that any of the three positions that can be taken has its ambiguity and its equivocation. But they must be overcome. And what is certain is that the saints, the prophets, and Jesus decidedly opted for an attitude that confronted them with the institution and confronted them with political perils: and so they were murdered, tortured, eliminated, because they did not preach an eschatological kingdom in such an ethereal way that it would declare them innocent before the system; they did not support the prevailing situation or the system. That's why they suffered poverty. This poverty is not the poverty of the poor as seen from without (the tyrant near the road in the parable of the Samaritan) but the availability of someone who "in-the-whole" raises questions about the whole. The person who has given up the values of the whole can move to the liberation of the poor. That availability does not consist of not having any individual goods and afterward having great collective goods within the system (this is a still better organized wealth). Poverty is availability to serve the "other one." That is the *anawim. Anawim* is the "flesh" that opens. The perfect poverty was that of the Virgin Mary. She says, "Let thy will be done in me." When she said this she opened herself to the word of God. She believed in the "other one" and on believing in the other one she opened herself and on opening herself she became pregnant, she produced the new, which was the son. This son of hers, brought up in the pedagogy of liberation, in the end will have to die on the cross. Mary will go to the cross with her son, the fruit of her womb.

The Virgin Must Be a Sign of Liberation

What role is assigned to the Virgin in the theology of liberation?
I'll answer this best by saying what place she has in my reflections. I

was in Nazareth for two years with Gauthier. When I think of Mary I think of the poor, ordinary, common village woman. I think how the Virgin of Nazareth lived with her son and taught him the Old Testament with her own interpretation: "He made the rich come down from their thrones and he put the poor up high." The Virgin, on subverting (*sub-vertere*), on putting down what was on high, is really a teacher of "subversion." The Virgin, who was the perfect teacher, had to be next to the cross of her son; this means that a perfect mother runs the risk that her son will die tortured and murdered by the arms of the empire. Besides, another question appears here—speaking of the Virgin: I think, for example, that on the question of liberation the first thing to be considered is the man-woman relationship: it's the liberation of the woman. Then parents-children: this is pedagogical liberation. (The Virgin was wife, mother, and teacher.) Afterward, brother-sister: this is political liberation. But they're all very united. And, by the way, in Latin America today there's much talk of the problem of woman's liberation and how this liberation of woman (including the religious woman) comes to play a role in the pedagogical liberation of the son who must be educated to be a servant and not a master (which the mother never was, because she was the slave of her man), and in that way, the son comes to be the equal of his father, that is, his brother, not to control him but to serve him. There is a correlation here between the great themes, I believe, of our theology of liberation, which is being organized. The Virgin, the Virgin of Guadalupe, for example, also has the figure of a mother of a new country; Hidalgo in Mexico began the popular revolution in the nineteenth century ("the land for the person who works it") with the banner of the Virgin of Guadalupe. The Virgin Mother is equally a political sign of liberation in Latin America . . . or ought to be one.

Some see it like this for the present. But bourgeois Catholicism and also popular Catholicism, what images of the Virgin do they have? How is the Magnificat still sung?

It is even sung at times at "campaign masses," attended by armed soldiers in well-organized squadrons. They sing, "He brought the rich down from their thrones," and they're quite happy. They certainly don't believe those words. They hear them as something they already know. They don't ask for interpretations. It's not a poor person who is speaking through them. It's a memorized doctrine, internalized in the system, made inoperative. They already have the kingdom. The future kingdom isn't possible. We're already in hell. Because hell is the false claim of a total anticipation of the kingdom; through "I am God" it is the serpent that is tempting Adam. . . .

Two Violences: The Dominating and the Liberating

When we were speaking of the critical function of faith in political commitment, you referred to the prophets and to Jesus: they had to die and they are going to die. But they didn't kill. How do you view the relation between faith in revolutionary commitment and bloody violence?

As we keep advancing we see more and more types of violence. There used to be talk of violating a girl, which involves the sixth commandment, as is seen in moral theologies. But, of course, you have to go farther back. Violence comes from life, from force *(vir, vis)*. Violence, like the passions, is ambivalent; it depends on what it's used for. If I use violence so that my son won't cut off his little sister's ear and I snatch the knife from him violently, that violence is good, just, and nobody can say anything. St. Bernard preached the Crusades to recover the Holy Sepulcher. And he's a saint!

But today we criticize him.

Well, I want to indicate how, within tradition, that was possible, even canonizable.

More in traditionalism than in tradition, according to your own concept of "tradition."

I agree. But there were even more interesting examples. Because, in fact, the example of the Crusades was that of an experiment in domination, in conquest. The conquest of the infidels was preached. But there's another type more in the line of the first example, and it's our struggle for independence from Spain. Of course, Spain probably doesn't see it that way, but in Latin American countries, a San Martín or a Bolívar struggles for independence. That's why there are two kinds of violence: "dominating" violence and the violence that I would call "defensive" or "liberating." "Dominating" violence is a violence that kills or enslaves. We might call it a dialectical violence. Whereas the defense of the poor, which is not my defense but the defense of the third person, is the right of the poor and not only of the one who takes up arms. To defend the poor is to defend them in their rights. In this case it's not only possible, it's obligatory. Then we have to see if it's appropriate to use one or another *means*, but this appropriateness is not now a question of principle, either moral or ethical, and even less of faith. To defend the poor is a duty. And to defend the weak, the child, is a duty. And this is just the situation of many of our peoples.

But there's more, something that deceives and confuses: the state of domination in an organized "whole" is one of violence, real but "implicit." As long as the dominated accept that violence, it's not exercised "explicitly." But on the day when the dominated become conscious that they are "other" than the system and that there could be a system that was just, that's when they rise up and stand. And when they stand up and try to march, then violence shows its teeth or its fists and "implicit" violence turns into "repression." That repression has its origin in the love that the enslaved or dominated had of being free. That is, that love is at the bottom of the process. Repressive violence is the fruit of *sin*; defensive violence is an act of justice based on love and it's liberating to the extent that it is aimed at the new whole and that, in itself, it does not propose the death of the dominator. That can happen, but it's not proposed. Whereas repressive domination proposes the death of the liberator and that's why we have martyrs and the death of Jesus. This means that one violence proposes the death of the witness, while the other wants the liberation of the poor. The liberator also wants to convert the dominator. That's why the blood of Jesus falls on the Romans, not to kill them but to save them. So this defense, which I would call liberating, is just, and it is a duty.

Nevertheless, there are vocations. Those who believe themselves called to a military vocation cannot elude this call. The church as such—because it does not propose to take over power, because as the prophet bears witness to the kingdom but cannot fall into the equivocalness of taking power or into the equivocalness of the use of arms— the church dies but does not kill. It would be necessary to make a distinction between the "hero" of the future homeland and the "prophet" of that future homeland and of eschatology. The church has, as a historical function, to be always the "prophet" of the future homeland and never the "hero" of the future homeland. That's why it has no armies. And that's why it hasn't today, praised be God, pontifical states. And if it had them at one time it was because Christendom confused things, and at that time it was possible to be a soldier but very hard to be a prophet. A St. Louis, with his weapon in his hand and yet a saint, is a completely ambiguous sign; if you don't agree, ask the Arabs and the eastern Christians. But, besides, he was a conqueror and not a liberator, a situation doubly ambiguous.

Which doesn't prevent Christians from taking up arms.

They may be heroes of the future homeland and politicians, but they are not, as such, representatives or signs of the church. The unequivocal institutional ecclesial sign is the kingdom. Jesus could have defended himself and did not choose to do so, because at that moment he would have fallen into a near totalization. Because those who take up arms today inevitably fall into the ambiguity of law that, even though it is just for the poor of today, it is repressive for the poor of the future. Every positive law—and there is no other, because the natural law is a limit that is in the foundation—every positive law always includes a measure of injustice. This is the question: those who struggle against someone, in a certain way, are not only conquering the dominator but at that very moment are already imposing themselves, today, on a possible dominated one. This does not mean that a Christian (even a priest or a bishop) through civic vocation cannot take up arms. On the contrary. Nonviolence is a Hindu, not a Christian, doctrine. So it's a question of distinguishing: the prophetic violence of the church and the violence (even armed) of the politician; the first, the church is obliged to exercise; and for the second, it is wise to know its suitability, but there is no opposition to it because of theological or biblical principle or "according to tradition."

Much More Than a Political Theology

Let's talk about Latin American theology. How was it born? How is it in relation to European theology?

I think Latin American theology appeared when we began to discover the conditionings that I would call political in European theology. We suddenly noticed that there was a thinking in European theology that had not kept its presuppositions in mind and, for that very reason, had not been able to include the area from where that conditioning was being generated. Very important in this was the work of Methol Ferré, a Uruguayan layman, who wrote Cardinal Suenens a critical article from Latin America in which he showed that on the basis of some statements by Suenens there was "one politics"; he raised the question of "two politics; two theologies."

In Europe there is almost always a double conditioning that takes place when theology is made: if it is a theology practiced by a certain social stratum of university professor, that theology implies an economic-political conditioning; when it is made from a European perspective, it assumes that the European is the only and ultimate horizon. So there are cultural and economic-political conditionings: one is thinking from the metropolis and including the periphery as an entity, as a thing; and this is being done from a certain social level or stratum or class. That's why, for example, when a "political theology" (which means the discovery of the critical function—I would even say the liberating function—of theology) is practiced—as in the "political theology" of Metz—on the national plane and it does not see that there are nations and groups of nations in the world in quite different situations, that some nations from the North Atlantic dominate nations in the south, it is reducing itself, it is in fact falling into a particularism that leads to falsification. It's not the same to think on a national scale and on an international scale. If the critical-liberating function is limited to the national field, the whole question of colonialism that has dominated the world for five centuries, that whole great problem of human domination over other humans, of nations over nations, of cultures over cultures, passes unnoticed into a theology that falls into a narrowing of the horizon and of the content of its theological reflection: it falls into a particularism with pretensions of universality. And what is serious is that it passes for the universality of Catholic theology. This is a mystification and theological domination, because the others (who are "others" and not parts of the "whole") come to be thought of from a situation that is not their real one; they come to be theologically alienated. They were already alienated religiously by a faulty evangelization imposed on them by foreign cultural molds, and now theology comes to think of and justify that alienation as something revealed.

On the other hand, if it is in the international field that the great sins are being committed, we're going to be able to rethink all the themes and questions of theology, but in its universal content and range, from the universal consideration of the content of sin and, therefore, in the universal range that the redemption of Christ has in our epoch. This in regard to the political conditioning of European theology. I could also speak of the erotic conditioning, which is no longer a conditioning of the "political theology" of Metz but of theology in general. In general, Catholic theology has always been done from the celibate point of view, by celibate males. As when Descartes says, "I think," it's always a celibate male who is thinking: the problem remains of seeing what will happen when a woman says, "I think." Besides, theology has always been thought out from the viewpoint of father to son. That is, one must now rethink a whole theology from the viewpoint of the poor, of the woman and the disciple, of the young man, of the son who suffers under a dominating pedagogy. This indicates that the "theology of liberation" is much more than a "political theology," because it implies the liberation of the woman, the son, and the brother. "I have done justice to the widow, the orphan, and the poor," say the prophets.

Spree Is Not Festival

What can Latin American theology contribute to the rest of theology?

From the experience that I am having with the dialogue, the contribution can be enormous. It can, above all, warn theology that the theological method is not a method that ponders what is already given as knowledge; it's not a "tautological" method but a method that we can call "analectic," that is, a method that asks *how* to be able to listen to the voice of the "others" who, at bottom, are the poor. The European must get to the point of knowing *how* to listen to the voice of the Latin American, the African, the Asian, and also the voice of the European poor, but in relation to the poor of the other worlds, for one must be willing to scan the universal horizon, and the liberation of oppressed Europeans will not be attained except by including them in the liberation of the oppressed of the Third World. We have had to listen for centuries and centuries to European theology (and so we can talk its language). European theologians are going to have to listen to the theologians of the poor countries, first, because then they are going to listen to the thoughts of their own poor. What we say of the liberation of the poor peoples must also be said about the liberation of the poor in Europe. And you have a Girardi, a González Ruiz; they have solved some of these problems, and they haven't done it from a Latin American, African, or Asian perspective; they've done it from a European perspective. But that same thinking on a universal horizon is going to acquire much greater clarity. And it will be possible to think also of the responsibility that the oppressed of Europe have in the oppression of the world's poor, because the oppressed of Europe also have their share of domination. And this also must be discovered, because otherwise even the oppressed of Europe, struggling for freedom, in doing so will dominate the poor on the periphery. The European theologian who can't see this point transforms national liberation into international alienation of the oppressed.

An example at the philosophical and theological level: in Europe (and in North America) they are seeking a way out of the trap of modernity, a way out of pragmatic totality, and they fall into the stalemate of the *homo ludens* (Marcuse): in *play* it is said that humanity achieves gratuitousness. For us, beyond the pragmatic totality that we endure is the gratuitousness of liberation; in the liberation of the poor and oppressed, Christian love finds gratuitousness in casting its lot for the other one, for the poor one: the adventure of staking one's life gratuitously for the liberation of the poor is the true image of the "festival" of the kingdom (the Passover of the passage through the desert of liberation toward the Promised Land) and approaches it, whereas the other play of *homo ludens* degenerates into wasting time together, or having to go on exploiting the poor to be able to go on playing, "amusing ourselves." The "spree" is not the "festival."

Cox's "festival" was probably Marcusian. Perhaps some European theology is in many ways closer to the North American than to the Latin American.

Kant says that immortality is necessary for happiness and virtue to coincide. And as he thought himself virtuous, this means that he was unhappy. And of course one must die to the totality of an organized whole in which the only possible existence is a tautological and bored existence, in order to cast one's lot into the adventure of the life that comes after the death of the totality. This adventure is risky, but joyful, and this joy is just what happiness is. In fact, Kant saw clearly that one must die, but he didn't understand that it was not a question

of biological life but of "totality." In essence, current European thinking is Kantian: it postpones happiness until afterward, until after the
work week, and then goes off to the country (and hence the civilization
du loisir); it means that in essence *life* comes after *this* life. And what
happens is that this life is not lived as an adventure. On the contrary,
one ought to risk oneself in the adventure of the liberation of the
"other." That's where there is a new anthropology and where the
culture of poverty can bring a new vision of humanity, where humans
live much more deeply as humans and show much more what they
are. To give a homespun example, I would say that Europeans at
times, or northerners, are required to eat less, and they give to this
much less energy and enthusiasm than does the person who doesn't
eat and wants to eat something. It's like a fat person who has to eat less
and go on a diet, but has no real enthusiasm for it. On the other hand, a
poor starving person who isn't eating struggles to eat. In this process it
is quite possible that the one who has the force is the poor one—the
force of resurrection, not the force of oppression.

To Evangelize, Become a Disciple of the People

*You have spoken about evangelization in Latin America with historical
perspicacity, with critical acuteness. You have pointed to the root of a
terrible falsification in evangelization. Is evangelization today also cor-
rupted by radical falsifications?*

Yes, of course. I've said that evangelization is also an analectic
service. At bottom, to evangelize is to give to those who are going to be
evangelized the critical ferment that will allow them to liberate themselves. In *content* it teaches them nothing, but it teaches them to
discover what they already are. First I have to listen to their revelation;
I have to put myself in the service, the discipleship, of the people that I
am going to evangelize, and only what they give me is what I have to
give back to them as prophetic criticism—break down their
alienation—in order to free them. Faith will enable them to deidolize
the ideological totality in which they find themselves alienated, and it
will launch them ahead again. In practice, I am not going to teach them
a content, a doctrine. I am going to teach them the operative-
interpretive revealed guideline. But because it is a guideline that God
has revealed to us to know how to interpret what he says to us, on
returning it to them now, judged by those guidelines, I return to them
what he said to me not as he provoked it in me but as a doubly
provocative situation. I provoke them to enter into the conversation
and relaunch the process. Then it is an "analectic" movement, in the
sense that the *"logos* comes from beyond-my-world." My *doctrine* is
not valid; what is valid are the principles that allow them to go beyond
themselves. At bottom, I teach them to listen also to the poor, although
they are poor. The poor liberate themselves by liberating other poor

persons. The rich convert themselves by risking themselves for the liberation of the poor. That is faith: to teach how to enter into commitment to the liberation of the "other."

It would be an error and a sin to believe that we are helping the Latin American church by sending missionaries who would impose a false evangelization. Would you raise doubts about European missionaries continuing to go to Latin America, or would you oppose only their going indiscriminately and with false attitudes?

I believe that it is extremely positive that missionaries be sent. To such an extent that I judge it very necessary that we come to Europe to "missionize" Europe. But for what? To learn and to teach. The Spaniard who goes in an attitude of apprenticeship, of service, and not exclusively of teaching, teaches those who are there that he or she does not know what the "others" are. Because those who are there believe they know what the poor person is, and that's a lie; they don't know. It is first necessary to have a true disciple's attitude on the part of the one who goes, to want to learn what a given people are. That is the best testimony for the others who are doing mission, so that they do not forget that they always have to listen. With this attitude one can do a great work. But afterward they can contribute their Spanish experience, although it's not that they are going to teach it from the beginning, but that, listening to those poor people and from their experience, they can enormously enrich the critical process of liberating faith. So, with a warning that one is not going to teach "content" but to give critical guidelines to an *existent* content that has to be learned first, we can say that it is very positive to go to other lands: for the missionaries because they learn, for the people because the missionaries serve them in their liberation, for the missionaries' native colleagues in mission because they are taught to learn. But afterward, if missionaries return to their own countries, they have a magnificent basis for enriching their own people. Every Christian community should have—and it was always like that in the church—people to send to other worlds to be missionaries, because it is to repeat a little the experience of Abraham in understanding himself as "foreign." "Foreignness" is the condition that makes faith possible, because it indicates the detotalized position, freed of cultural bias and alienating ideologies, and allows us to hear the voice of the poor, the historical voice of God. All this is to take very seriously the description of the "last judgment" (absolute judgment of history) of Matthew 25.

Audacious in his criticism and audacious in his proposals, Enrique D. Dussel speaks with such decisiveness and rapidity, makes such extraordinary reflections and associations, that one feels involved in his feverish undoing and redoing, and one asks for time to put oneself at a distance and to reflect.

A Conversation with Segundo Galilea

Born in Santiago de Chile in 1928, Segundo Galilea was ordained a priest in 1956. He became a pastor in his native city and was director of the Chilean Journal Pastoral Popular. *From 1962 his life has been devoted to works of pastoral renewal in Latin America by means of courses and publications. He taught at CIDOC in Cuernavaca, Mexico, and was director of the Latin American Pastoral Institute of the Latin American Episcopal Council (CELAM) in Quito, Ecuador. He has since been a professor in the same institute, in Medellín, Colombia. He has published* Hacia una pastoral vernácula, *Toward a Vernacular Pastoral Approach;* Para una pastoral latinoamericana, *For a Latin American Pastoral Approach;* Evangelización en América latina, *Evangelization in Latin America;* Contemplación y apostolado, *Contemplation and Apostolate;* Espiritualidad de la liberación, *Spirituality of Liberation.*

I remember that we were struck by a punishing, pitiless sun on that afternoon. With a straw hat and in shirtsleeves (a very rural shirt, blue and without pockets), Segundo Galilea looked like a sunburned peasant, an Indian, from the aquiline profile of his face.

I must confess that I admired Segundo for his simplicity and for his sharp clarity of thought about the burning problems of faith, pastoral work, and the church. In writings of his that I had recently read, I found for my questions discerning answers anointed with the gospel.

Although he had warned me that he had little time for talk, and that he feared he would not answer me with the composure and subtlety that he would have wished, I approached him with great hopes of listening to meaningful answers.

I knew that the rhythm of our conversation would be deliberate. I knew

63

*that the words would be staked out with silences and puffs of smoke from
Segundo's pipe. This man, to talk, thinks a lot while he quickly uses up his
pipe stuffed with fragrant tobacco; and he speaks frank, simple, transpa-
rent words, pronounced slowly in a low voice.*

Lack of Evangelization and Solidity

*Give me your analysis of the crises and weaknesses of faith in the churches
of Latin America today.*

I believe that the dangers and the changes that faith confronts in
Latin America, the crises, occur also, with variable shades, in western
countries. But in our case the problems are sharper and more adolescent. In general, through lack of evangelization and of the solid back-
ing of a Christian tradition, both the common people and the most
educated classes are less prepared for the crises of faith.

It seems to me that the current crisis facing Latin American faith is a
general one. In the masses I see the crisis of a faith that was tied to a
traditional religion, to a popular Catholicism that, because of politicization, industrialization, or urban immigration, is in a state of crisis
and many will not have resources to overcome it, unless the popular
pastoral programs change profoundly. What I say should not be interpreted as a process of secularization or massive popular de-
Christianization. No. I believe that this occurs in certain ideological
groups, but that the Latin American world of the laborer and farmer,
although removed from and often allergic to many aspects of the
church, remains very religious and very Christian. It's only that this
Catholicism is precarious, as they say now, and the changes I refer to
are revealing its ambiguity critically.

In the more elite groups, consciousness of social changes and of the
revolution is so absorbing that, especially among the young, they
wonder what good faith does in revolution, in social changes, what
good do Christianity and the church do; and if they get no answer,
they are ready to abandon faith or to make it incidental. Here there is a
great prospect for de-Christianization.

Another element of crisis, in the most cultured classes, is a certain
anemia of spirituality. I believe this is something extremely serious.
Latin American Catholic spirituality was very traditional up to fifteen
or twenty years ago. Even among the elite. And now, as a result of
Latin American forms of secularization, of social change, and also of
church reforms, the traditional forms of spirituality and of expression
of faith have been quickly abandoned and no one has known how to
create anything new. Frequently a so-called liberty and secularization
conceal a real inability to pray, to live the faith, and to confess the
faith. One sees it in the most cultivated circles. There is a kind of
anemia of faith, because of anomie and an inability to seek new forms.

One knows very well what one must not do, but a new expression of faith has not been created. This is often tied in with the new experiences mentioned above.

Another element of crisis for the faith in certain groups—I think of the university groups—is the influence of Marxism. Of a Marxism badly digested, of a Marxism that becomes reductionist and that is not well considered, and that goes beyond the elements useful for criticizing capitalism. I mean the following: many young people, college people, students, have in various degrees taken to a Marxist analysis of society. I don't want to go into the problem of whether it is possible to separate the method of Marxist analysis from its philosophy and its political ethics. The facts speak of the difficulty of introducing this dichotomy. Because on adopting this tool of analysis, many students have also adopted other philosophic, religious elements, and have finally found themselves in the dilemma of practically having to choose between "two religions." That tool has sucked them in. For a long time Marxism was taboo in all Christian circles, but now certain leftist youths have discovered it and become fascinated. They haven't digested it critically and this has led them into a crisis. I don't know if it will be a problem peculiar to this generation (which is the first to have this type of contact with Marxism) or if the problem is going to continue. My impression is that the temptation of Marxist Christianity is typical of this first period of contact, and that coming generations will have a better knowledge of the limits of Marxism and will discover forms of Christian life more in keeping with its challenges.

What are the greatest challenges confronting the believer today?

The believer today faces the challenge of a "new experience" of faith, within a new situation; and the Christian is left quite lacking in experience as well as in theology. Hence the ambiguities. It's about a new way of living the faith. In this sense, the faith that confronts social changes and revolution is the faith that confronts a qualitatively new analysis of reality (the perspective of liberation); within this framework and itinerary the political dimension of faith must be emphasized as one of the crucial adventures of Latin American believers. Likewise, another challenge is in trying to recover for faith "its works," with which faith becomes "praxis." With this the faith of believers begins to acquire new categories to which they were not accustomed: history, the oppressed neighbor *(especially!)*, concrete commitment, the future, etc.

To Reformulate Faith and to Recover Its Critical Power

What tasks do you consider most urgent today for an authentic pastoral program of faith, for a true evangelization?

Evangelization has two great challenges at this time in Latin America. The first challenge is the problem of the repatriation or reformulation of faith in a society in rapid change that is taking on revolutionary consciousness. Preaching, catechizing, and Christian formulation in general were not prepared for this. And there is a sudden appearance of this challenge to evangelization and to the pastoral program of faith: to manage to reformulate faith in such a way that it will survive in the atmosphere of social change, of new culture and revolution, even in Marxist atmospheres; to achieve not only its survival but even to be a valid interlocutor that supplies something of its own and that means something in this situation. We must recover the "subversive" element in faith, its critical dimension (in all senses and at all levels), its radical originality as critique of historical models and systems, its incentive toward historical verification, its capacity for turning the believer into an "unsettled one," a wanderer, at the same time that the believer is committed to the present task. It's also a question of restoring to faith its unifying sense of history and of salvific action. Let faith be the "destructive" element of all the dualisms (ahistoricism, disincarnation, etc.) that endanger the message and its historical efficacy.

I see the second challenge at the level of the Catholicism of the people. The question is how to recover the Christian values that are at the heart of the Catholicism of the people wrapped up in ambiguous attitudes, feelings, customs, and rituals. How to purify everything Christian so that it will come to be a liberating force authentically enrolled in the whole process of liberation. A serious challenge, because of the difficulty of the task and because of its importance for the Latin American church, given the great proportion of Christians to be found in this popular Catholicism.

How do you view this task of the pastoral program of faith in the Catholicism of the common people?

For me it can be synthesized like this: the Catholicism of the people has an interpretation of Christianity that is predominantly religious or "sacral." To be a Christian is to perform sacred things and acts. The problem is in giving it, through evangelization, through the criticism of the evangelical faith, a "nonsacral" interpretation of the message of the gospel. That is, to secularize the "sacralized" religious vision of popular Catholicism. What I mean is that it must be made clear that Catholicism does not consist only in relations with rituals, saints, and God but it includes and requires the proper relations with work, with all human duties, and that it is authentically Christian and religious to commit oneself to others, to better the human and social conditions of a neighborhood, etc. For this is part of the message of the gospel. It's important also to point out, as tasks of purification, the pastoral activities through which one gets to discover the real "age of faith" of the people, and to start there: a "re-creative" criticism of the current pastoral activity, to emphasize the task of making the people grow in their faith. Any evangelization of the "faith of the people" will have gradually to unblock it and purify it, to make it free and liberative of others. In this sense the process of liberation in Latin America is also applicable to the Catholicism of the people and it can make of it not a burden but a dynamic principle in this process.

"I've told you I have very little time." Too little time for the many interesting things that this man can tell us. But that is the way it has to be. The conversation with a theologian of the people, who has many responsibilities, who practices theology in shirtsleeves and in free moments, must be as short as this.

A Conversation with Giulio Girardi

Born in Cairo in 1928, Giulio Girardi entered the Salesian Society of Saint John Bosco in 1942 and was ordained a priest in Turin in 1955. He earned his Ph.D. at the Salesian University of Turin in 1950 and then studied theology in Rome at the Gregorian University (1951–53) and in Turin at the Salesian University (1953–55). From 1958 to 1969 he was professor of philosophy in the Salesian University in Rome, from 1969 to 1973 in the Institute of Science and Theology of Religions of the Catholic Institute in Paris, and from 1969 to 1974 at the International Institute Lumen Vitae of Brussels. From these three centers he was dismissed successively for "doctrinal reasons," while continuing to give (since 1969) a course in philosophic anthropology in the School of Philosophy of the Catholic Institute in Paris. In 1977 he was suspended a divinis *by the Holy See and expelled from the Salesian Order. Among his works is* Marxism and Christianity: Dialogue, Revolution, and Atheism.

Until 1967 Guilio Girardi wrote on "Metaphysics of the Exemplary Cause in Saint Thomas," "Phenomenology of Judgment and Absoluteness of Truth," "Description of Essences and Ontology." . . . Since 1968 he writes on "Marxism and Christianity: Dialogue, Revolution, and Atheism," "Christian Love and Revolutionary Violence," "Christianity, Human Liberation, and Class Struggle." . . . This contrast suggests a certain jump. ("I have seen myself obliged to change my intellectual projections, opening them to unsuspected horizons.")

At this hour, who is unaware of the steps in the journey of Girardi? His thought, his options, the conflict with the church institutions, the marginalization. ("I have been the object of three successive expulsions on the part of university centers where I used to teach: in 1969, from the Salesian University in Rome; in 1973, from the Catholic Institute in Paris; in 1975, from the International Institute Lumen Vitae, affiliated with the University of Louvain.") His numerous books and countless articles, his lectures, pronouncements, and papers are there, within anyone's reach, in several languages. And there is the last ecclesiastical obstacle to his journey: the suspension a divinis and the expulsion from the Salesian Order, which struck Girardi in 1977.

He is usually available, as he was for me that sunny March morning in Paris, when we ate together in a self-service restaurant and I told him at the end of the meal that I wanted to interview him, that I would not leave without taping a conversation with him. He did not refuse. He tightened his agenda for the afternoon.

I had arrived twenty minutes before noon at the enormous building on Avenue Reille that is headquarters for courses and conferences with scholarship holders from the Third World. Girardi was still in class. From outside, sitting in the corridor, I could hear a girl with a soft Latin American voice: "What is specifically Christian in the revolution? Mustn't it be criticism of the revolution itself?" And Girardi, in French: "No, no. Criticism of the revolution belongs to every authentic revolutionary. It can't belong exclusively to the church." I did not know then that that was a preview of our own dialogue.

It is twelve o'clock. The class has ended and I go into a great auditorium where black, oriental, and Latin American hands are removing the simultaneous-translation headphones. In the back, at the teacher's desk, Girardi is gathering up books. His smile and his glance are, as always, cordial and a little timid. "We'll eat together," and he shows me two tickets. He leads me to the basement, to the end of a long line of young people of different races who are entering a gigantic and already filled dining room. After juggling trays and briefcases, we eat quickly, harassed by those who surround us and stare at us until we get up, which is what they are waiting for so that they can sit down to eat, and we go up again to an empty classroom. We are alone now, the professor and I, with the tape recorder between us. Giulio speaks a faultless Spanish, precise and filled with nuances.

Faith, a Place of Alienation or Liberation?

The way the church is living through the changes in the present world, what do you think are now the gravest threats or dangers for faith?

The way of identifying the threats to faith depends a lot on the position in which one finds oneself. Contradictory answers can be given, depending on the way in which each one conceives of Christianity, of faith. Depending on how one conceives it, one will make a very different analysis of the situation and of the contemporary crisis.

As far as I can see, the gravest dangers for the church and for Christian faith today are those of rejecting the demands of secularization and of revolution.

Explain yourself.

Today there is a whole movement that doesn't deal purely with ideas but is embodied in the structures of today's society and penetrates the contemporary mentality. It is the secularization movement, in the face of which the church can take either an attitude of defense or an open attitude of renovation. To the extent that it takes an attitude of defense and that, therefore, it prolongs its Constantinian form, although with new forms, at times more hidden, there is prolonged in the modern world the contradiction between the human being and God, between human fulfillment and faith, and, therefore, faith continues to be lived and fulfilled as a place of alienation. This danger is evident in all the sectors of secular life: in particular, facing the human sciences, where it is very clearly seen that the church, the dominant religious mentality, is afraid of confrontation with psychoanalysis, with the sociology of religion, with the sociology of culture, with the economic analysis of society, with a whole series of new demands that cannot be accepted without questioning a certain type of Christianity and without therefore seeking an alternative that will accept as an essential dimension the recognition of the autonomous value of the secular.

Another sector in which this confrontation occurs is the political, where there is once again the same danger that the church will take itself as the measure, as the criterion of the value of the various societies, of the various political proposals, and that it will not have the courage to accept the demands of an objective analysis of society. Here also, to the extent that the church goes on thinking that it has its own solutions, which it sees as based on the Scriptures and on tradition, to that extent it will go on rejecting the contributions of a scientific analysis, the contributions of the political experiments of the militants, and it will therefore go on being a place of conservation and therefore of alienation.

So, as a first danger, I see this rejection of the great historic trend which is secularization. And on the other hand, although it is fundamental to achieve this transformation of Christianity, that is not enough. Because the secularization movement remains quite ambiguous, remains open to a whole series of secular values that may be contradictory and among which one must choose. A purely passive attitude in the face of the secularization movement could lead the church (it seems to me that it is often in fact leading it) to a situation of new conformity, to a situation of opening up that is not critical enough. There is a kind of opening up to secularization that is liberal in character and that consists in the church's accepting today more or less the values of the French Revolution, but, supporting the bourgeoisie in turn, opposing the new transformation, which is the socialist transformation. There is the other danger that I see today for faith: that the church stay outside or in opposition to the revolutionary movement, to this whole transformation of thought and society, which sees a whole liberal regime in a state of crisis. Once again, the church would adapt to a regime when it has been surpassed by the progress of secular consciousness. There is danger today that the church will adapt to the liberal regime at the moment when there is an urgency for a transformation of society in the socialist sense.

Do you mean that today the place of faith is revolution?

I wouldn't say that it's the place of faith, because it seems to me that everything that is human is the place of faith, but I believe that it can be said that it's a privileged place in the renovation of humanity. It's the place where the new humanity is being prepared, and to the extent to which faith is not found in this place, to the extent to which the church places itself in opposition to this project of human renovation, to this extent it seems to me that it would lose the great historic opportunity that the present epoch offers it.

If the church now places itself on the side of the social and political revolution, won't this justify those who accuse it for that reason of a new opportunism, a new clerical abuse of faith?

I believe that first we must see at what moment the church places itself on the side of the revolution. If the church places itself on the side of the revolution when the revolution has won, when it has achieved power, then we may, without doubt, speak of opportunism; and it's probably what is happening in the socialist states, where the church is making concordats now because power has been imposed and the church has to reckon with it. On the other hand, when the church puts itself on the side of the revolution at a moment when it is far from power, in the opposition and with the oppressed, the church finds itself in its place and takes its risks. No risk is taken by making concordats with those who are in power; risks are taken when an alliance is made with people who are opposed to power, because in this case persecution is accepted through love of justice, which is the most authentic tradition of the church, a tradition that is forgotten every time the church fails to be persecuted because it is living in alliance with power. And it then forgets what Christ said: "As they have persecuted me, they are going to persecute you." And we do not know another kind of presence of a truly prophetic church. Each time the church finds itself accepted by power, the question must be raised of knowing to what extent it continues to be faithful to its prophetic mission or is being a victim of opportunism.

Where revolution wins and seizes power, what must the church do: collaborate, keep its independence, take a critical attitude?

I think that to the extent to which that revolutionary power goes on being a liberating power, the church will have to establish a certain alliance with this power. But the form of this alliance has to be profoundly new. A way must be found to save the liberty of the church and of the power. To save the liberty of the church has no other meaning than to make the church a place where one goes on seeking freedom in the face of this new power. The church does not have to seek a privileged relation with this new power, it does not have to seek for itself a freedom that is not the freedom of all people. Then, to the extent to which the church participates in the freedom that belongs to everyone, to that extent it can establish a type of collaboration with the power, precisely because in this hypothesis the power ceases to be an oppressive power. On the other hand, to the extent to which this new revolutionary power turns oppressive and offers the church a privileged position in its oppressive regime, the church will have to reject the offer in order to be always on the side of the oppressed, to be always on the side of those who are struggling for their freedom.

Must We Stop Being Christians to Be Revolutionaries?

But is it necessary to be a Christian to bring about the revolution? Won't the revolution have to be made–where and when it is necessary–on the basis of human and political responsibilities and not necessarily from faith?

I think that to make the revolution you have to be a person. It's not through being a Christian that you're a revolutionary, and many revolutionary militants are not Christians. Nevertheless, the problem does not consist in knowing whether faith is necessary to make the revolution. The problem consists in knowing whether revolutionary militants, by reason of being revolutionaries, will have to stop being Christians, or whether they will have to invent a new kind of Christian experience.

What do you think, Giulio?

It seems to me that Christians mustn't look in the gospels or in faith for the solutions to their political problems, the reasons for being revolutionary; they must look for a way of living harmoniously their militant experience and their experience as Christians. Now then, this experience cannot be realized in such a simple way, precisely because the experience of faith is burdened with a whole past, with a whole relation to an institutional church committed to the established order, which makes combining the Christian experience and the revolutionary experience in one's life very problematical. Christians cannot in a coherent way live their faith and their revolutionary commitment *without* a very deep transformation of the meaning of their faith and the meaning of their relation to the church. It seems to me that the experience of revolutionary Christians is precisely one of the privileged places in the transformation of theology, in the transformation of Christianity in the world of today.

You lead me to think that the problem consists in knowing whether Christians, by being Christians, have to be antirevolutionaries, whether revolutionaries cannot be Christians. And some say (not the most reactionary, for we know why these say what they say) that if you try to live faith in the revolutionary experience in a very committed way, as true revolutionaries, you run the tremendous risk that faith itself will lose its transcendence, not only in relation to the church (a change that you affirm to be necessary) but in relation to God, to Christ, and to fellow humans.

I think that risk exists, but we must see the reason for the risk. We must see why this is in fact happening: that many of the Christians who commit themselves to the revolutionary struggle gradually stop being Christians, and if they don't stop being Christians, they stop considering faith as the center of their experience and come to consider it as something marginal. I believe that this depends a great deal on a given way of thinking and living Christianity, which has been the "traditional" way, and that therefore this could change profoundly from the moment that the kind of faith, the kind of interpretation of Christianity, the kind of theological foundation that is given to the revolutionary commitment is profoundly renewed.

In Search of Christian Specificity

Would you point out essential, specific differences between Christians who want to commit themselves to the revolution in total fidelity to their faith and the Marxist revolutionary?

The essential differences, for me, do not consist in a type of behavior that would be typically Christian and another that would be typically Marxist, although it can be said that the cultural climate in which the Christian and the Marxist have been formed can also have a certain influence on behavior. But the fundamental difference is in the sense that the Christian and the Marxist give to their revolutionary commitment: what for the Marxist is the construction of a new history in which the realization of humankind is achieved, for the Christian is the realization of a new history that forms part of an integral history that also has other dimensions, and other presences: in the first place, the liberating presence of Christ resurrected and of a new kind of relation among people which is founded on the death and resurrection of Christ.

And this Christian specificity, these other dimensions of history, that presence of Christ resurrected as liberator and the kind of human relations established in his death and resurrection, do they limit the revolutionary action of the Christian in comparison with that of the Marxist or of other people who don't believe in Christ?

It seems to me that this imposes no limit that is not found in the human exigencies of the building of a new society that, in fact, will never be truly new if it is not founded on overcoming the forms of egotism, violence, and oppression that are part of this society. Faithfulness to Christ, then, demands faithfulness to the true exigencies of the revolutionary commitment.

Other ideologies can also demand complete faithfulness to the true exigencies of the revolutionary commitment. So wouldn't there be a difference between acting out of a revolutionary ideology and acting out of the experience of faith in the resurrected Christ?

I say there is no difference, for this reason: there is no difference because of believing in the risen Christ; there may be differences based upon diverse analyses of society, on diverse human plans. But it's not really the fact of being Christian, of believing in Jesus Christ that brings with it an analysis of society and a plan of liberation that is anything more than what can be deduced from a reflection and a search that is properly and honestly human.

You persuade me again to think that instead of looking to find out if faith imposes limits, one must look to see if it opens up passages, exigencies, greater spaces on the horizons of revolutionary action. For I think that belief in the resurrection of Jesus and in his liberating presence, and the consequences that this has for life, love, and death (like that new kind of human relations that you referred to before), open up new horizons, new riches, and new exigencies to the hope of liberty and to the struggle for its attainment.

"To Be More Deeply Faithful to Love"

For many human ears (because of education, ideology, or whatever), to hear "revolution" is like hearing "violence" and "blood." There are different ways of approaching the problem of violence. There are ambiguous, abrupt, equivocal ways. Some say: "Violence cannot be chosen in the name of Christ, but there are circumstances where violence is inevitable or is already provoked; in the name of Christ you may not kill, but you may kill in legitimate self-defense."

Yes, it's absurd to say, "I am killing in the name of Christ." And, beyond that, we must say that that very way of approaching the problem is ambiguous, for it makes us think that Christians are expecting to get, from their relation to Christ, from their reading of the Bible, the concrete orientation for their revolutionary commitment. I believe that Christians, whether they opt for violence or nonviolence, can never justify fully this option by basing themselves on a reading of the Bible or on their relation to Christ. What we must say, in a more general way, is that the inspiration that Christians get from the contact with Christ, this demand for freedom and love, drives them to seek the truest means for a revolutionary transformation, which are precisely nonviolent means. The inspiration lets them take the risk of a violent commitment precisely when the exigencies of love seem in fact to impose on them this recourse as a lesser evil, if institutionalized violence is so strong, not only for them but for all of society, that they cannot objectively choose between violence and nonviolence but have to choose between two kinds of violence.

The love that in the contact, through faith, with Christ becomes universal, helpful, and sacrificial, absolute and limitless, would be what is specifically Christian in the revolutionary commitment, wouldn't it?
I wouldn't say that what is specifically Christian is universal love, because I think that any authentic revolution has to be based on love. I would say that the contact with Christ gives to love a source of inspiration, an exceptionally strong foundation, which the Christian probably cannot express or communicate to others.

I believe that in this we are trying to say the same thing, although you are trying to give more nuances. I wanted to start from the fact that faith in Jesus Christ gives to the Christian's love a peculiar, specific inspiration and I was going to ask you whether that "Christian" inspiration of love based on the very love of Christ that led him to die and not to kill, to be violated and not to violate, would not point out to the Christian this same path of dying without killing?
I don't think so. I think that this would be a very literal interpretation, and therefore mistaken, of faithfulness to Christ. Because although the personal mission of Christ was expressed this way, Christian fidelity to the love of Christ has to guide Christians, not to a material imitation but to a search for the ways that, in the new situations in which they find themselves and with their new tasks, they have to invent to be more profoundly faithful to love.

Where and in whom will Christians find the criteria of discernment to be more profoundly faithful to that love? For there is room for subjectivism, for relativism, and this is very serious.

I believe you won't find anywhere absolute criteria that will give you the certainty of not being wrong, and that this risk of being wrong has to be taken because you can't be a person without taking the risk of being wrong. This risk you don't have to take alone, you have to take it in community. And this communitarian Christian reflection may be one of the places where, among militants, the word of God is listened to and listened to in a creative way, knowing that it has no solutions for our problems but that in the face of our problems it has an inspiration for the solutions that we must undertake under our own responsibility.

It's getting late for Giulio. Our conversation continues down the street, as far as the subway station, into the subway, until we separate at the Trocadero Station. I can testify that Giulio is transformed when he talks; his timid air, almost of a shrinking mystic, becomes resolute through sincerity and passion. I can well imagine the passion with which he defended the meaning of his struggle in the press conference held in Brussels on January 25, 1975, following his expulsion from the Lumen Vitae Institute: "I am more and more convinced that my life can have no other meaning than to contribute, even though very slightly, but with all my strength, to solve this immense problem: the cause of the classes, exploited peoples and continents that are struggling for their freedom. Those human masses, systematically deprived of the product of their labor, their culture, and their means of subsistence constitute humanity's gravest problem." And I shiver at the utter sincerity with which this man confesses the limitations of his stand, limitations that he recognizes with a lacerating and lucid consciousness: "I've had to admit that my criticism of the church and of society is due also, in part, to resentment and to a desire for revenge. I've discovered that the underlying revolutionary option is not only a political attitude but is also influenced by a psychological necessity. The 'parricide' that occurs in it is not imposed only by the 'contradictions of the system' but also has roots in an extremely complex personal crisis. I've also discovered that the liking for power (cultural, religious, political) and the notoriety that an enterprise of such sweeping nature brings is not alien to my deep psychological motivation. After all, persecution is without doubt a suffering but also a pleasure, a desire for which I have sometimes detected in myself." Passion and sincerity. I believe that Giulio is deeply sincere when, accepting his limitations, he takes on the struggle with all its conflicts: "Whatever may be the limitations of my personal capacity for discernment, this is ultimately the only norm at my disposal. . . . There exists a personal responsibility about truth that is necessarily solitary because nobody can be replaced either by other people or by God. This is valid above all for that fundamental truth that marks the life sense of each one and constitutes one's personal and historical plan. Such a responsibility is very demanding. . . . But the option for freedom, as I try to live it, is not a solitary adventure, for it is equivalent to a class option, by reason of which it is no longer only my personal criterion that enters into conflict with that of the official church: it is that of the exploited classes and peoples who, in the midst of their struggle for freedom, run into the resistance of the church and denounce it as an ally of the oppressors." Giulio lives out his search and his struggle with "hope" (hope that "the point of view of the oppressed is the one closest to God"; hope lived in "an act of confidence based solely on a bold faith in Christ the liberator" and on "an act of confidence in the masses of the people, whose revolutionary potential, today repressed, allows us to believe in a different future for society and for the church"). I see clearly that Giulio is like that, and that he will seek and struggle like that as long as he lives. And the latest "punishment" of the church perhaps confirms and consecrates—paradoxically and painfully—his path and his struggle.

A Conversation with
José María González Ruiz

González Ruiz *was born May 5, 1916, in Seville, Spain, and was ordained on August 15, 1939. A doctor of theology and a bachelor of Sacred Scripture, he studied at the Gregorian University and at the Biblical Institute of Rome. He is canon reader of the Cathedral of Málaga and has been professor of the New Testament at the Instituto Superior de Pastoral of Madrid. Among his works we may cite* Atheistic Humanism and the Biblical God *and* The New Creation: Marxist and Christian?

When I was talking with Central European theologians I noticed that the Spanish theologian best known to them is José María González Ruiz. This will surprise nobody who knows anything about his activity in connection with Vatican Council II, about his frequent contacts with numerous theologians and thinkers, about his participation in colloquies, meetings, international dialogues with believers in other religions and nonbelievers (Rome, Vienna, Prague, Geneva. . .). José María has been, among us, a front-runner of the "dialogue." From the "desert" of his harsh previous life, he arrived at the dialogue as at a promised land that furnished him, from then on, with his horizon and his humus. I see him thus in this revelatory confession of his: "As a Christian dialogist, I brought from those enriching contacts throughout old Europe this nagging interrogative that I think I couldn't honestly avoid: are we Christians guilty of perverted mystery? . . . The apex of the dialogue has been the confrontation, alone and naked, of each one with oneself. With respect to Christian faith, believers—if they have been sincere dialogists—have seen themselves

78

*stripped of all the rationalistic and apologetic justifications and have en-
countered a tremendous reality—marvellous and terrible—which is the
gratuitous God." Is this not the flavor of all the thinking of González Ruiz?*

This was not the first time I talked with José María, nor was it the last.
One among many, that meeting has not made history. There remain—and
this is what is important—the words of this singular man.

To talk with José María is a joy to be savored whenever possible. "Come
and let's talk," he says to you over the phone. "Come for coffee." "Can you
come for dinner?" He is an accessible and cordial man, intelligent and
extremely well informed, sharp, ironic, witty, a brilliant coiner of happy
expressions that popularize theology. And he always adds to the meat and
potatoes of a conversation the taste of wine or a dish he himself has
prepared.

I have oriented our conversation to the matters of faith that I cover with
other interlocutors, but in relation to the thought of José María and to
certain expressions from his writings. He listens, agrees to answer, and
writes down the questions because he prefers to answer calmly and in
writing.

Faith Is Not a Bank Account

*What is happening with faith? With respect to it there are such contrary
attitudes among Christians that you could say that today it is understood
and lived in very different ways, and some people fear that faith is being
lost.*

Faith is essentially a free option of people, and gratuitous on God's
part. It's a dialogue between God and people, but it is God who takes
the initiative. Authentic believers have full consciousness of the
gratuitousness of their faith, and at the moment of truth they can't give
a *reason* for it; they believe, and they cannot say the opposite. That's
why true believers are more understanding about the phenomenon of
atheism: if for them faith were the result of a rigorous investigation,
they would not understand why other people do not reach the same
result. But since they have that profound experience of the gratuitousness of their faith, they are understanding toward their atheist
brothers and sisters.

Now, then, in a climate of "conventional Christianity" it frequently
happens that by "faith" something else is meant: it's a kind of conviction that justifies the whole vital and cultural universe in which the
individual moves. That's why, when, for one reason or another, that
universe crumbles, we see those "believers" clinging desperately to
the elements that constituted that universe, believing that faith is
really going to disappear. Well, now, it's certain that *that* faith is going
to disappear, but true faith, by no means. The latter—the authentic
faith—will develop more easily in a climate of resistance, which will

facilitate the option for gratuitousness. When the "believer" is practically forced by society to be a first-class citizen, the phenomenon of "faith" is perfectly natural—but not that of true faith: the climate favoring the dynamics of gratuitousness is lacking. Let's not forget that the "golden age" of Christianity was in the first centuries, when to be a Christian was a mortal sin according to the security regulations of the Roman Empire.

Today, what are the gravest risks of falsification of the faith?

For me, the gravest is the attempt to enclose faith in a formula and eternalize it that way. The great medieval theologians used to speak of the "God always greater": that is, human comprehension can never exhaust all the wealth of the revelation of God. And by "revelation" I understand what the Bible proposes: not only the manifestation of a given supernatural knowledge but God's vigilance, which is manifested precisely in the sign of freedom from all kinds of slavery. In the preamble to the great revelation of God on Sinai, apropos of the promulgation of the Decalogue, appears the declaration: "I am Yahweh, your God, who has brought you out of the land of Egypt, from the house of bondage" (Ex. 20: 2).

As a result, what would be today the most urgent tasks of the church with regard to faith?

Simply to live it. Faith is not a deposit that is owned, like a bank account, but a life that develops in the presence of that God who shows the power of his arm "bringing the mighty down from the throne and exalting the humbled" (Job 5:11; 12:19; Ps. 147:6; Lk. 1:52). If the church does not live through that vital risk of true faith, it runs the risk of losing it and replacing it with a so-called faith.

Our Churches Become Idolatrous

What roles is it going to be impossible now for faith to play in this world in transformation? What functions will faith have to perform tomorrow? What gods or demons is faith going to encounter, and what exorcisms is it going to have to cast upon the coming world?

Naturally, true faith is faith in the only absolute, in the only God. When faith has been degraded to "faith," then it has abandoned God and has turned to the gods, although it goes on talking about God, in name only. At times our churches become idolatrous but they hypocritically hide their idolatrous condition. The first thing that an idolatrous church must do is to recognize its guilt, as was done—at least officially—by the Catholic church in Vatican Council II: ". . . in this genesis of atheism believers themselves can have no small part since, with the neglect of religious education or with the inadequate statement of doctrine or even with the defects in their religious, moral, and social life, they have veiled rather than revealed the genuine face of God" (*Gaudium et spes* 19).

Erich Fromm, who honestly confesses that he is an agnostic, knows how to value the revolutionary force of faith. He writes:

What is idolatry? What is an idol? Why is the Bible so insistent on uprooting any trace of idolatry? What is the difference between God and idols? The difference is not primarily that there is only *one* God and *many* idols. Indeed, if man worshiped only one idol and not many, it would still be an idol and not God. In fact, how often has the worship of God been nothing but the worship of one idol, disguised as the God of the Bible? The approach to the understanding of what an idol is begins with the understanding of *what God is not*. God, as the supreme value and goal, is *not* man, the state, an institution, nature, power, possession, sexual powers, or any artifact made by man. The affirmations "I love God," "I follow God," "I want to become like God"—mean first of all "I do not love, follow, or imitate idols." An idol represents the object of man's central passion: the desire to return to the soil-mother, the craving for possession, power, fame, and so forth. The passion represented by the idol is, at the same time, the supreme value within man's system of values. Only a history of idolatry could enumerate the hundreds of idols and analyze which human passions and desires they represent. May it suffice to say that the history of mankind up to the present time is primarily the history of idol worship, from the primitive idols of clay and wood to the modern idols of the state, the leader, production and consumption—sanctified by the blessing of an idolized God [*You Shall Be As Gods* (New York: Holt, Rinehart and Winston, 1966), p. 43].

From all this it is deduced that a "faith" whose object is an idolized god cannot play any positive role in a new world, to which a great part of humanity aspires. And even when, in an effort to create a new world and a new humanity, our contemporary militants have found themselves obliged to dethrone God, he is not the God of Abraham, Isaac, Jesus . . . but that idolized god that has been venerated in our sumptuous temples sponsored and frequented by the oligarchies. That's why faith has to hurry to cast exorcisms everywhere; the idols of our time have to be exorcised, including those idols that we have sacrilegiously dressed with the sacred ornaments of the only God. We live in a satanic world, and no breach is needed to let Satan's smoke seep into us, since our own structures of oppression are substantially satanic. Even more, if we Christians fulfill our duty of exorcising the

capitalist world in which we live, we shall have enough moral authority to go on doing our job in a possible socialist world, when in it
appear also—of course!—some new, as yet unknown, idols.

*You have stressed more than once the paradoxical contrast that exists today
between the western theory of the "death of God" and the interest of
certain militant atheism in the problem of God.*

In fact, under western affirmations about the "death of God" there
is a tacit emphasis on the superiority of humans: God dies so that the
superhuman may be born. It is the old rivalry: God and superhuman
are incompatible. On the contrary, a certain "atheism" (which, as I
have just said, is at bottom nothing other than the rejection of an idol),
on having rediscovered humankind in its own dimensions, is
psychologically more prepared to listen to that mysterious voice of
God. Recently the French Marxist Roger Garaudy acknowledged that
his Marxist calling has brought him again to the acknowledgment of
Christ and to the expectation and hope of resurrection. The fact that
now among Christians themselves there is a constantly widening
attitude of adoration of God alone and therefore of rejection of all
human idols, at whatever cost, is having a great impact on those fierce
militants, the last of whom no longer declare themselves militant
atheists and at times have no objection to revealing their deep nostalgia for Christian values.

*You say that there have been many "Christianities" and that we are now
passing from one to another. Is it inevitable, this step so relative and so
relativizing, to go from one to another "ism"? Can we hope to overcome the
"ism," or is it still premature, or will it always be impossible in history?*

The passage from one "Christianity" to another is never an absolute
one. This is the tragedy of all great movements: by reason of their own
magnitude, they are always exposed to deterioration and distortion.
Nevertheless, it is always possible to go to the great reference points to
find out what is authentic and what isn't. It's what St. Paul called the
"discerning of spirits." In the very writings of the New Testament we
frequently see attention being directed against the "pseudo." Even
more, in the parable of the wheat and the tares, Jesus tells us expressly
that in the ecclesial area there will always be tares and that we won't be
able to pull them up by the roots until "the end of history." That's why
all dogmatic assertion is useless: rightist or leftist. There has been and
there still is a triumphalism of the left which, on the basis of the
indubitable revolutionary phenomenon of Vatican Council II, believed that everything was now done, and expected too much from the
pope, the bishops, the ecclesial institution. And on seeing that the
revolution did not impose itself drastically by means of a new leftist
"holy office," they felt disappointed and some have even left the

church. We really are at an important moment of transition, and I, frankly, feel optimistic, but I am careful not to be dogmatic: a true ecclesiology will always be the ecclesiology of the "Son of man," not that of the shattering Messiah dreamed up by the good Palestinian guerrilla fighters who were contemporaries of Jesus.

But the rightist triumphalism hasn't died either. Aren't the old integralist attitudes—more or less rejuvenated—reborn precisely when it is planned to implement the promulgated renovation? Don't we still have faith subjected to the immobile religious order and to the bourgeois abduction that that "order" protects?

I believe I've just answered that. We are subjected—and we shall go on being subjected—not only to the bourgeois abduction of faith but to new kinds of abduction already looming on our horizon. The struggle never ends. We have scarcely finished one battle when we must be thinking of how to undertake the next one. But it's true that the battles won suppose a positive advance and fit us for a better fight and, above all, one more full of hope.

A New Way of Looking at Faith

You are more optimistic than I. It seems to me that one battle hasn't ended—or won't end—before we're forced to cover other fronts. For the old fanatics haven't died—or will not die—when other new ones are born. Yes, even at the official and hierarchical level some dynamic historical exigencies of faith have been formulated. But they remain formulations, like a renewed orthodoxy that is bitterly contested as much by the most advanced progressives as by the old orthodoxy. And the general religious praxis continues to be relegated to the preservation of established situations, to the maintenance of the "religious order," and it even turns, on the part of some, to the restoration of forms and customs that seemed outmoded. Aren't we living through a new stage of heteropraxis in which people say what has to be done but don't do it? Hasn't the church, on renewing some doctrines, got into a new and more serious contradiction because it doesn't do what it says?

Certainly the church has got into a new and more serious contradiction. Thank God. If it weren't for that the ecclesial institution would not awake from its centuries-long sleep. The contradictions, which we are all suffering in our own flesh, I interpret as God's punishment: we must remember the fierce invectives of the prophets against the people of Israel. Well, now, I believe that the placidity of the old, religious praxis has been broken forever. This is evidenced by the unmistakable signs of uneasiness, at times hysterical, shown by certain groups that up to recently found themselves in peaceful possession of the "truth." Up to now, the various attitudes that appeared in the bosom of our Spanish Catholicism were only that: attitudes. At the moment of truth they all professed the same theology. But not any longer today: the fact is that a new way of looking at faith, radically different from the one that was common up to now, carries with it an irresistible dynamic, the consequences of which we can still not state fully, because very little time has passed. Every institution has an irresistible tendency to adapt its praxis to its theory. Now as the new "theory" in our church has no reverse gear, the logical thing is for a necessary adaptation of the praxis to emerge. There will certainly be a struggle. Not all the battles will be won, but I believe that the war will be won.

But some Christian believers are again accused of being heretics and atheists. Is it a question of the simple repetition of an old mechanism or do you see new perspectives and new causes?

As an "old dog," I believe that things are going better. We used to be accused much more of being heretics and atheists. And there was nothing doing: everything happened in the sacred shadow of the hierarchical mystery. The poor heretics didn't even have the possibility of knowing what they were accused of, or who were their accusers. Now things have changed. Even the ex-holy office has new norms for dealing with accusations: in the first place, the accused must be informed, given time to reflect, a possibility of defense, etc. This is all straightforward, compared with the old days. Yes, today anybody can dare, in an extremist journal, to thrust you into the hell of heresy or atheism, but it's scarcely worthwhile to defend oneself from those accusations, given the slight prestige that such publications have. What continues to be shocking is that our own hierarchy doesn't take this more seriously, preventing the extreme ease that some people have of sitting in *judgment* on the orthodoxy of any Christian. In my opinion there ought to be a great freedom of theological opinion, but no one should be allowed formally to *condemn* one's opponent, except by counterposing the opponent's ideas, and that's all.

To Abandon Faith Is Counterrevolutionary

Aren't we still committing sins like "eschatological impatience," "triumphalistic spirituality," and "historic passivity" when the opposite sins are springing up, such as the identification of the kingdom with certain "novelties," the death of all spirituality, the immanent historical activism?

I would say that "eschatological impatience" is sharpening today precisely in those desperate extremist circles. On the contrary, the identification of the kingdom with certain "novelties" I wouldn't say occurs very frequently. It's rather what you say next: that absorption of the kingdom for a renovating but immanent humanism. That's often the case with our Catholic ex-militants who have even abandoned the faith *in order to* become full members of a revolutionary movement. This attitude must be seen under two aspects. In the first place, one must be very respectful of what goes on inside the conscience of each person; if the abandonment of one's previous "faith" corresponds to a sincere change of attitude, I have nothing against it. Now if you establish the *thesis* that to become a full member of a revolutionary movement you *have to* abandon your faith, I believe that is a profoundly conterrevolutionary affirmation. Let me explain: if I really feel myself a believer and I don't succeed in "getting rid of" faith, I must understand that my revolutionary commitment will be truly so if, far from diminishing or obscuring faith, it stresses its importance. I remember the Exodus now: the Israelites were asking the pharaoh's permission to withdraw to adore their God. The pharaoh refused, because he knew very well that the God of the Israelites was a God who reveals himself in the freedom of the oppressed, and therefore, those "spiritual armies" would rouse the consciousness of that subproletarian people to fight for their own freedom. That's why he refused tenaciously. And in fact that's the way things happened: the Exodus event was a legitimate child of a deep spirituality.

To understand this better, one must sound out the reaction of the "adversary." In fact, the adversary is more tolerant of ex-believers who have wound up in revolutionary movements than of believers who, starting from their faith and after having prayed intensely, throw themselves into a freedom movement. This irritates the adversary enormously because it takes away his or her monopoly of religion.

Faith Vaccinates Every Revolution

For you, what is "to carry out the saving gesture of God"?

Why, very simply: to come away from our meeting with God in prayer, ready to enlist wherever in an effective and positive way there is a real search for the freedom of humankind. This naturally imposes on us an attentive study of the reality that surrounds us; prayer does not take the place of this study but it does stimulate us powerfully to it. This study we must share with all those who are undertaking it seriously, whatever political label they wear. I have to say in all honesty that my atheist or non-believing friends who are committed to this search, and to the consequent struggle, are the ones who have given me the best advice, and they are precisely the ones who have always told me not to commit the folly of abandoning my faith, my membership in the church, and my position as an official minister of this church. They have a fine sense of smell for the revolutionary potentiality of a "theology of liberation." And I would be so bold as to say that they feel a great nostalgia for Christian values. I have had with them the best "spiritual conversations" of my life. It seems paradoxical, but my experience is very rich in this regard.

You have reflected and written, and you have talked a lot, about the social, political, and revolutionary dynamism of faith. So that you can sum up your conclusions I am going to ask you some questions about this. Can we say that the social, political, and revolutionary commitment is a dimension of faith? To what extent and why?

Of course the social, political, and revolutionary commitment is a dimension of faith, as long as this commitment goes steadily in the direction of human freedom. In fact, my faith conditions me previously, as I face the other human beings with whom I coexist. In the first place, it tells me that "God created man in his image and likeness in order that he have dominion over the birds of the sky, the fishes of the sea, and the beasts of the earth" (Gn. 1:26). That is, that person is a kind of vice-creator, who cannot be controlled by the surrounding world, but must put into it a certain order according to the person's loyal knowledge and understanding. In the second place, it tells me that all human beings have the same importance to God and that therefore everything that produces an island of preference in human coexistence goes contrary to the plan of the creator. Finally—to come down to the essential—it tells me that all people must be brothers and sisters. Logically, when I go out into the street, after having heard this God who tells me these things, and find myself in a world of islands of privileged ones, where some human groups control others and prevent them from fulfilling themselves wholly, I feel myself obliged, by virtue of my loyalty to God, to rebel against this world and to enlist in the ranks of those who struggle against it. That's how we explain that the "revolution"—that is, the effort of poor people to free themselves from this oppression—is a privileged place of faith. In a little book of mine I have tried to show that "God is at the grassroots": that God has taken the fancy of choosing the human "grassroots" to reveal himself from there to the learned and powerful ones who believe themselves in possession of the divine secrets.

What would be the specific role of faith in the social and political commitment and in the revolutionary struggle?

This theme has already been studied from the very heart of the revolutionary struggle. There can be revolutionaries with different but convergent motivations. The Italian Marxist Lucio Lombardo-Radice, in a discussion with the German Communist Max Friedrich, answered sharply:

Let comrade Max Friedrich and the others who think like him confront the new facts like revolutionaries and Marxists. Camilo Torres has a *weltanschauung*, a conception of the world, that is not that of materialist-dialectic philosophy but of Christianity, understood from a *certain theology* ("the love of God coincides with the love of neighbor," to use Rahner's phrase); from *this* concept of the world is received the stimulus to become a revolutionary, adopting Marxism as the science of the revolution; *after* this acquisition, he lives and dies as an admirably *complete* man: Christian and revolutionary (*Socialismo y libertad*, 1971, pp. 259 ff).

To go from a "laboratory specimen" of Marxism to the real battlefield, I think it will be very useful to reproduce some paragraphs from the friendly conversation that Fidel Castro had in Santiago de Chile in the spring of 1972 with a large group of priests:

PRIEST: "And to be a Christian you have to be a Marxist?"

CASTRO: "It happens that there's a great coincidence. There may be some differences in the field of pure philosophy, which is not the fundamental problem. Of course, one problem is faith; the other is social. And what do we understand by 'Marxist'? This is the problem. Well, Marxist in economics? You can be a Christian and a Marxist in economics—in Marx's thesis—and in politics and in everything and not get into the field of what we'd call philosophy; which, besides, isn't ever what's being debated. [*Laughter*] Class distinctions may disappear and a Communist society may appear. Where is the contradiction with Christianity? Just the opposite: it would be reestablishing contact with the Christianity of the early times, in its purest, most human, most moral aspects. I believe that with what you are doing you will win the masses and you will win supporters for your positions. Gentlemen, you really do know the customs and habits of the bourgeois, the rich. You know this. There's nothing Christian about them, from any point of view. It's even true, and you know it, that when they deal with humble people, they do so as a great favor, it's condescension, paternalism. It's the way it is. There's no real sincerity in such treatment, because that's the way it is: it's in the mind and it's everything. You know about frivolous life in general, at least the life that we've known, and I believe that it's the same in many countries. It has no real human content, and it can't have any. You can't be a wild beast, a devourer of men, and at the same time be a Christian. In the arena you can't be both the Christian and the lion." [*Laughter*]

As we see, we're at the beginning of a new human experience. But we already suspect what is to be the specific Christian contribution to the process of liberation. In addition to the stimulus of hope, Christians bring to the process of liberation their *dialectical enthusiasm*, that is, their generous and total surrender, tempered by the experience of danger. We Christians know that the "kingdom of God" will arrive fully only beyond the limits of history: our contribution will be a kind of vaccination against the cancer of every revolution: triumphalism, whether it is called Bonapartism or Stalinism. Ah, and above all, we cannot forget that Christ is the pinnacle of humanity. Christ had been abducted by capitalist bourgeois society. We Christians do a great service to the people by rescuing Christ and putting him back at the service of the true people. Naturally, without impositions of any kind. Christ himself, in spite of us, but not without us, will go to meet them.

The Tactics of the Conquered

Is there any place for violence in Christian action or does faith imply an absolute preference for nonviolence?

Every day I am more astonished at the time that we Christians waste asking one another these questions. It seems that we start with the assumption that things are going to occur *in rerum natura*, as we have dreamed them in our archaic and venerable scholastic laboratories. Well now, if there is anything clear in the whole gospel message it is precisely that insanity of God when he submerged himself in the contaminated waters of human history. St. Paul goes so far as to say that "God made Christ a sin" (2 Cor. 5:21). Is it possible to go through life avoiding all kinds of contamination? It's clear that the Christian ideal is the total absence of violence, and for that reason violence is never sanctified, not even the violence that the oppressed see themselves *obliged* to use to free themselves from oppression. But in most cases the option facing us is not violence or nonviolence but *this* violence as opposed to *that* one: if I don't join in the violence of the oppressed I am automatically collaborating with the violence of the oppressors. In these cases—which are so real—Christians cannot waver: precisely because of their aversion to violence in general, they will choose the violence of the oppressed, since this violence aims to suppress the source of all violence, that of the oppressors, established and institutionalized violence. But today we do know that in many cases the oppressed cannot permit themselves the luxury of using violence—liberating violence—precisely because it is foreseen that it will not be liberating, since the establishment is already prepared and forewarned to nullify the efforts of the humble. And then we have to fall back on the only possible tactic: the tactic of the conquered: "to turn the other cheek." At times a good nonviolent campaign more easily disarms the powerful oppressor than a whole brave army of guerrilla fighters. But this belongs to the specifics of strategy, which we must share with all who struggle.

I Don't Believe in a Christian Revolutionary Who Doesn't Pray

I have heard more than one make this statement: "The revolution is something prior to the ethic of Christian faith, prior to existence in Christ. You have to participate in revolution, but it must be prior to faith." What do you think?

It seems to me a stupid inferiority complex, but above all an alarming lack of faith. God appears before us in any place and at any time: in bourgeois society and in socialist society, at moments of success and of adversity. I think this is a new attempt at "leftist apologetics." God has no need of our defense. We run into believers in the most unlikely places, even in the Vatican palaces, as happened with John XXIII.

Don't you see ambiguities and risks of lessening the faith, of utilization, falsifications, and new clericalism, in applying faith to social, political, and revolutionary commitments?

Of course I do! The struggle must be renewed; in any situation the kingdom of God will always be an eschatological goal; here—in history—there will always be wheat and tares, although the proportion and quality of both seeds changes with the times. In respect to this I think it fitting to recite here a poem of Ernesto Cardenal, a Nicaraguan, an old revolutionary fighter, later a priest, a great poet and (above all) a great believer:

"... WORLDLY WEALTH" (LK. 16:9)

And as for wealth, why, just or unjust,
Goods well-gotten or ill-gotten,
   all wealth is unjust.
All goods
   ill-gotten.
If not by you, by others.
Maybe your deed is all in order. But
did you buy the land from its rightful owner?
And did he buy it from its owner? And the other one? etc., etc.
Maybe you could trace your title to a royal title,
   but
was it always the King's?
Was it never stolen from anyone?

And the money you now receive legitimately
from your client, from the Bank, from the National Treasury,
    or from the U.S. Treasury,
was it never ill-gotten? But
don't for a moment think that in the Perfect
    Communist State
the parables of Christ will be quite antiquated
and Luke 16:9 will no longer be valid
    and wealth will no longer be WORLDLY
and you'll no longer have to share the wealth!

How to avoid this risk? Simply by having faith. And faith is a
meeting with God, where God takes the initiative. I don't believe in a
Christian revolutionary who doesn't pray. Not at all.

We Have to Restore Faith

*In the face of current tasks of evangelization, for you what would be the
basic objectives of a true proclamation of faith in Spain?*
    I believe that the main thing we have to do with faith is to restore it.
Let me explain: faith is like an old and valuable mural on which have
been slapped several layers of vulgar and wretched painting. We have
to strip faith of all the superstructure we have been slapping on it since
the days of Recaredo, passing through the "Catholic" kings and the
Emperor Charles, until we get to our latest Numantine enthusiasms of
believing ourselves to be the "spiritual reserve of the West." I always
dreamed of the collapse of that artificial "Christendom" that I had to
endure from childhood. I always believed that, once "conventional
Christianity" evaporated, some minority groups would be left, true
believers. But much to my surprise, to the rhythm of the collapse of
Christendom groups are appearing that are quantitatively greater
and qualitatively superior to any I had imagined. That's why it happens that, contemplating the *same* phenomenon, some of us declare
ourselves frankly optimistic and others cannot hide their bitter pes-
simism. It's the old German joke: the pessimist says, "The bottle's half
empty," and the optimist says, "The bottle's half full!" They are both
seeing the same reality, but their point of departure is different. My
greatest fears concern the possibility that our hierarchy and our clergy
and militants will attempt a reconstruction, a kind of Christendom
with its face washed. No. We must let the collapse be complete. Only
over a "Hispania" flat to the ground can we continue to proclaim the
authentic gospel. Of course I know that this ideal will not be achieved,
because there will always be sin. But I believe that we are at a decisive
historical moment. Only a pure faith and an insistent prayer from the

"remnant of Israel" will succeed in making the future of the gospel in our country really promising.

The Gospel Cannot Be Marxist or Christian-Democrat

Do you consider that "Christians for Socialism" is a clever evangelical "slogan" for faith today? Why? In any case, what slogans would you propose for faith at this moment of human history?

In the first place, I don't dare to propose any "slogan" for faith today. God forbid. I have spent my whole life stating the phenomenon of faith. It is something free that comes down upon us without our knowing why or how. Faith—God—will go on being like a thief: it will come and go when least expected.

Coming back to the business of "Christians for Socialism," I have defined my position on that phenomenon at various times and in various places. I have criticized it and I go on criticizing it, but only for *structural* reasons. I think that if today we put together those two terms, "socialism" and "Christianity," it will be very easy some day for the ecclesiastical hierarchy (which since the time of its founder, Jesus, has continued to be tempted by the demon named "power") to think that the time has come to pull out of its sleeve a powerful and impressive instrument in a socialist society that can come down on us when we least expect. I recall an earlier movement: the "Movement of Christians for Democracy." They were stupendous people; they didn't claim to create a separate political party; they were only trying to raise the consciousness of Christians so that they would lose their fear of what was up to then considered diabolic by the hierarchy itself: "democracy." But what happened afterward? Democracy went from being an ideology of change to an ideology of power; and then the ecclesiastical hierarchy *occupied* (with its mediocre and servile men) a structure innocently created by some heroic Christians. All you have to do is read the work *De Gasperi, uomo solo,* written by the daughter and secretary of that great Christian and democrat Alcide de Gasperi : I wish he hadn't put that cursed little hyphen between Christian and Democratic! Who can tell if the same thing won't happen with the current "Christians for Socialism" movement?

Nevertheless, I have the greatest respect (and almost veneration) for the brave Christians who are struggling within the Marxist world and with their own weapons. To experience the relation between Marxism and Christianity as a concrete version of the relation between faith and politics does not mean to experience a fiesta or to go on a tourist trip; it means to experience a tension and a conflict. And this not because Marxism is necessarily a "perverse" ideology, as the bourgeois ideology of a certain church tries to make us believe, but simply because

Christianity is not satisfied with any system of thought, whatever it is. Christianity is an attitude permanently critical, face to face with humankind in its historicity, with its powers, its struggles, its laws, its temples; Marxism is the *absolute cult* of that same humankind, in its historicity, with its struggles, its laws, its temples. When people declare themselves Christian and Marxist, they ought to be conscious that they are not proclaiming the fashionable *dernier cri*, they are not making a simple and almost obvious statement; they are placing themselves at a crossroads, they are taking on a tension, they are confessing themselves to be immersed in a conflict. That's why a statement like that can never be made in a spirit of superiority, with vanity, or with the integrist's supposition that there is no other road; that this is the only way to be Christian and that therefore all those are mistaken who do not sail in these same waters. We must respect other itineraries, allow time for situations and consciousness to mature, avoid conflicts with others in the faith, since what matters in the church is not to launch new fashions but to help people grow and to propose new signs of coexistence.

Now, moreover, it is useless to deny that the church (or *certain* churches) has not only been content to be the space of faith but has identified itself—more or less—with a specific philosophy or *weltanschauung*, and that this philosophy has come to be cleverly manipulated by the ruling class, in such a way that "faith" seems almost the patrimony of the interests of this master class. It thus happens that often the anathemas that the church launches at Marxist "philosophy" are not launched from the pure and naked faith (for that would be quite acceptable!) but from the "other" philosophy, which is a rival to and incompatible with the Marxist vision, and not for reasons of faith but for pedestrian reasons that smell a good deal like true "materialism"—a fact that an authentically Christian mysticism cannot accept.

To be more specific: the pastors of the church ought to view "with fear and trembling" that risk run by some wonderful Christians when, out of love for the downtrodden, they plunge into that world—clearly dangerous, like all "worlds"—of Marxist socialism. If the pastors have faith, they would use most of their time praying, night and day, for their faithful and talking affectionately with them, letting their faces be lashed by the new and unlikely experiences that they bring. I call to mind St. Peter (Acts 10) when he was sent to Caesarea in Palestine because in that church something was happening very much like today: the "Marxists" of that time (the pagans) were being accepted into the church without ceasing to be pagans (that is, without becoming Jews). Peter went, observed humbly, and confirmed that the Spirit was also flowing over those "cursed" pagans without their having gone previously through the ritualistic purification of circumcision. And he had nothing more to say: if the Spirit was acting like that, who was he, no matter how much of a "pope" he was, to criticize? We can see that this case typifies our modern problem: faith was confused with a "philosophy" and even with a "religious mood" as glorious as Judaism was. And so the pagans were condemned not because they opposed the faith but because they belonged to "another" philosophy. It is certain that paganism was very dangerous. But what happened? The entrance of pagans into the church produced two healthy effects in two directions: (1) it purified paganism and relativized it, accepting from it all that was acceptable; (2) it relativized "religion" itself, which, shutting itself up in Jewish nationalism, had "reduced" itself to a small enclave and had lost its universalist élan. Why not believe that that dangerous risk of our Christians who are moving around there (around Marxist socialism) is not going to produce the same salutary effects? I believe (I say *believe* in the deep sense of the faith) that the results can be very positive. Christians immersed in the Marxist world will relativize it, will help it to come out of the impasse of a cult closed to humanity and to reality (and with this they are going to make it more "Marxist," I say). At the same time, they are going to do a great deal for this church, so identified with that world sacrilegiously called "Christian," where we see in full vigor (disguised as honorable virtues) the three classic temptations that Jesus endured and that the church continues to endure.

There will naturally also be many silly acts, much nonsense, many mistakes. But I am sure that an attitude of *trustful and pastoral* attention toward this kind of Christian will be very positive for the future of our faith. The sad reality of these recent years gives us testimony to it: the best, the most eager, have left us completely, and have "secularized" their Christian hope exchanging it for a short-term hope. With this they have also done a double harm: to the faith and to the revolution. I am convinced (not scientifically but through the gift of faith) that without hope for resurrection the world may be able to take a few steps forward, but it will become weary at once. Our world now lives on the inertia of a hope (which it clings to, although secularized)—but on the day when there is nothing to hope for and nothing to fight for?

To sum up: my opinion is that the bishops should not make many declarations in this direction, that they should let the Spirit manifest itself, that they should be attentive to the surprises of the Spirit, that they should talk with their Christians with humility, with receptivity, that they should act always according to the person and not the law. The gospel cannot be Marxist or (much less) Christian Democrat, and it is sad to observe how some bishops are going around (behind the scenes) making propaganda for the political party (logically "confessional") that is going to guarantee the survival of that hybrid function, where the "pastoral" element is obscured by the dimension of "state functionary," even though it be the "new deal."

In a word: faith has no other way out than—faith. I mean that we can't appear before God and say, "Look here, God, I'll believe in you if 'faith' leads me to the left . . . or the right." No, true believers stand before God, listen, and sign a blank check for him: will they be reactionaries or will they be revolutionaries? Only a posteriori can believers show that their faith led them always to commit themselves in favor of human beings, as they are.

Ah! Don't let me forget: just as it was a stupidity to demand that the pagans stop being pagans and become Jews in order to receive baptism, so also it continues to be a major stupidity, for example, to demand of Roger Garaudy that, to be a Christian, he stop being a Marxist and become—a Thomist! Then "faith" would really have no way out!

We have talked at length about this matter, terribly important at present and with an uncertain future, which González Ruiz judges more promising than threatening. José María does not dodge issues. He lives honestly and openly. "It would seem to me absurd to take a progressive position for the sake of being progressive. What's more, to progress is really annoying, because it involves abandoning positions within which one feels comfortable, especially when one has reached a milestone as serious as the half century." This singular Andalusian canon is not a snob. He is a believer as much in love with the church as he is free in facing it.

A Conversation with
Gustavo Gutiérrez

Born in Lima, Peru, June 8, 1928, Gustavo Gutiérrez studied medicine four years at the University of San Marcos in Lima. He was ordained in 1959 and received a master's degree in psychology from the University of Louvain, Belgium, and in theology in Lyons, France. Consultant to the Peruvian National Union of Catholic Students (UNEC) and member of the National Secretariat of the Sacerdotal Movement (ONIS), he is also professor in the Department of Theology and Social Sciences at the Catholic University of Lima. He is a member of the doctrinal reflection unit of CELAM (Episcopal Council of Latin America). His most famous book is A Theology of Liberation.

The name Gustavo Gutiérrez exploded with great force among us about 1970 or 1972. For many he became overnight the man of the theology of liberation. There are, as evidence, the seven quickly successive editions of his book of the same title translated into the major languages.

When I approached him I discovered that Gustavo is not a theologian who made himself overnight. And as I penetrated into the various lines of Latin American theological reflection, I saw that Gustavo is not the only man of the theology of liberation, although he is one of its pioneers and his is the most widely known name in Europe and America.

In Gustavo I was amazed to see so much depth, so much sharpness, and such overflowing humanity in such a small body. In his face with the features and complexion of a Peruvian Indian, in his figure and his careless way of dressing, and in his overflowing cordiality, I saw the plain man of the people. In his speech I observed a powerful thinking, agile, bold, and confident. He speaks from the soul and coins words with a brilliant intelligence that dictates from experience with the strength of conviction. I believe him capable of transmitting humor, irony, tenderness, and indignation, and he can be biting (even without wounding) because he has the art of effective humor.

He kept me waiting. I saw him arrive perspiring, wiping his brow with a big handkerchief. "Forgive me." With his great briefcase of dark old leather in his hand, Gustavo seems to me even smaller. "We have very little time." Anyone else would have begged me to skip it, and I would have softened, but Gustavo, with his powerful agility of mind and word, is capable of recording a conversation brilliantly in spite of this weariness and the lack of time and place. We are in the open patio of a residence hall invaded by students who come and go. Soon Gustavo will return to Peru; this may be my last chance and I will not give it up. I shall suppress questions. We shall reduce the topics of conversation. Facing a key person in Latin American theology, facing the most popular name in the theology of liberation, it is essential to talk about his theology. A few innocent questions and others not so innocent. Then, if he does not cut me off, I will sound him out on the questions that I ask everyone.

Now We Think Through Faith from within Our Experience

Latin American theology: what is its originality?

I must confess that I don't much like the expression "Latin American theology." In Latin America there exists a theological reflection that springs from the concrete circumstances of our social reality and of our church, of our Christian community. And this reflection is called "Latin American theology"? I'm not against it, but it seems to me that for it to be that it must first be just plain "theology": that is, an understanding of faith, a reflection on faith (I believe that this is theology). Latin America is the context in which it takes place. The experience of that church, of those Christian communities, is not that of communities that move in distinct historical coordinates, and this is what gives that theology a certain peculiarity. For a long time it wasn't so. In Latin America people didn't think or even try to think with their own heads and they copied a theology that came from completely different contexts. Recently we're trying to think from our own Christian experience and *that* is beginning to be called "Latin American theology."

You ask me what it can have that's original. For me all theology has a certain claim to universality, in the sense that the experience reflected upon by a group of Christians is offered to the church community to see if other Christians recognize themselves in any way in that kind of reflection on faith. That's the way I would also see our theological reflection. I would say that the only original thing it has is what's original in all theologies: that is, reflecting on faith by starting from specific circumstances. Give me a single example in the history of the church in which a theology has not started from specific circumstances. All of them. What happens is that we forget it and that we have an idea a little "eternalizing" about theology: we think that theology, a given theology, has existed forever and that it is valid for all times and places, but that's not so. For me theology is the consciousness that a community or a Christian generation has about its faith at a given moment. Theologies are called upon to succeed one another: they are successive understandings of faith. And I believe that today in Latin America there is an effort to think through our Christian existence on that continent in revolutionary process, and that's what we offer to the rest of the church as an attempt to think through the faith. And it seems to me that other Christians who live in somewhat different circumstances will find in that reflection some points in common and others not.

In Latin America All Is Not Theology of Liberation

Can all of Latin American theology be summed up as the so-called theology of liberation?

I believe that is a somewhat glib label. Maybe I have personally contributed a little to that. But I believe it's true in the sense that the basic experience from which the theology of liberation starts is that of Christians committed to the revolutionary process of the liberation of Latin America. So yes, in a certain way. Nevertheless, it's stretching things a little. I believe there are many examples of native and original reflection in Latin America, and that by forcing them only slightly they could all fit under the label of "theology of liberation." I wouldn't reduce things so much. Frankly, it seems to me that the matter is a little broader and I believe that theology of liberation is an expression—in my opinion, an important one, but still an expression—of the theology that is born in the Latin American context. I will also tell you, quite sincerely, that in spite of having made a slight personal contribution to that theology of liberation, I'm beginning to feel that the term is getting a bit worn. It seems to me that the point of departure is not sufficiently perceived and it is interpreted through a theology somewhat more classical and traditional, or it is a little mythified. In short, it's somewhat inevitable; expressions run that risk.

Can the theology of liberation be justified and applied in any place?

I think so, but with different nuances according to the varying realities. The attempt that is being made in Latin America corresponds to our very specific circumstances. It seems to me that it has valid things for the universal church, but the Christians who are living in other situations must see with discernment and clarity what can be useful to them in this offering.

I Reject the Expression "Theology of Revolution"

What does the theology of liberation have to do with the theology of revolution? Are they two names for a single theology?

I'm glad you ask that question because the theology of liberation is frequently interpreted in the perspective of the theology of revolution. Their names frequently lead to their being paired. I should like to mark out clearly their distance apart. And I would say that the difference is fundamentally this: the theology of revolution (I'm going to be sketchy but I hope not to falsify things) starts from the fact of revolution and seeks in the Bible and in theological reflection to justify the revolutionary commitment of Christians. It searches in the Bible for themes that refer to a situation of historical mobility: it will seek texts to prove that a Christian has no need to be always in agreement with the established order, it will seek prophetic themes, and texts will also be seen in which violence appears in the Bible or in theological reflection, etc.; but all this without questioning the reading of the Bible, our interpretation of the Bible, and our theological reflection. Well now, it seems to me that the theology of liberation has a different point of departure. I would express it this way: the commitment to the liberating process, to the revolutionary process, brings Christians into a different cultural world and makes them live a quite distinct reality, parting from which they begin to live and to think through their faith in distinct categories. I believe that is the theology of liberation. Someone said to me, "It's a theology not so much in order to move toward commitment and to motivate it as a theology of committed Christians." It has something of that but it seems to me a somewhat facile formula. I wouldn't accept it completely.

What I would like to stress above all is that the point of departure of the theology of liberation means a rethinking of our faith, starting from that world to which Christianity has been brought when it committed itself revolutionarily. It's not a question of elaborating a theology from which can be deduced a given political action. For me this would be a Christian ideology and not a theology. I would reject the expression "theology of revolution" because it seems to me that it makes bad theology on the one hand, and on the other hand it seems to me that it softens revolution.

Would you say the same about "political theology" and the "theology of violence"?

About the "theology of violence" I would say the same as about the "theology of revolution." Basically the same, with some nuances that are not worth mentioning. The so-called political theology, it seems to me, has another perspective. Political theology tries to show the political implications of the evangelical message. For that reason I would not apply to it what I have said about the "theology of revolution." Political theology does not claim to be a theology that justifies the Christian's political commitment but, rather, claims to see the political implications of the announcement of the word and of the function of the church in the world. It is not the perspective of the theology of liberation, but neither does it coincide with that of the theology of revolution, and I see in it greater theological seriousness than in the latter. I might perhaps make a critical observation: political theology was born essentially in Germany, in a political context very different from the one in which we live in Latin America. I believe it responds to the context of an advanced industrial society, but nevertheless it seems to me that political theology does not always keep in mind that its own conditioning reflects on the society to which it belongs. It seems to me also that its notion of politics does not have the scope and the perspectives that it has among us, just because our thought is based on the reality of countries that are underdeveloped. These are differences that seem to me important.

Allow me a detail. Without sarcasm. The theology of revolution was made in Germany. There are people who think that the Latin Americans are the ones who are very interested in the theology of revolution. Nevertheless, check a bibliography and you will see that it is basically the work of Germans. And everything published in Latin America is a translation of German authors. This seems to me symptomatic.

You Cannot Put Faith on a Shelf

You reject the expression "theology of revolution" also because it "softens revolution." But you are all accused of improperly mixing faith with social and political revolution. There are those who say that they are things that have nothing to do with each other and that it is a grave error to try to make revolution from a basis of faith.

Well, I believe that revolutionary commitment is not made from a basis of faith. And in the first place let's say that to speak of "faith" is an abstraction. What exists in reality are people who believe, people who have faith, that is, people who accept the word of the Lord. And I don't see that people can commit themselves to anything so total and global as revolutionary commitment and say that their faith is not committed in this commitment. If they are even going to give their lives out of solidarity with the exploited classes, I don't see how any one of them could say, "All right, but my faith does not enter into this

commitment." I don't know what that means. If they enter into solidarity and into this commitment with everything in them, then their
faith enters also, their belief in the Lord, their love for the Lord. And
this doesn't mean that they make revolutionary commitment on the
basis of faith. They make it on the basis of what they are as a totality,
and faith is a fundamental dimension of their existence. You can't put
faith on a shelf. I think that if faith remains outside their commitment,
it's a fraud: it's a matter of not wanting to commit this concrete living
faith (the faith that the believer has, not faith in the abstract). To want
to "preserve" my concrete faith from my commitment is a kind of
pretense of "purity" in faith that definitely devalues and devitalizes it
totally.

It's not a question, then, of committing yourself politically on a
basis of faith: I commit myself with everything that I am: that is,
analyzing reality scientifically, living within given circumstances,
loving other human beings, loving the Lord within my commitment.
That's it. And that's what I believe we in Latin America are trying to do
and what committed Christians are doing there. And what is involved
in the claim that faith doesn't enter into commitment is, it seems to
me, at bottom not so much to want to preserve it as to want to keep it in
a kind of state of "purity" that will allow some Christians not to live
committed as believers, as if that were really possible or allowable.
Faith operates through charity, and charity leads us in Latin America
today to commit ourselves in solidarity with the exploited classes. Not
simply from a basis of faith, I insist, but from scientific analysis also,
within our specific circumstances, with everything that we are.

*There are some who say that it's not necessary to make a "theology of
liberation" to get to where you get, that one can reach the same conclusions, attitudes, and commitments from "absolute" theology if one is realistic and consistent. Or does the theology of liberation perhaps have other
basic statements and other principles that "plain" theology doesn't have?*

I believe that to the theology of liberation we must apply the traditional way of seeing theology. It springs from an experience of specific
Christians, an experience that has led them to place themselves in a
different world, and it's a reflection on that experience. If you tell me,
for example, that you have no interest in Thomistic theology (pardon
the comparison, I am conscious of the distances) because with the
Augustinian you get to the same place, that would seem to me
stupid—because St. Thomas lived in a different cultural and political
world, worked with a different set of instruments, and therefore made
a theology that is distinct, which does not do away with the great
intuitions of Augustinian theology. It's as if you also told me that the
theology born in the twentieth century, Rahner, etc., has nothing to
offer because St. Thomas has already said it all. Of course he had dealt
with the same themes, but a contemporary theology embraces a dif-

ferent cultural world. Well, this is what the theology of liberation does: it takes a different set of instruments to reason with because politically committed Christians in Latin America live in a different cultural world that leads them to live and think through their faith in a different way. And this doesn't mean the abolition of whatever efforts the church has made to think through the faith, but it does mean that we must assume there will be some splits in styles of thought, as has happened so many times in the history of the church.

The Faith-Reason Encounter Nowadays

Some say that with your theology of liberation all you do is add mysticism to sociology and political action, and in particular—they say—to socialism and Marxism. Others say you "sacralize" the revolutionary struggle.

I'll answer the second objection first. I think that those who say we sacralize the revolutionary struggle confuse the theology of liberation with the theology of revolution. That's why they think it's a sacralization. This confusion is very common. And, of course, if the theology of liberation is reduced to the theology of revolution, that objection is valid. Since I do not accept that reduction, I reject it.

As for the first objection, I believe that to think that we are adding a mysticism to political action is not to have understood what we are trying to do, or we haven't been able to express it well. I don't believe this theology is like that. I think it is authentically theology: that is, a reflection upon faith in very concrete and very precise circumstances. What is certain—if you'll allow me to get into more precise and technical aspects of theology—is that we use for this theological reflection something that up to the present moment has not had sufficient acceptance in theology: the social sciences, for example. I'd like to say two things about this.

First: for me the fundamental contribution of Thomas Aquinas to the history of theology is to have made the faith-reason encounter. To say this is to say nothing new; everyone knows it. But the form in which that faith-reason encounter was carried out in his thinking was in the encounter of philosophical faith-reason, and much more concretely Aristotelian philosophical faith-reason. Well, now, what is important is not that there has been a faith-Aristotelian philosophy encounter, faith-Aristotle, but faith-reason. This is what is valid and permanent. Since Thomas Aquinas, theology has gone on being, in part at least, a philosophical faith-reason confrontation with other philosophies, that of the twentieth century, for example, and we have in Rahner an existential philosophy, at moments personalist. All this is legitimate, but as a central nucleus there always remains the faith-reason encounter. Well, in our times human reason has forms different from philosophy. At the time of Thomas Aquinas human reason had only one expression, the philosophic, and specifically the Aristotelian. Today human reason has other forms: the human sciences and social sciences are forms of human reason. How to make the faith-reason encounter nowadays without keeping in mind, besides the philosophic aspect, other dimensions of human reason like those sciences?

Of course that seems a little strange to philosophers of rather classical training, fundamentally philosophic. It seems to them that it's like baptizing or theologizing sociology. It's more or less what it seemed to the theologians of the time when Thomas Aquinas (again I beg pardon for the comparison, I am conscious of the disproportion) began to use Aristotelian philosophy: they also said he was baptizing philosophy, that that was something that had nothing to do with what was religious, that it was a philosophical system—and thought up by a pagan. And it's because the theologians of that time weren't accustomed to use philosophy. A different style of commentary was made on the Sacred Scriptures and that was the first reaction. I believe that the objection is repeated because Christian thought has not yet assimilated what the human sciences mean for theological reflection upon humanity.

All History Is One

How does the theology of liberation understand the "autonomy of the temporal" and "secularization"? It would seem, at first sight, that the theology of liberation goes counter to the common theological conviction about the "autonomy of the temporal," which is seen as very sound and is confirmed and favored by the fact of "secularization," and recognized positively by theology.

I believe that the notion and mentality behind the "autonomy of the world" has its little history. Where does it come from? It seems to me that it comes from the time when the temporal appeared as subordinate to the spiritual power (a clear and typical case, always cited to illustrate this, is the famous *Unam sanctam* of Boniface VIII). And being thus subjected to the spiritual power, the temporal reclaims its rights, the political reclaims its rights through a series of historical events that we know well. And also thanks to Thomist theology which, starting from Aristotle's notion of "nature," gave it a theological foundation. From then on there begins to be talk of the autonomy of the temporal, an attitude of defense: to defend the temporal in the face of the spiritual, of the religious. I believe that this reaction is very sound, yes, because it goes against all clericalism. We have learned that the human world, the temporal world, has its own consistency. The birth of the modern sciences, physical as well as human, gives us an autonomous field of knowledge in which theology has not a word to say.

What happens with that in the perspective of the theology of liberation? I believe that it does not leave this evolution to one side but that, once assimilated as evolution, it does not maintain a belligerent attitude, decidedly adolescent, but adopts, rather, the tone of the unity of history and recognizes that that unity is complex. And within the complexity of history, it recognizes what, in the vocabulary of an earlier theology, was called the "autonomy of the temporal" and speaks of "proper control of the political," "scientific rationality," etc. I believe that that is not forgotten. The statement is simply made and stressed, fundamentally as old as Christianity itself, that history is all one because there is a unique vocation, and that the heart of the one human history is the saving work of Christ. This does not suppress the autonomy of the temporal; we do not have a bellicose problematic with religious power. To say that human history is a history of salvation because it is the one specific history in which people give a yes or a no to Christ is not to suppress the autonomy of the temporal. The problematic is different, but the vocabularies get mixed up and then things become confused.

With respect to secularization I would say something similar. It seems to me that secularization also appeared initially as an effort to break away from religious tutelage, from spiritual power as well as from religion made into an ideology. I would say that a good secularization leads us to distinguish clearly among the sacral, the religious, and the salvific. Let's try not to cross up vocabularies; it seems to me that this is important. There are moments in the evolution of thought that are thresholds: you go through a doorway and words take on another meaning, and if you go on using them as you did before you crossed the threshold you create confusion. I would also say that I have reservations about talking of secularization in Latin America in the same terms in which we talk of it in Europe.

Under the Pretext of Defending the Faith, They Devitalize It

Finally, some questions about faith and our time, questions about which I'm taking a poll of the personal views of my interlocutors. They are questions of general scope; you can be specific: what major dangers do you see today for faith?

"Dangers" for faith? I must confess that the expression disturbs me a little. In general it is not part of the vocabulary of the sectors of the church with which I feel identified. It is a vocabulary that strikes me as rather foreign. With this warning, I will say that I consider that what fundamentally devitalizes faith is trying to save it by leaving it within the narrow limits of an excessive spirituality. The fear that some have that Christians are losing their faith makes them place themselves as tangentially as possible to the questions of this world, to the discovery people are making today of what it means to take over history, to their capacity to transform the society in which they live, etc. And then, under the pretext of defending the faith, they devitalize it. I believe that it is precisely the best way to lose it.

What are the tasks of faith, of believers, in the world today?

It seems to me that the task of those who have faith, that is, who accept Christ as the Lord of their existence and the Lord of history, is to understand that they have to live their faith in a commitment of love for others, basically, of love for the poor, even more basically, of love for the marginalized in our society. It seems to me that it's along this path that faith can find a great vitality.

I would also say that the greatest task that believers have is to express that love for people with their own testimony, to make their faith operate through charity, as the apostle Paul says. And today charity makes great demands of us, different from what it demanded of us some time ago. For me the greatest task, then, would be to live faith as a praxis, as a behavior, as a love for fellow humans. Within this great task, of course, there is room for more specific options.

One of those options is no doubt political commitment. Does faith have any original and specific contribution to make to it?

It seems to me that the fact that I have faith, that is—as I said—that I recognize Christ as Lord of my existence and Lord of history, gives me a way of seeing people and seeing history which is a contribution to *my* political commitment—and through my commitment, to the revolutionary process in general. In this sense faith does bring something to that political commitment—not in the abstract but through the believer who is committed. Let us stress that into that political commitment there enters a very great respect for the true realm of the political and for the scientific rationality implied in that true realm of the political.

Faith Is Already Ideologized

Do you see in your situation and in your commitment in Latin America risks of new ideologizations of faith?

I believe that there are real risks. I believe that the danger of an ideologization of faith is very great. I would even say that it is not just a danger; it is a fact. Christians committed to the revolutionary process for liberation in Latin America have discovered that ideologization already exists and that it is a factor of the ideology of the dominating classes in Latin America. So it is not that Christians committed to revolution run the risk of ideologizing the faith, but that faith is already ideologized in Latin America. That these revolutionary Christians, on trying to oppose this ideologization may run the risk of making some other ideologization is quite certain. But I insist that the danger does not begin with them.

To Announce Love Is to Go to the Root of Social Evil

What demands on evangelization are made by the fact that faith must be a praxis, a behavior, a commitment of love to fellow humans?

It demands that it revise its content and its form. I believe that, if we keep in mind what I tried to say a moment ago, evangelization, the announcement of the Good News, changes in perspective and in style. If you permit me, I would like, coming down from high or abstract language, to tell you specifically what I think that, in this perspective, evangelization must be in a society like the one I know, in which I live: it seems to me that, among us, Christians are becoming very clearly conscious that to preach the word of God necessarily has a political dimension. I say political "dimension" precisely because I don't believe that any one of us thinks that evangelization is to be reduced to politicization. I speak of "dimension." Evangelization has other dimensions but there is an irreplaceable political dimension. And we think that to preach the love of God and the response that we must give it in love for fellow human beings must go to the very root of the social evil that we have in Latin America. When the bishops in Medellín say that the situation in Latin America is a sinful situation they are putting their finger on the sore spot. It is a sinful situation because at the root of every misery, injustice, alienation, exploitation that we live through in Latin America there is sin. To preach, to announce love is to go to the root of that social evil and this, it seems to me, leads us to an evangelization tremendously committed to the situations in which people live.

Latin America is an example. I don't believe that what I have just said applies only to Latin America. I'm convinced that it has broader application.

Gustavo answers rapidly and without faltering. One senses that he not only has perfect command of these themes but that he has often faced these same objections. "I have accustomed myself to endure them as inquisitorial accusations and I am by now tired of hearing them as excuses." So they accuse others and excuse themselves who ride on Medellín's shoulders and want to eliminate the theology of liberation, although the most they achieve is to test it. The same effect results from the concerted repression that now reigns in almost all the Latin American countries: with the people, they subject the theology of liberation to captivity. Since there is not a theology of hope but a theology of the cross, so there is not a theology of liberation but a theology of captivity. "It's the same theology. Captivity is a propitious situation for exodus and liberation." Night has fallen over Lima and the darkness makes me think of the shadows that here and in all Latin America lie in ambush for "liberation." But "there is no night so long that it does not end in dawn."

A Conversation with Hans Küng

Hans Küng was born March 19, 1928, and was ordained in 1954. He obtained his licentiate in philosophy and theology from the Gregorian University of Rome and his doctorate in theology from the Catholic Institute of Paris; he also studied at the Sorbonne. In 1959, he was assistant professor at the University of Münster and since 1960 he has been a professor at Tübingen University where he teaches dogmatic and ecumenical theology and is director of the Institute of Ecumenical Theology. Of his works we mention only the ones most translated into other languages: The Church; Signposts for the Future; Structures of the Church; On Being a Christian.

Küng was not in Tübingen. "He's probably in Lucerne," they told me. (I remembered: "He has an imposing chalet next to the lake.") At the university, second-semester classes had not started. "He may be traveling in the United States; it's not easy to keep track of Professor Küng." (I remember again: "They say he has a luxurious villa in Miami for his vacations.")

Years before in Spain I had heard such things about Hans Küng that the image I had formed of him was disagreeable. They told me he knew scarcely any theology, that he posed as a rebel to attract attention. They told me he was rich (through his family) and that he had several houses in Switzerland, a splendid, lakeside chalet, a luxurious yacht, an enormous car, and several secretaries who wrote for him the books on which he put his name. They told me he had an impressive villa in Miami and that he was a man with no soul, mundane, with the pose of a Hollywood star. To hear that then in Spain was to see the devil. And since that time, dreaming the impossible, I conceived the evil desire of interviewing Hans Küng to induce him to show off. "He won't receive you," they said. "He's hateful and he charges money for interviews."

Years later, a German television report on Hans Küng presented him with such artificiality that his posing was clear to me. And the ironical laughter with which an ecclesiastic of the church bureaucracy in Switzerland greeted my projected interview confirmed that monstrous image hatched in Spain.

That phantom lasted until I exchanged impressions with Hans Küng by telephone in order to arrange the interview. Then the false image began to melt away. And when I found myself with him, next to the lake (not the crowded and elegant Lake of Lucerne but the Lake of Sursee, which is solitary and austere), I found no trace of the imagined monster.

Scandal has sullied the name of Hans Küng, not the scandal of his position and his teachings but the scandal of the denigration with which he has been disfigured in high ecclesiastical spheres and in the low depths of clerical gossip.

I am not going to make a defense of Hans Küng. I shall not canonize him or declare him infallible. He neither needs it nor claims it. I shall offer the new image that I have formed of him in direct contact, telling plainly what I heard and what I saw.

You cross the small town of Sursee, lying on a hill with the hospital above, and at the top you see the three houses next to the lake. It's just as Küng described it on the phone. The plain that you glimpse from the hill is immense, dark, fertile, and it edges the lake, which is also enormous and solitary. It has not been easy to come upon Professor Küng. When he withdraws to Sursee to write, he lives in the most secret and inaccessible solitude. Nobody except his closest friends know the telephone number of his refuge, which appears in no directory. All inquiries, all contacts, lead to the telephone of the man who acts as his secretary, protecting his privacy: his own father. And he does not give his son's telephone number; only his own address. You have to write to him, explain to him, give him your number, and wait.

Küng did not delay in calling me. We understood each other in fluent Spanish. He explained how to get to his house in Sursee, and here we are, Antonio Ibáñez and I at 2:30 on this sunny March afternoon. (Antonio is a good traveling companion along the Swiss roads.) We approach the houses along the rustic dirt road that crosses the countryside, and from the balcony of the last house there is Hans Küng waving to us. When we get out of the Volkswagen he has already come down and he offers us his hand with a smile. His handshake is friendly and as strong as his athletic body.

"You've come very promptly." He has light blue eyes. "Is it hard to find this place? We're completely alone here." When he smiles widely his face is covered with furrows dark as the earth that we have been walking on. "My parents have owned this land for many years, and they built these three houses." His high forehead draws attention, crowned by hair, tough, straw-colored, rebellious. "In that last house my parents live, in the next one my sister with her family, and this one they gave to me so that I can

work or rest in solitude, but near them." They are simple houses, especially this one of Küng's: limited space, two stories, without visible display, like thousands of houses or chalets of middle-class people in Switzerland and even in Spain. At the door I see Küng's car, which is not the "enormous" car they said but a normal-sized car, inferior to other priests' cars that scandalize nobody. And I see that his "luxurious yacht" is a simple motorboat.

We enter the house: a corridor, short and almost bare; at the rear, the stairway to the left leads to Küng's study and bedroom on the second floor. We sit in a modest living room with a few pieces of functional furniture and some brightly colored abstract pictures. He serves coffee, a liqueur, and biscuits, and while we're sipping, we talk about his books. He is hurt and surprised that Infallible? *is not allowed in Spain.*

"How do you manage to write so much?"

"By hiding myself away here. You know how hard it is to find me and interrupt me. I believe that like this, retired in this hiding place, I can do my best service to the church and to people."

"Some people claim that you have a great number of secretaries who write the books that bear your name." We laugh, and all the furrows in Küng's weatherbeaten face are charm and laughter without a trace of self-defense or resentment.

"Some people claim that? They say so many things! . . . To have a secretary who types is normal, isn't it? Here you can see to what extent I work alone. And in the books you can discover if it is or is not a single mind that has written them."

Küng is vivacious, agile in his reactions and his gestures, fond of detail, attentive to everything and very cordial, with his smiling, blue eyes. No façade, no pose, no arrogance. He has received us with simplicity, with cordiality, with complete openness. And up to now (I can swear it) he has not put a price on this interview. I am disarmed.

Jesus Is the One Who Criticizes Our Church the Most

From your broad critical reflections about the church, you can clarify for us a little the current crisis of faith and its causes. The view of it in different sectors is ambiguous. For example, isn't what many describe as lack of faith really a crisis of confidence in the church?

I believe there are several aspects and causes of the current crisis of faith. Of course, the credibility of the church has decreased a great deal in post-Council times. Credibility, which at the beginning of this pontificate was perhaps the highest since the time of the Reformation, is now very low, and this influences the credibility of its message. When those who present the message lack credibility, the message they present is not trustworthy. And so the current crisis of leadership and confidence that we are suffering is one of the principal causes of the crisis of faith. At the time of John XXIII we were faced with changes as radical and profound as now, and perhaps greater, but we had no crisis of confidence. Now we have some partial progress, but we are paralyzed by a grave crisis of confidence. I should like to make a second point. In the very doctrine of the church, traditionalism tends again to dominate. In Vatican Council II we have seen that we advance only when we achieve an aggiornamento in doctrine, not only in discipline but also in doctrine. But now again, in Rome and elsewhere, we are trying, as before the Council, to defend the formulas more than the content. We ought to be more concerned about the content of faith than about formulas alone, recognizing of course that formulas do have their importance; but if we are content to maintain the formulas by repeating the traditional doctrines in a way that people of today don't understand, faith reaches a crisis.

With your permission, I'll point out some other causes. Of course, everything is mutually involved: ecclesiastical doctrine has remained far behind the evolution of human society. Today there is a series of problems that are fundamental for people, which the church is not succeeding in solving at all well. I think that with our *Quadragesimo anno* ideas (so to speak), we are forty years behind the times and we are hardly keeping pace with the validity of what was already, forty years ago, evident to human society: tolerance, religious freedom, recognition of other religions, better relations with the Jews, problems of war and peace, social improvements in the working class. Why must we always be backward, always out of step?

And where is the collaboration between the hierarchical ministry of the church and the theologians and thinkers who are not out of step?
There is no collaboration between the leaders of the church and the theologians. And this is another of the causes of the crisis. There was collaboration during the Council, and therefore things progressed. Theologians and bishops worked together, professors and pastors. It now seems that in Rome they're thinking once more as if they could run the church without heeding the evolution of theology. The Pontifical Commission of Theologians has no influence on the evolution of the church or on the progress of Rome. The Congregation of the Faith does not face its positive task of propagating the faith, but is living again in the times of the Inquisition. The Inquisition has become more discreet, more timorous, slower, more wary, more regulated, but it still operates by inquisition and with methods that have nothing to do with Christianity. For all these reasons, there is no mutual confidence between theology and the leadership of the church in Rome. In this lies one cause of difficulty for the progress of faith.

But what is most decisive in the current crisis of faith?
That we have remained very far behind the gospel and so we have lost sight of what Christian faith is really based on. We have made of Christianity an ideology, a very agreeable one, above all for those who

have power in the church and in society. We have forgotten that our faith is based on the message that Jesus Christ has brought and that Jesus Christ himself is the basis of faith. We suffer from a decentralization of faith; we are concerned about many secondary things and we do not have clear priorities. That's why we can't tell what's the center and what's the periphery; that's why we today can't proclaim the essential things that faith can do to really help people. We must admit that the forefront of criticism of the church, the most severe criticism that must be made of the church, does not come primarily from modern society but from Jesus himself, because he would not agree with much that is taking place in the church. It is Jesus who most severely criticizes our church.

Let Us Return to the Gospel and to People

Can everything be negative today? Allow me the simplicity of asking you if, considering the crises that we are suffering today, you are a pessimist?

All things considered, I am not a pessimist. Quite the contrary. And it seems to me that the whole crisis of faith can be surmounted if we manage to overcome the crisis of confidence and of leadership in the church. Today's crisis is fundamentally a crisis of leadership. Everywhere I've been in the world, I've noticed that if there was a good parish priest in the community who preached the gospel well and was concerned with people's problems, their crises of faith are not alarming. Today everything depends a great deal on each individual, on each parish priest, on each seminary teacher, on each bishop. And a great deal will also depend on our having once again a pope who can proclaim the faith today in a confident, positive, and constructive way in the church.

What are the most positive aspects that you see in the present evolution of the faith?

Above all, two things that are linked with the dangers. First, that today everywhere in the world theology, Christians, even many bishops, and the church in general are concerned about the real problems of humankind. In this there is an enormous difference with respect to the time before Vatican Council II. They are trying to help overcome the social miseries of people, whether problems of South America or of Spanish workers in Switzerland, or other problems. It is certain that there is more talk than there is action with respect to these things in all countries, but a concerned awareness has occurred. Very slowly the church becomes conscious that it has to concern itself about the needs of today's people, although social problems aren't the only ones that should concern it. Certainly in today's society, which tends to stress comfort, it is extremely important for humanity to know where it comes from, where it is going, what the basis of its life is, what its ultimate standards are. About all this many are concerned today more effectively in the church. And I think also that, in general, preaching and catechizing have improved. To sum up, today we are closer to people than we were twenty years ago.

And a second positive element that I see in this same context is that now we concentrate more on the essentials of faith. We know that not everything is equally important. We know that many things have evolved in the course of two thousand years and that not all that was important for past times is equally important for us today. We tend to concentrate on the more important things. We see that what it's all about is the message itself. We are witnessing a concentration on the gospel, which we haven't seen for a long time in the church. And if, just because of that, many new questions have come up that are now creating a certain confusion, I am sure that in the long run all this will have a positive effect. Now we're noticing everywhere that many Christians, many parish priests, many teachers do not see themselves any longer tied to some of the problems of the past and they discover a new security that did not exist twenty years ago because they are concentrating more on the true basis of the gospel. This seems to me to be what is most positive in the current evolution.

What Is Decisive Is Jesus

Let's look ahead. How do you see the future of faith in the world of today and in the coming world?

I am convinced that Christian faith will endure in the world but I also believe that it will change profoundly. Christian faith cannot go on being the same if it doesn't change frequently in its formulation and its outward forms, as John XXIII said. The future will be determined by the fact of concentrating on these two aspects that I have already mentioned. On the one hand, we shall have to concern ourselves even more to discern the future questions and problems of individuals and society. On the other hand, we must concentrate on discovering more profoundly what is truly the essence of the Christian message. What seems to me most hopeful for the future of the church is that today everywhere in the world there is a new and keener realization that Christianity is Christ. We have recovered a strong sense of Jesus. Even today's young people are discovering it. Many people at the church's edge discover that what is really decisive is Jesus and that with respect to him what is important is not only to adore him but to follow him. Today we are not simply interested in christological dogmas but in Jesus himself: what did he think? What did he do? What meaning does he have for people today? We are interested in the man Jesus who lived as the son of God and as an individual man, who suffered and died, who found his meaning in God, his eternal life in his Father. What this means for us is what can be a sign for the world. What Jesus means for the future of humanity is more decisive than many more or less dogmatic doctrinal questions from the past.

The Hierarchy: More Than Lords of Our Faith, Servants of Our Joy in Faith

You know that in every country the institutions of the church are undergoing a crisis, and the response has been contestation, contempt, indifference. How do you see the future of the institutional church?

In my book *The Church* and also in *Infallible?* I have tried to set forth what could be the function of the institutional church. It will have no future if it tries to see its meaning in itself, if what matters to it is its own power, its force to perpetuate itself. The institutional church and, in particular, the episcopacy, the papacy, have a permanent function inasmuch as they are at the service of the faith. They should not be "lords" of our faith, they should be "servants" of our joy in faith. But up to now, in many countries and above all in Rome, we perceive little joy and receive little joy to confirm us in the faith. This should be the authentic task of the hierarchy wherever there is a bishop, to be able to give joy in the faith to clergy and faithful. In that way no one would doubt the meaning and the evangelical efficacy of the episcopal ministry. Wherever the pope can make the church happy in its faith, no one will question what good a pope does.

We have seen that this is possible and I am convinced that this will go on being possible in the future. And so the task of the hierarchy will turn to clarifying the grave questions that I formulated a while ago as perspectives on the future of the faith and the church: what are the needs and hopes of people and society today, and how can we respond to them, and expose clearly what the Christian message is and what Jesus means for today's church and society? This is what we ought to be hearing, especially from the bishops. The pope must talk about this more. We hear too much of other things and too little of these that should be the heart of Christian preaching. Perhaps I should add to this that it has been joyfully noticed everywhere that the Spanish episcopacy has recently managed to open its ears to the needs of the people and to give answers that inspire hope. They have managed this better than other episcopacies, in central Europe. I wish that elsewhere bishops were as open and brave as some bishops have recently been in Spain.

As believers, what basic tasks should we have today with respect to the church and the world?

The general tasks of believers I would not describe in any other way than as we have said with respect to the church in general. Thus, all Christian believers and communities have the task of concerning themselves with the needs and hopes of all people and societies of today, and the task of fathoming what the gospel means for oneself and for everyone else, and of announcing it in a credible way. It would be necessary to find everywhere various pastoral forms of overcoming the retardation of those baptized in the faith, of helping adults abandon the baby shoes of faith. Most have learned a catechism that corresponded to another time and then they have become adults in life and they don't know what to do with their childish catechism. The bishops, parish priests, and clergy ought to devote themselves in great part to clarifying for people what it means today to believe in Jesus Christ. Homilies ought to be directed to showing clearly what *is* decisive in faith, and what is *not*, what endures and what is conditioned by time, what are the variable aspects of faith and what are the permanent ones.

Believers, according to their capacity and preparation, must also contribute to this immense task of clarification. Among the Christian laity the intellectuals would have to concern themselves today not only with the evolution of the investigation of space and the evolution of science, of economics, of technology, but also with the evolution of faith. On the other hand, there are many books and journals to read and reflect on, and I believe also that the average, indeed the simplest, man and woman has something to contribute to the present meaning of the Christian message, to the essentials of faith in Jesus Christ. This must not be left only for the experts, well trained culturally and theologically; in dealing with questions on the faith and the following of Jesus, simple people frequently understand them and solve them better than do theologians concerned only with abstract doctrines and ideas, with "theologies."

To Each Country Its Theology

I'd like to know what you think about the theology of liberation that is coming from Latin American theologians?

I don't believe I have enough knowledge about the de facto situation in Latin America to be able to form a judgment sufficiently ample and precise about that theology. So I should like to answer this question cautiously; others could answer better than I. It seems to me that liberty, liberation is something fundamental and essential in the Christian message. And there is no question that the biblical notion of liberation goes beyond the strictly religious and has social implications. There is no doubt that Jesus himself proposed a deep and real liberation and that his whole message can be considered in this light. It seems to me that this is basic, germinal, for the theology of liberation.

And in each country there must be a translation and expansion according to the demands of the specific social situation. In Switzerland it will be different from in Spain, and in Spain it will be different from in Latin America. That's why it seems to me important that we European theologians not think that we can always tell the Latin Americans what they have to say there. In Latin America each country has to develop its own theology as a function of its corresponding situation. And in my opinion, the theology of liberation in Latin America has enormously important things to say, not only in Latin America but indirectly to us also, because also among us Europeans the church would thus have much more to contribute to the liberation of humanity.

I would only point out certain limits and differences with respect to other theological concepts. It does not seem to me that a theology of liberation can be identical with a theology of revolution. "Revolution" is a word with many layers, with numerous meanings, and it would have to be defined exactly. Jesus himself was not a social and political revolutionary—according to any precise meaning of the term "revolution". It may be that revolution is necessary in a country, as it was perhaps necessary in national-socialist Germany to make the revolution that was not made and that couldn't be made, unfortunately. But we must be extremely careful with respect to Jesus, because something may be necessary that is not therefore the most positive from a Christian point of view.

I believe there are leftist theologians who exaggerate when they think and say that, at bottom, a Christian has to be a socialist and that a socialist is necessarily a Christian. Theology will proclaim an evangelical liberation when it does not limit itself to repeating what others, Marxists or non-Marxists, say; when it proposes according to each case what Jesus himself would say; when it also proposes the values and aspects of liberation in the evangelical message that are not spoken by the leaders and militants of the rightist, leftist, or centrist parties. We must clarify and profess the demands that Jesus makes on liberation so that it will not be a false or deceptive liberation but an authentic liberation of people.

I myself would like to reflect more about all this, and especially to know more about Latin America. For that very reason, what I have said is not any *ex cathedra* definition but some exploratory thoughts that I propose with caution.

Let Our Church and Our Theology Be More Christian

You are a critical theologian and also, perhaps for that very reason, a theologian criticized. The Roman proceedings against your books, the interdict, the warnings, your unshakable attitude toward Rome, and the official repercussions of all this, scandalously orchestrated, have unleashed passions both against you and for you. Some say the worst about you; others, the best. Sincerely, what do you intend with your theology and your critical attitude?

I propose to contribute as much as possible to make our Catholic theology and our church a little more Christian and therefore a little more ecumenical and, of course, much more human.

Do you not also want popularity, leadership? And isn't your theological approach very partial, too institutional and unpopular? And, according to some of your critics, will you not destroy the Christian side of theology and of the church by making it so ecumenical and human?

In the first place, I assure you that it has never occurred to me to be popular or a leader. I have never thought of having in back of me a concentration of the masses. And this is so even though, with my theology, I always have to serve above all the people of the faith. I do not really make my theology for the hierarchy of the church. I am no court theologian. But I have never wanted to be a disputatious and progressive theologian in a partisan and popular sense. I have always tried to state my criticism and my dialogue in such a way that it can be understood in even the most conservative and traditional church circles (in the good sense of the words "conservative" and "traditional"). In substantial and decisive issues I'm not a destructive progressive, I'm not a revolutionary; on the contrary, I'm very conservative. I want only to be able to be a servant of the Christian message for all people and not merely for a group, a sector, or a party, whatever its inclination.

In the church we have our home and our spiritual fatherland, where will be kept for us, in an active, current, and living way, the essentials of the gospels, what is decisive in the Christian message, the faithful and living memory of Jesus. My theological aspiration is to contribute to the church in this way, concentrating on the essentials for us, on what is the substance of the Christian faith, on our being permanently sure with regard to it, without constantly being upset and frightened when learning again and again that we are clinging to secondary and accidental things on the edge of the essentials of faith.

I should really like the leadership of the church to concentrate on this, on what in essence concerns us all. We should thus all come to know that changes in the church are possible and necessary without any essential change to the church itself; on the contrary, may the church be always the safeguard, witness, mother, and home of the essence of the gospels, which makes it the church of Jesus. It's not a question of Catholics becoming Protestants or Protestants Catholics but of both of them making themselves more Christian. It's not a question of opening a path to violent revolution, since the church must remain substantially what it is. It's a question of reforming all that keeps the church where it ought not to be, all that prevents it from being evangelical and even makes it antievangelical. For that reason, on becoming substantially evangelical the church will also acquire a more human face. What is most Christian is most ecumenical and most human. It is precisely the less human and the less ecumenical side of the church that is the less Christian. And that's what blocks off the church.

Nevertheless, while certain streams of current theology direct their criticism toward the world and society, you cultivate a theology critical of the inner church, of its institutions. And today it's said that this is a stay-at-home criticism, sterile besides, because the institution is not worth it. It's said that this is a waste of time, that you've got to let the present structures and institutions collapse all by themselves and that critical theology today must go out into the street, with the workers, into politics.

I don't think it's necessary for us all to do the same thing all the time. I leave to each one their own field of work and criticism. I've done what I myself can do. Besides, it seems to me that each one of us theologians must be modest and not believe that we can pass judgment on all the world's social and political problems from a comfortable house in Switzerland or Tübingen (and I mention these places to speak of myself). I believe problems must be viewed from within each country. In the third place, and this would be my definitive answer, it seems to me an error to isolate criticism so much, inwardly and outwardly. Very often the church is not able to give an evangelical and liberating judgment on social situations because it is orientated inwardly, because it is not critical of its own attitudes. That's why it is indispensable to change the internal situation of the church to make it capable of being more positive, more critical, and more liberating toward society. Society itself today hopes—concretely—that the church will face up to its own problems. Frequently the solution to society's problems cannot be faced by the church because the church has not faced its own problems. So, when we have overpopulation in many, many countries, specifically in Catholic countries, this problem cannot be faced positively by the church. Why not? Because the teaching of the church does not accept birth control. And why doesn't it accept birth control? Because we are maintaining a continuity, an authority, and an infallibility in the teachings of the church that are purely literalist, that are not based on the Scriptures and that today are being pushed aside. If the pope hadn't seen himself tied to the teaching of his predecessors (who can say nothing that will respond to the new problems), he would have given a different answer in *Humanae vitae*.

So, then, church reform is frequently the basis for contributing to the reform of society. The reform of society also helps in turn to reform the church. But I think we must begin on certain things by ourselves. I'm not impressed by a community or an institution that is always talking only about others and that doesn't begin by criticizing itself and applying to itself operatively the gospel message. We have more than enough people in the church who always talk about what society ought to do, but we don't change a thing. We talk about democracy in society and we don't have democracy in the church. We preach justice in society but justice has no place in the church. We talk about peace in the world and we have no peace in the church. That's why I think that intra-church reform is still a central matter and a necessity if the church is to speak and function better in the world.

Just one final word: I see no guarantee in that apocalyptic dream of those who say that you have to let everything collapse in order to build something else, somewhere, new. Anybody waiting for this will have to wait a long, long time and I believe it's better to propose and look for a radical reform than a revolution that destroys everything to begin from zero.

I see that you're a reformist, not a revolutionary. You have described yourself as a conservative in what is substantial and decisive. But those that we call "conservative" label you and fear you as a terrible revolutionary, and the revolutionaries scorn you and accuse you of being a mere reformist, a person they classify contemptuously as conservative and integralist. Among the criticisms directed at you I imagine that the honest ones don't bother you. But sincerely, are there criticisms that hurt you?

Without question. There are criticisms that astound me. I receive so many messages of support that I can endure the negative and wounding criticisms. I can state that there are no offenses or insults that I haven't already received. Now, what bothers me is that things aren't stated objectively, that people try to answer theological questions with moral arguments and with personal arguments. They don't answer the theological problems, they attack the person. All this has little to do with real Christian dialogue and discussion.

What annoys me above all is that in Rome there's so little readiness to understand that criticism of the institutions and teachings of the church is a positive effort, not negative or destructive. It bothers me that critics are so seldom thought to have good will, that there is absolutely no understanding of their concerns. I blame no one. At times, Roman officials don't know all that's being done, don't know theology well, and make judgments about what they don't understand. Of course, I consider the Inquisition a defective method of criticism, and the worst way to discover the truth. The Inquisition can suppress people, but not convert them.

I try to concern myself as little as possible with all that kind of criticism, and I hope not to be too much impressed by it. I have gone on and I shall go on working positively without worrying about that kind of criticism. I have received so much support from theologians and nontheologians all over the world, from parish priests and from the laity, men and women, that I *know* for whom I am doing theology. We have to keep going ahead. Today's theologians must commit themselves in their theology, with all their strength, to the people, and especially the poor, of every description. Today's theologians have in the first place the obligation to serve the Christian message, and speak out *opportune, importune*. Who is right in certain cases only the future will tell. It doesn't matter to me if I'm right on such-and-such a question. It matters to me that truth makes its way until it prevails by itself, also over me.

A person's own history helps to make clear that person's attitude toward life and work. Can you tell me something of your own story, of your personal itinerary?

I have said several times, and it is true: I feel myself fortunate to come from a traditional Catholic background. My family is a deeply Catholic family. My schooling was also Catholic. And I go so far as to say that my theological training was ultra-Catholic. I studied philosophy and theology in Rome. I was seven years studying in Rome. And after finishing my studies I went back to Rome repeatedly, and during the four years of the Council I spent several months there. So I have a good knowledge of Catholic theology and all the traditional Roman doctrine as well as the praxis of the church and the Roman system.

The first years I spent in Rome passed very calmly in a quite traditional atmosphere. But it was precisely my Roman experience that obliged me, in the second half of my student years there, to face a doctrine, a praxis, and a leadership in an absolutist church that, under the admired Pope Pius XII, condemned the worker-priests and disqualified many theologians, especially in France. I had to ask myself, with greater and greater frequency, if that kind of theology, which seemed to be the only kind accepted and admissible for the church, was or was not valid for our time and if the kind of organization and discipline that I was experiencing there could serve for the people and the church of our time. I must state, nevertheless, that all those experiences, questions, and doubts that tormented me never made me doubt my Catholic faith, never shook the Catholic bases of my faith. Ever since then I have tried to resolve and transform, always in a constructive way, those fundamental questions that tormented me. Ever since then I've been working on the basic objective, as I told you, of my theology: to make our church and our Catholic theology more Christian and therefore more ecumenical and more human.

I must add that ever since I was a student in Rome I have had contacts with and dedication to parish work. I am more of a parish priest than some people think. When I was studying in my Roman school I carried out parish activities with Italian colleagues. And it was precisely this first parish activity that introduced me to conflict. Later I was a counselor to Swiss girls who were studying in Paris. Afterward I was vicar of the so-called Court Church in Lucerne, then spiritual director of a school in Münster. While I was in Münster, and now in Tübingen also, I always had, in addition to my teaching, a pastoral commitment. Now I regularly serve the local hospital of Sursee—the liturgy, the sisters, the patients.

I awkwardly thank Hans Küng for this conversation, so different from the aggressive interview I had imagined. He brushes aside my thanks and smiles with the air of a boy. He says he won't correct the transcription or revise the editing of what he has said to me. He leaves it in my hands. "I wouldn't have time, and I trust you. Improve my style, delete words and repetitions. Polish the text but don't mutilate it." He gives us some inscribed ("cordially") copies of his Infallible? *translated into Spanish in Buenos Aires in 1971. On leaving his house I see in the hall a switch to turn off the telephone and another to turn off the doorbell. "At times you have to defend your solitude and seclusion to be able to work." Near the door he has on the wall a popular Andalusian mosaic of folk dancers. "I like flamenco and I like the way Antonio was dancing a few years ago." After our affectionate farewell, back in Zurich, I confess to my companion my shame, my indignation, and my joy. In Hans Küng I have seen the exact opposite of what the evil tongues say of him. Anyone who can read without overwhelming prejudices needs no further commentary.*

Nevertheless, I want to add something to establish a decisive trait of the real Hans Küng: I wonder who would not sign, with sincerity, the profession of faith in the church, of love and permanence in it, that Hans Küng signed when everything was so black for him that some friends, with incitement in their voice, and many enemies, with a tone of rebuke, asked him: "Why do you stay in the church?" "The alternatives—another church, no church—don't persuade me: breaking off leads to the isolation of the individual or to a new institutionalization. Any fanaticism shows that. I cannot defend a Christianity of chosen ones who claim to be better than others, nor do I defend the ecclesial utopias of those who dream of a community honestly moved by the same feelings. I have received too much in the community of faith to now abandon those who have made a commitment to me.

"Why do I stay in the church? Because I, as a member of the community of faith, am part of the church, which is my spiritual homeland. The church for me is the place where the memorial to Jesus Christ remains alive in spite of all the difficulties, in spite of all the mistakes. As long as the church goes

on being this place, I will never, never try to leave the church. Why do I go on in the church? Because with my faith I have hope *that the reality of Jesus Christ is stronger than all the abuses that happen in and with the church. That's why it makes sense to take a decisive stand* in *the church; that's why it makes sense to take a very concrete stand in the ministry of the church, in spite of everything. I don't stay in the church* although *I'm a Christian: I don't consider myself more Christian than the church. No, I stay in the church* because *I'm a Christian. I remain in the church because the reality of Jesus has convinced me, and because the church community in spite of every failure has been the* defender of the cause of Jesus, and it *ought to go on being so."*

I insist: who among his enemies, his judges, and his slanderers would not want to sign this confession if he could do it with the sincerity and clarity with which Hans Küng signed it?

A Conversation with
Jürgen Moltmann

Born April 8, 1930, in Hamburg, Germany, Moltmann is a Calvinist of
the German Reformed Church, and once served as minister for five years in
the small town of Bremen-Wasserhost. He is married and has four children.
He studied at the University of Göttingen, where he received his doctorate
in 1957 and was "certified" in theology. Professor of the history of dogma
and of dogmatic theology at the Ecclesiastical School of Wuppertal (1958–
63), he also taught systematic theology at the University of Bonn (1963–
67). He is at present professor of dogmatic theology at the University of
Tübingen and is editor of Evangelische Theologie. His most widely known
work is Theology of Hope. We also cite The Experiment Hope; Hope
and Planning the Future; Man: Christian Anthropology in the Conflicts of the Present; Gospel of Liberation; The Passion of Life: A
Messianic Lifestyle; The Crucified God.

The day was rainy. Cecilio and Luis drove me from Winterthur, Switzerland, to Tübingen, one hundred seventy kilometers. We had plenty of time
to visit the city, which spreads over valleys and hills in its industrial,
residential, and university sections, but whose old center, on the river and
the hill, is a handsome living museum of streets that go up and down, lined
with ancient Bavarian houses.
We photographed Jürgen Moltmann's house, his daughters in the garden,
and Moltmann himself during the conversation, violating his modesty.
Now, with the photographs before me and hearing his voice on the tape
(he has a low but gentle voice, slow, with soft cadences that carry his
irony), I can look back on the meeting in even the tiniest details. The street
climbs a hill with chalets on both sides. The two-story house, white and

121

gray, is surrounded by a rustic little garden, and is also the seat of the Institute of Ecumenical Missiology of the Faculty of Theology of the university. Moltmann's four daughters (ranging from about seven to twelve years of age) were playing in the garden. They wore slacks; one of them was hanging from the stair railing; we caught them by surprise in their uninhibited spontaneity.

The room where we talked was a very functional living room, plain and light, with a low table and two corner sofas, bookshelves, small television set, large record player, two or three modern paintings. Close up, Jürgen Moltmann has a young face, and his glance shows great intelligence; in his bearing and in his eyes he radiates an evident but unpretentious luminosity. Whether smiling or serious, he is pleasant, well mannered, timid, so unaffected as to seem aloof (he didn't like our taking so many pictures and it embarrassed him to talk about his writings, but he agreed to do it). It's probably of no importance, but I was struck by the fact that the room had two colors, white and blue; walls, doors, and bookcases white, chairs in white wood, with blue upholstery; in the corner where we sat a large white carpet covered half the blue floor. And Moltmann (blue eyes) wore a white shirt and a blue tie.

Moltmann opens our conversation.

I belong to the generation that experienced for itself the end of World War II, the destruction of a state with all its institutions, the tyranny and the shame of one's own country, and a long captivity. . . . I began to study theology in the English concentration camp. Repatriated in 1948, I studied at Göttingen. In 1945 there had surged up in Germany a "theology amid the rubble": God was seen as the only stable element in the midst of the collapse of the human world. In faith we found a refuge for the abandonment of the age. We found ourselves "in despair and yet consoled." Under these circumstances, we were leaving Kierkegaard and studying dialectical theology and we liked the theology of the cross of young Luther.

But after 1948 in Germany they reorganized the evangelical church, which, in its "confessionality," did not correspond to what the theologians had thought. From the experience of God "in the world's abyss," we went on to the elevation of God as "Lord of the church," who was installing himself in the security of "Christian society." The evangelical student communities protested. Following Bonhoeffer they were trying to get out of that blind alley into which the church had got itself and more toward the "pure worldliness of faith." With the help of Paul Tillich they were working on the dialogue between worldly questions and theological answers. They were protesting against the "Lord of the church" in order to find God in fellow human beings. But everywhere fruitless opposition was spreading between clericalism and laicism, dogmatism and commitment, and there was a repetition of the struggle between neopositivism and the critical theology of Bultmann.

These arguments always left me cold. On the other hand, since I had begun to study I was fascinated by the new biblical theology that Gerhard von Rad was fashioning on the Old Testament, and that Ernst Käsemann was fashioning on the New Testament. After studying Karl Barth's *Dogmatics*, it seemed to me impossible that any other systematic theology could be worked out thereafter, because he had said it all. I had thought the same about philosophy after Hegel. The Dutch theologian Arnold A. von Ruler freed me from this error in 1957. With him I learned the field to be explored in eschatology and the missionary initiative of Christianity.

And it was then that Ernst Bloch appeared on my horizon. He was still teaching as a Marxist philosopher in Leipzig. I remember very well spending a whole vacation in Tessin with his book *Das Prinzip Hoffnung* (the Hope Principle) without noticing the beauty of the Swiss mountains. I asked myself: "Why has Christian theology avoided this theme that really ought to be its own theme? What is the place of the primitive Christian spirit of hope within current Christianity?" I then began to work on my *Theology of Hope*. Out of biblical theology, the theology of the apostolate and of the kingdom of God, and the philosophy of hope, came the patterns of a tapestry in which everything fitted together well. I didn't want to be Bloch's heir or to establish any competition. I was thinking of a treatment in Christian and theological traditons parallel to the philosophy of hope.

But when, years later, you wrote The Crucified God, *some said it was a denial of your* Theology of Hope. *What relation do the two books establish or involve in your thought?*

In the introduction to *The Crucified God* I wrote that there is no contradiction, no denial of *Theology of Hope*. The theology of hope is founded on the resurrection of the Crucified One, and the theology of the cross is founded on the cross of the Resurrected One. The two books are two aspects of the same thing, the two faces of a single coin. I must add, of course, that there are differences. And they are there because in the intervening thirteen years I had changed, experience had made me undergo changes; people are not stones, and I do not remain unchanged. When I wrote *Theology of Hope* I was nursing a certain enthusiasm and a short-term hope that the changes I desired were going to happen soon; Vatican II had come and there was hope for a great reform in the Catholic Church; at the World Council of Churches there was a spirit of optimism and a hope for a leap forward in the ecumenical movement; in Czechoslovakia a socialism with a human face was beginning and there was a student movement that began with enthusiasm. Then the spring went by quickly and we saw how strong was the resistance against which we would have to fight, in the church as well as in socialism, as well as in the western world. That's why in my second book I became more critical with regard to the excessively optimistic hopes that things can improve very quickly.

I must stress a second aspect: *Theology of Hope* was received with great enthusiasm and interpreted as support for the "happy American life," like support for the activist life that believes it is preparing a continually better future. I then told my American friends: "When I come back again to America, I shan't speak of resurrection and hope but of the cross, this is more necessary." Meanwhile we could see the mess in Vietnam. After the Vietnam War people wondered what was to come, and they tried to look for a better future, forgetting the past, but that's not the way to act: you have to face the truth even though it hurts: you have to have consciously the experience of the cross in your own life, also in the political life of the people. Therefore, for me there's hope for a new future only when you accept the past with all the guilt wrapped up in it and with all the crucifying experiences that it includes. That's why I think that *The Crucified God* has more hope than *Theology of Hope*. The signs of destruction multiply and our hope must stop being childishly optimistic. It must become mature and firm in the common resistance to the pawns of death. Hope is faithfulness to the resurrection and therefore it is perseverance in the cross.

God Is Suffering Now in History

Then where shall we seek God today? In strength or in weakness? In human possibilities or in human impotence? In human failure or in hope? Bonhoeffer went so far as to say that it's not a question now of seeking God at the edges but at the center, not in negativeness but in human possibility.

But at the end of the book *Widerstand und Ergebung (Letters and Papers from Prison)*, Bonhoeffer says that "the Christian participates in the sorrow of God in the world"; that is, he seeks God in his own weakness, not at his edges, and not in his strength, but seeks God in the sufferings of Christ in the world. God is not an idol that represents force. What does Bonhoeffer understand by this formula? Here I very gladly accept Bonhoeffer's lead. He understands that in the grief of the scorned, of those who have become the guilty in this world, in the community of these persons, is where we must seek God. This is something very different from looking for God in a "religious" way. Most of the natural religions and political religions seek God as a strength, so that our strength may become still stronger with the strength of God. But if God reveals himself in Christ crucified, then we must try to find God in his grief in the world, and seek communion with God through communion with those who suffer most in the world. That's why I believe we must not ask where God shows himself active but where God suffers in history. Because not only does humanity want to become free, not only does nature want to become free, but God also wants to become free, because God suffers now in history. This will perhaps help us to mistrust a little our activism and our optimism fascinated by success. This will make us more realistic in relation to the hope that we have for the liberation of humanity, the liberation of nature, the liberation of God.

And what shall we do with the festival, joy, and play, Professor Moltmann? You have also written Theology of Play.

Well, I don't see the world so negatively, as if it were only a world of suffering and sadness. In this world of internal and external oppressions there are also constant anticipations and signs of joy, of happiness, and of freedom. If there weren't these signals we wouldn't suffer with the misery of the world: we would be so absorbed by the misery that we wouldn't notice it. Only in the positive do we suffer the negativeness of the negative. That's why we must look for and tend to the positive in joy, in life, which I see preferably in noneconomic, nonpolitical areas, in the area of play, festivals, celebration, and joy. I don't consider this alienation (if it's authentic) but a sampling of liberation. That's why we must perform our religious services, our liturgy, more festively, more lucidly, more aesthetically, to offer an alternative to this world of work and consumption in which we live. It's not a question of a tranquilizing replacement but of a real alternative. We Christians must invest more fantasy in liturgy so that believers can feel the experience of liberation and expansion. The idea of festival seems to be current again; from Taizé came the slogan of the festival with Jesus. And this festival must be enjoyed not only on Sunday but as a daily occurrence. One can say that the life of Jesus was a festive life. Jesus was not a great penitent who suffered in a sickly way for the misery of the world; nor was he a rebel or a revolutionary; his life was a festival, a festive life. This concept is much more important than worrying whether our world is conservative or progressive.

Nevertheless, we must admit that the way of organizing amusement and festival is industrialized; for example, in the construction of German hotels in Spain ("Festival, games, and joy"). This is business. And so we do not enter a sphere of freedom but an arena of pressures and of impositions. We must seek how to reach forms of festival and joy that are forms of liberation. I believe the countercultures of our society have suggestions and indications to attempt a happy life without commercialization. Of course, not by trying to flee from the problems of our world, but by making a search for breathing space and spirit to use ourselves better in the reform of the world. If you don't have these breathing pauses you can be left without spirit, from so much political commitment, and be done for.

Do you concur with Feast of Fools, *the "Christ-Clown," of Harvey Cox?*

No. I know Cox well. And I think highly of him. He's a theologian of culture, and he sees what there is in culture and tries to interpret it. As a European Protestant theologian, I am more absorbed by the Bible and I try to extract what corresponds to biblical testimony. I would be reluctant to apply to Christ a title like "clown" or fool. Although it's true that Christian faith is a madness in this world. I prefer to speak of "festival" rather than refer to the clown or the buffoon of the court or of society. Basically, I think the same as Harvey Cox. Nevertheless, I believe that what we think doesn't all have to be projected in a new image of Christ. From the true story of Jesus we can extract figures and titles much more profound than a clownish figure.

Your answers, Professor Moltmann, harmonize the theology of hope, the theology of the cross, and the theology of play. What do you think of the theology of liberation?

According to what little I know, there is more than one theology of liberation. There are two or three. There is the theology of black liberation, which is against racism. There is the Latin American theology of liberation, which claims, rather, to be a socioeconomic liberation. And there is a theology of women's liberation.

If we compare these three theologies, we see that they have all argued about which of the three brings true liberation, and they have done this in the form of a negative metaphysics: they have argued about when and how all that misery began. The theologians of liberation most influenced by Marxism assert that everything began in the exploitation of person by person. Black theologians assert that it began with the domination of one race by another race. And the theology of women's liberation, with the submission of woman to man. It seems to me that this is a senseless discussion, like that of those philosophers who argued about where the first matter came from. The problem lies in seeing how these three liberation movements can cooperate, for without a liberation from economic exploitation there is no liberation from racism and there will be no women's liberation. And vice versa. The three kinds of oppression—workers, blacks, and women—are interdependent and it can be shown how one form of oppression moved to the other.

We theologians have the mission of integrating those movements into the total liberation of God. If we name God and want to elaborate a theology (every theology must name God), we must consider God as the One who achieves total liberation, as the totally liberating power. We must wait and aim at total liberation, the liberation of everyone and everything, not only the liberation of the proletariat, of blacks, of women, but of everyone and everything. A few steps have been taken toward that integration.

Contradictions in Latin American Theology of Liberation

Let me bring in here something of what you wrote to José Míguez Bonino about Latin American theology of liberation, pointing out contradictions, disparities, and forebodings, in the search for dialogue between Latin American and European theologies.

The Spanish review *Iglesia Viva* (The Living Church) published my "Open Letter to José Míguez Bonino on the Theology of Liberation" [Eng. trans. in *Christianity and Crisis*, March 29, 1976]. In it I wrote especially about some equivocations that have hindered the reciprocity that is necessary between Latin American and European theologies, and I postulated that dialogue had to be carried out in a mutual criticism that would be constructive.

"The theology of liberation in Latin America wants to be a native theology, freed of European tradition and North Atlantic theology, to confront Latin American experiences and tasks which are properly its own. This is a necessary step in the historical process of liberation, as can be observed in Africa and Asia. The more rapidly it occurs, the more and better will European theologians learn from the others. But when European theological imperialism collapses, it cannot be replaced by theological provincialism. For the imperialistic collapse to make sense, it must lead to the building of a common theology of world scope, which will overcome the fragmentation of western theology. Tendencies toward a provincialism limited to only a few angles of vision are already evident. It's not good to reinforce them from without by a policy of noncommunication.

"African theology appears to us to be something authentically new, for the genius of African thought has been unknown to Europeans since the time of Aristotle. Japanese theology, thought out in a Buddhist context, guides western activists to a constant restatement of their interests and their way of thinking. But nothing similar has so far come from Latin America. We listen to severe criticism of western theology, and, in general, of theology as such, but what such criticisms really offer us is no more than part of the thinking of Karl Marx and Friedrich Engels—as a genuine Latin American discovery! We have nothing to say against Marx and Engels except that both, one born in Trier and the other in Barmen, form part of European history, and their thought is not only not an obstacle for us but, rather, an advantage. Neither of them is unknown to European theologians. And as for the criticism that Latin American theologians level against European theology, you get a contradictory impression: you first see yourself strongly criticized, to discover later, to your surprise, that the critic ends by stating the same thing that you had already said, even using the same words. It may well be that the relations between

European and Latin American theologians are still unconsciously affected by the relation between the metropolis and the colony, between the mother church and the daughter church. It would make more sense to work together for the construction of a new theology, rather than try to beat one another in a race toward the 'left,' the 'right,' or the 'center,' stepping on one another's heels."

Another problem touched on is that of the utilization of Marxism by Latin American theologians:

"The history of Latin America is visibly different from that of Asia or Africa, more deeply marked by domination and the history of the European revolutions. The socialist revolution of the proletariat remains on this horizon, whereas China (which was only briefly, and never completely, dominated by the West) very early found with Mao its own road toward socialism. In the writings of the theologians of liberation scarcely any statements of their own are found. These theologians recommend that theologians all over the world use the Marxist analysis of the social classes to be able to tread the soil of the history of their peoples, but they do not themselves carry out this analysis in the history of their own people; rather, they limit themselves to citing some fundamental concepts of Marx, and in such a general way that you scarcely get to learn anything about the struggle of the Latin American peoples. What you do learn about is some of the fruits of the readings of those theologians. In them, you can read more about sociological theories of western socialists than about the story of the life and sufferings of the Latin American peoples. You feel morally obliged to choose for the oppressed, against their oppressors, accepting Marxism as the authentic voice of prophecy on the situation.

"Analysis of the historical situation of the people is one thing, and something quite different from the declamations of seminary Marxism as a *weltanschauung*. Anyone who accepts sociology as a substitute for contact with the people who work and suffer is sociologizing about the people, but doesn't understand the true history of the people as their own history. Marxism and sociology by themselves don't lead a theologian to the people, only to collaboration with Marxists and sociologists. Naturally, neither do mere moral appeals and biblical quotations about the poor lead the theologian to the poor. Pure theology as well as theology enriched by Marxism and sociology remain within their own ambit. The authentic change, the one really needed, we still have facing both the 'political theologians' of Europe and the theologians of Latin American liberation. Together we can, as I see it, venture into a turning toward the people."

Finally: "*Orthopraxis* is a dangerous word if with it we try to dogmatize and lay down a uniform praxis of life. In the diverse political situations and in the diverse historical epochs in which we in fact live, the just and proper thing that we must do offers different appearances.

The goal, nevertheless, is the same for all: a human world society, in which people will no longer live confronting one another but will feel solidarity with one another. Latin American orthopraxis will have another face than Western European orthopraxis. What is important is that the perspective be the same within the differences. Shouldn't a reciprocal recognition be possible, and with it a reciprocal acceptance of criticism?"

Underdeveloped Christian Hope

What dangers do you see today for the survival of faith?
    I have the impression that today there exists a double danger for the survival of faith. One is the dwarfing of faith (I call it the "little faith") and the other is superstition.
    The "little faith" is found especially in Christian churches where people, afraid of freedom and lacking in courage, are suspicious of one another, are afraid of the world, and stand back. Others abandon the church, causing the lament to be heard: "You too want to leave?" and the impression grows that those who remain are the "little flock," the last of the faithful and righteous in the church. I believe that this fear, this "little faith," is a real danger that today threatens the survival of our faith.
    And then there is superstition. Nonbelief, total atheism, does not exist. But it is possible to believe in idols instead of believing in God. Those idols, in which many people place their confidence, formerly existed under the form of divinities of nature and they exist today under the form of nationalism, imperialism, capitalism, and, what is lamentable, even under the form of socialism; they assume the function of a "superego" for the person and replace freedom of faith. Those idols are depriving people of their freedom.
    Faith always wavers between the "little faith," on one hand, and superstition, on the other. If faith wants to free itself of these dangers, it must make a radical reassessment of its own origin and go back to the history and memory of Jesus Christ. We find in the New Testament that faith implies an unheard-of liberty. It says in the Gospel: "everything is possible for God," and then also, "everything is possible for the one who believes." This creative freedom of faith is stymied by the fear that shrinks faith and by superstition.

What positive and negative aspects would you stress in the form and rhythm with which today we tend to live our faith?
    Let's begin with the negative aspects. One negative aspect is that in certain sectors the survival of faith tends to direct itself toward the past and it clings to ecclesial, moral, and psychological traditions that have been able to survive up to now but that no longer can survive, and you

little fa ——————————————— superstition

FAITH

don't open up the promised land through those traditions. The faith that looks backward and wants to preserve only what is old is a negative aspect of the faith still living today among us. I consider as very positive in the present survival of the faith everything that is an opening of faith to hope in the promises of God. I don't know if this is a subjective viewpoint motivated by my preoccupation with the theme of hope. I believe we have to make it explicit and vigorous, and develop much more our underdeveloped Christian hope. This energizes faith. Hope disposes the believer toward change. Hope is oriented toward what is coming tomorrow. In hope we count on the possibilities of the future and we do not remain imprisoned in the institutions of the past. Hope for change, for transformation.

Another important aspect could be defined today with a single word: "love." Up to now we thought of love in the Christian community as a relationship among Christians: "Brothers and sisters must love one another," it is said, and we have frequently said that "works of love must normally be shared with those in the faith, not with unbelievers." We also understood love as extraordinary activities of Christians, like "works of charity": to give to the needy something that belongs to us, etc. But we haven't understood clearly the meaning of political love and social love. This has to be developed and lived, and this can happen only if the community changes. In Protestantism we have had a preacher and a community that listens to the preacher every Sunday, and in Catholicism a priest and a community that shares in the priest's mass. But what task do lay persons have in their work lives? The border between love and hatred lies in the terrain of politics, of social work, of medicine, of education, etc. If we do not discover the charisms and the gifts of each one of the laity in the community, we cannot hope that love will awaken in what is political and social. We can't hope that it will always be the clergy who take the lead and commit themselves politically and socially; we can't allow the laity, who are always and naturally immersed in society and politics, to wait for the clergy to take the lead in these fields. Lay persons have to discover and live out, in their place, in their profession, their Christian mission. It seems to me very positive in the current survival of faith that there exists a whole series of action groups, of peace groups, charismatic groups, that are trying to fulfill that radical obedience of love in the life of this world. The church has to learn from these groups; the official church must not reject them as heretics.

Called to Be a Liberator

What functions should faith perform in our time?

I must begin by saying what I understand by faith: in the past one understood by faith participation in the religious life of the church. I understand faith as a personal experience of liberation brought by Jesus Christ. This experience can be mediated through the church by preaching and the sacraments. But I would insist that faith is the experience of a liberation from fear to hope, from indifference to love, from inner and outer pressure to freedom. If this is so, if faith is that personal experience of freedom, then the function of faith in our time must be to free other people from their circumstances of inner and outer pressure. The name of Christ would have to be translated as Liberator; he who has come to free people and the world from sickness, misery, hunger, sin, to free them from their inhumanity, to share in the freedom of God. If this is true, then every believer is called upon to be a liberator for others. And this in each task and through the gifts that each one has: mothers for their children, doctors for their patients, etc. Today we see people enclosed in various circles of inner and outer oppression. About those diabolical circles of unjust domination we could say many things. We can speak globally of a diabolical circle of economic domination by humankind and also of the diabolical circle of political domination by dictatorships and of the diabolical circle of cultural alienation: persons do not know who they are but see themselves shaped by the images of other people; there is also the diabolical circle of psychological apathy; and finally there is the diabolical circle of the ecological crisis, through which we lead to death our whole life system: we commit suicide.

If faith is an experience of liberation and if the believer is assigned to the liberation of others, the believer has to get into those diabolical circles and, according to individual possibilities and strengths, free others from them, work so that those systems of domination will be violated, suppressed, overcome in such a way that they will be oriented toward life. It seems to me that the specific task of faith is to give new courage to people, to waken in them an interest in life, because if there is today a serious human weakness it is general indifference, apathy, insensitivity to life. Faith wakens an interest in life because it implies a participation in the interest that God has put into this life. Sociologists say we have gone from a society of consumption to a society of depression. Cold despair seeps in everywhere. Therefore, to give new spirit to people today, to do something for our own freedom, and to attempt the freeing of others—it seems to me that this is a most important function of faith in our time.

Identity of Faith Is Found in Jesus Christ

So that we believers may faithfully fulfill this function we must successfully overcome the grave crisis of "identity" of faith from which we suffer. How shall we achieve this?

I have written about the double crisis of faith today: a crisis of

relevance and a crisis of identity. The crisis of relevance is shown in
the fact that today many Christians don't know why they should
believe or what things faith could change in their lives. It seems as
though, for many, to believe or not to believe—in a Christian
sense—would change nothing in their lives: so why believe? Many
wonder what the church really means in their personal, political, and
social lives. It is clear that the church is becoming more irrelevant
every day. This impression is held today by theologians themselves
and by church people and they therefore try to make Christianity more
relevant in the different spheres and to make it significant for people
today. And the more they try to make faith relevant for life in this
world, the more they fall into a crisis of identity of faith, because if you
work in favor of social justice, you see that other people are also
working in favor of justice and are doing it better than you, and the
question arises, "So why am I a Christian?" The crisis of relevance and
the crisis of identity are interrelated in a dialectic way. You have to
find the point at which both crises can be resolved. You can waver
between personal, social, and political relevance on the one hand, and
identity on the other. There are church groups that say, "We are
guarding the identity of the Christian faith because we are preserving
tradition, the Bible, the confession of faith, the institution of the
church," and they complain about those who commit themselves
socially and politically in the name of Christ and say that is a negative
politicization of the church. And on the other hand, there are progressives who say, "What do we care about the identity of the Christian faith? We have to confront what's facing us, overcome the misery
that surrounds us."

I believe that the relevance and the identity of the Christian faith are
found only in Jesus Christ. And for me the solution of the crisis of
identity and relevance of faith is in concentrating on Christ, since
what makes the faith Christian is not really a tradition and a church
but the experience of the real liberation of faith through the life and the
person of Jesus Christ. If this faith is concentrated in the person of
Jesus Christ it is identified with him just as Christ is identified with
believers, and then they find their identity and their own relevance for
today's world, they enter into the messianic work of Jesus Christ,
which is to free people from inner and outer slavery; they enter into
the way of Jesus, which is the way toward the cross, and they thus are
introduced into the messianic suffering of Jesus. It seems to me that
we shall get out of the crises of identity and of relevance of faith only if
we concentrate deeply on the origin of faith, on Christ himself.

Sufferings Are the Signs of the Spirit Today

Where is the Spirit at work today? Where are there signs of the Spirit?
I shall have to answer from our Protestant tradition. It says that the

Holy Spirit speaks only through the word and the sacraments. It proceeds from the Father and the Son, therefore it is the Spirit of Christ. Nevertheless the reformers, especially Calvin and Zwingli, have also said that there is, besides, an action of the Spirit in history itself, in humanity, and we must also understand those signs of the Spirit. For Zwingli these signs were the great thinkers, the poets, the heroic figures of antiquity. Nevertheless I would begin by speaking, with St. Paul, of the negative signs of the Spirit. According to Romans 8, the Spirit is not only in believers, in the church, in the Christians, in their prayers, in their hopes and their inner lives, but the Spirit sighs also in the enslaved and oppressed creature. If you take this into consideration, you discover a universal action of the Spirit, or rather, a universal suffering of the Spirit. The Spirit suffers in oppressed creatures. If we apply this, we shall have to recognize that sigh and that suffering of the Spirit of God in the cry for bread of the hungry, in the cry for liberty of prisoners, in the mute sob of violated nature. Therefore we must not ask, as Latin Americans often do, where is God active in history, but where does God suffer in history. God suffers through his Spirit in human history.

Community and communion with the Holy Spirit have to be a community and a communion with those who suffer and are oppressed. And if we look closely we shall see that the signs of the Spirit are especially clear in people who have been condemned to silence, in those who have been condemned to hunger and death, and in the devastated human environment, in mistreated nature. The special signs of the Spirit in our time are the afflictions, the silence, the suffering and economic, political, and psychological oppression. If we recognize and take seriously these signs of the Spirit in our time, we then understand that we can live a Christian life, a messianic life, a life for liberation, only in communion with the suffering of the Spirit in people who suffer, who are oppressed, who are hungry and mute.

They Abandon the Church through Love of Christ

Among Christians there is a widespread distrust of the institutional church and its official representatives. We hear of contestation, of indifference, and even of "abandonment." How do you view this institutional crisis of the church, Professor Moltmann?

The abandonment that the church is suffering, especially by youths and militants, is certainly a very significant phenomenon today in all the churches. One can speak of a partial abandonment of the institutional church by the Spirit, since there are people who leave the church-institution through love of Christ. Today things are being said like this that I heard in Chicago: "If somebody wants to be a Christian I don't send him to church but to the slums; there he will find Christ"; that is, the person will find the Christ who suffers in the world. There is therefore an emigration from the church in the name of Christ, in the name of love, and in favor of the people who must be liberated. In this respect the church must change. The temporal structuring of the church has been crystallized in the institutionalization that is being abandoned today because Christian churches in the "Christian countries" have cultivated a bourgeois religion and a political religion. This is perhaps the case in Spain, where to be a good Spaniard one had to belong to the church: the church and Spain were the same thing. I think this is not a precisely evangelical way of creating and maintaining an ecclesial institution that is authentically Christian. Nevertheless, in the wake of recent changes, we don't try to politicize the church today but to christianize church policies, since up to now what we can call church policies were not always Christian. We can't complain if we hear criticisms against the institution, the power, the money, the treaties with the state, the concordats. It's mostly a question of Christian criticisms that a church that relates itself to Christ must face and answer; it can't just reject them. In this sense, I would like a church that, within society and the state in which it lives, was more critical, that maintained a critical freedom.

And there is another kind of emigration from the church. For example, there are those who believe there are other ideologies, other forms of replacement of religion, that are better than Christianity. It would be like talking of emigrating from the church toward what Christians would call "idolatries." And it also happens (for example, among us in Germany) that people leave the church because they think there are too many older people in it and they don't want to be old, to stop being so active, give up success, etc. They should be told, "Consider the kind of society and company Christ chose: the psychologically disturbed, the marginalized, the elderly, the weak." The society that Jesus drew around himself was far from an active vanguard of illustrious heroes and helpers of humankind; they were the poorest of the poor, despised by everyone. You have to take this seriously. You can't change the church into a club for successful executives; that "church" would automatically cease to be Christian. This kind of emigration I can't approve of; it's not an emigration in the name of Christ.

What possibilities, what chances, do you see for the church?

It's impossible to calculate exactly the possibilities that the church still has of renewing itself, radically, of converting itself into an authentic church of Christ, in this time of so much change. I cherish hope for the church but it's a hope that's contrary to any reasonable kind of hope. It may happen that we will see divisions and schisms within the church, as happened in the past. This is sad, very regrettable, but the resistance and the reaction of those of "little faith," the clinging to the old, the fear of change, is so great in certain groups that the calculation of possibilities for a positive global change cannot be very optimistic. But if it cannot change, we would have to leave that institution and create a new one. Nevertheless, what I regret in those who leave the church for the sake of Christ, for freedom, for love, is that they too quickly join other groups and many let themselves be absorbed by and converted into fellow travelers of the Marxists. They should try to set up new Christian communities that have no real reason to call themselves "churches," a worn-out label. Since the church began to unite with the state under Constantine, we've had a double form of Christianity: the great churches of the masses, very static, closely united with diverse forms of society and state) and radical groups—in the beginning monastic orders and later heretics and rebels who couldn't become monks and who were thrown out of the church. This double kind of church has always existed and we'll also have to reckon with this in the future. A great organization has to accommodate itself to the average opinion of its members if it doesn't want to lose them, and therefore it can't change radically or too quickly. The radical groups (and when I say "radical" I'm thinking of groups that want to choose a radical following of Jesus Christ in social and political life) must be accepted by the church as pioneers. The church needs their renovating influence if it does not wish to die in the tranquillity and lassitude of the masses. One might gloss over this emigration from the church, accepting these groups as in the past other groups were accepted (the Jesuits and Franciscans), although there was some doubt at the beginning whether to recognize them as a renovative group or throw them out of the church.

Christian Faith Cannot Be Apolitical

Profesor Moltmann, for you what are the proper relations of faith with political commitment, with revolution and violence, with the class struggle?

I'll try to give a brief—and therefore very incomplete—answer, because we could talk three days in a row on these themes.

First: as opposed to all the other religions of the world, the Christian faith has been political from the beginning. The Christian faith was political because Christ was crucified for political reasons, was crucified as a traitor. The memory of that political death of Christ forces faith to follow Christ in his messianic work of freeing humankind also on the political plane. There can be no apolitical faith in Christianity.

Faith and revolution? The word "revolution" has become a slogan. First, you have to be exact about what you mean by revolution. It is understood as a change in the very foundations of a system. Whether Christian faith can be involved in a revolutionary way depends on whether or not the foundations of the system in which we live are to be changed. I believe there are many societies where the foundations of social and political order have to be revised and changed because otherwise we could not overcome the inhuman effects of those systems. In such cases there is no reason why Christian faith should be afraid to act in a revolutionary way. Otherwise it can do nothing, in such cases, for the freedom of humankind. I should nevertheless like to add that it seems to me very shortsighted to see this only in relation to the capitalist system. In socialist as well as in capitalist societies we are in need of a much more radical revision of the bases of our life systems, beginning with the economy and going as far as value judgments and the way of giving meaning to life. This revolution depends on a deep conscientization. And we must not let other people supply us with the word "revolution." We ourselves can describe the elements that change a life system in a revolutionary way. We Christians must go ahead with imagination, without running to join other groups, seduced by their use of the word "revolution." At any rate, there are some who are too easily impressed.

The problem of violence, it seems to me, does not have to be reduced to a specifically moral problem about violence or nonviolence; it's a problem within the just exercise of political power. You can state the problem of violence in the context of the right to resistance. It's not a question of knowing whether violence or nonviolence is immoral; rather, we face this other problem: how can we take a meaningful part in the exercise of legitimate political power? There are states where the government violates its own laws, and not only once or occasionally but routinely. In this hypothesis one has the right to resist because the government no longer has the right to exercise political power and in this case the power again reverts to the people. There are also governments that promulgate laws contrary to the constitution, and not just occasionally, for example, during a war, but permanently; and in such a case you have the right to resist. Finally, there can also be a government that writes a constitution that is contrary to basic human rights, and in this case also you have the right to resist. It's not then just a question of knowing if there's violence or counterviolence, but of knowing if the legitimate exercise of political power is carried out justly or unjustly in specific circumstances. I think that the discussion about violence must be viewed in the context that I have outlined and not only in isolation.

Finally, faith may find itself entrenched in a class society. The dictatorship of one class of people over another is also a form of tyranny. In this case struggle is necessary not only to promote self-affirmation but to overcome tyranny. I believe that Christian theologians have to restudy the history of the theology of the right to resistance. In a tradition of the reformed churches, at the Scottish

Conference of 1560, for example, it is set down as an exercise in love for fellow humans to repress tyranny and help the oppressed to free themselves from it. And I believe there was a Spanish theologian (Molina?) who spoke eloquently against tyranny. This is not therefore so foreign to Christian tradition; what we must do is to rediscover it and apply it to current forms of tyranny, of exploitation of person by person, of oppression of person by person today.

Without Justice There Is No Reconciliation and without Reconciliation There Is No Justice

In all that range of just and necessary relations between Christian faith and political and social struggle, what role does reconciliation play?

It has been said that Christianity is a religion of reconciliation and that it is oriented toward reconciliation. In the New Testament this is certainly an important aspect of Christianity. Now, reconciliation is usually understood as an act that refers to a past situation, aimed at ending an enmity, a rupture, a hatred still going on. But what comes next? According to the theology of the apostle Paul, what must come is a life in justice. Therefore, reconciliation and liberation imply each other. The church cannot limit itself to bringing reconciliation after the conflicts. The church must also bring a new justice for the liberation of the world. Without liberation, without new justice, the church's message of reconciliation becomes "appeasement," as the English would say.

But vice versa: without reconciliation, the new justice and liberation could easily become terrorist, as we're seeing every day in the struggles for freedom. The struggle for a new justice at times brings on forms of struggle that produce injustices and tyrannies. Therefore, every struggle for freedom, every struggle for a new justice in the world, needs reconciliation. In any struggle for freedom and justice, injustice may be brought in: military or violent means are used that are in conflict with the objectives pursued: freedom, love, justice; more than that, they are even a mockery of these objectives. That's why the struggle for freedom and for truer justice needs reconciliation. Every human action in history is ambivalent and ambiguous, and it therefore has need of purification and reconciliation.

I had a discussion with the Marxist Machovec in Prague at a time when there was a lot of talk about Stalinism in socialist countries. I asked him, "How can you help alienated people to overcome alienation without introducing another alienation?"

He answered, "That's a good question," but added, "And how can you, Christian sinners, struggle against sin in the world without commiting a new sin?"

"It's a problem of grace," I answered.

And he said, "Then we would have to secularize the doctrine of grace of St. Augustine and apply it to our problems."

Every human act in history is in need of reconciliation. That's why we can't abandon the message of reconciliation but have to relate it continuously to justice and freedom.

That "new justice," does it exist in churches that haven't yet been reconciled? What is the relation between our schisms and the cross of Jesus, the Christ?

I answer briefly: in the World Council of Churches we have a great number of different churches. In the Utrecht Session it was said, "We become a community to the extent that we place ourselves underneath the cross." This can have a double meaning: first, the more we return to Christ, the more we concentrate on the cross, the more ashamed we shall have to be of remaining separate. It's not a question of asking ourselves why we are separated but why we are still not united if we put the cross in the center.

The second meaning is that to the extent that the church is persecuted and oppressed from outside, to this extent it recognizes its communion with the cross and its being a community beneath the cross, and it subordinates the differences that can occur among the people who live in the church. This second meaning was a strong motivation for the movement in Germany: the new community relationship was born in the concentration camps, where people of different beliefs saw one another placed beneath the cross and recognized a community of faith in persecution. So I imagine that a reconciliation would also be possible today between the conservative groups and the so-called progressives in the church: beneath the cross; first, in the sense that both concentrate on the cross as a center of their Christian faith, and second, when they see threat and persecution coming from outside.

We have repeatedly heard the voices of the children in the garden. The cat came into our sitting room and Moltmann's wife also came in, pursuing it. "I would like to know and experience how the grace of God comes to be a reality in a normal human life, with the small joys and great sufferings that people have. In my personal theological reflection, I ask myself how I must live, suffer, and behave according to the Bible and as a Christian." If I must confess what I have seen in the face of this man, the theologian Moltmann, in his eyes, in his look, and in his voice, I will say that I have seen simplicity, sincerity. "On the other hand, all my theological labor is in the service of overcoming the false alternative created between an unreal God and an atheistic reality, between a faith without hope and a hope without faith."

All of Tübingen, with its winding streets and its charming medieval houses, with the darkish banks of its river, is lit up by a mellow and peaceful setting sun.

A Conversation with Karl Rahner, S.J.

Karl Rahner was born March 5, 1904, in Freiburg, Germany. He joined the Jesuits in 1922 and was ordained in 1932. He received his doctorate in philosophy in Freiburg (1934–36), where he was a student of Martin Heidegger. Receiving his doctorate in theology from the University of Innsbruck (1937), he became Privatdozent *in dogmatic theology at the same university. When the Nazis invaded Austria, Rahner took refuge first in Vienna and then in a small town in Bavaria. When the war ended he taught in Munich until 1948, when he returned to teach in Innsbruck. During that period he was very active as a lecturer and writer, beginning the editing and publication of a great number of collected works. In 1964 he was called to succeed Romano Guardini at the University of Munich. In 1967 he was appointed to the Chair of Dogmatic Theology at the University of Münster, where he received a licentiate degree in 1972. His writings are almost uncatalogable in their quantity and variety. In addition to the important collective works that he has edited, we cite* Theological Investigations *(14 vols.);* Hearers of the Word; The Spirit in the World; The Shape of the Church to Come; Meditations on the Sacraments; Opportunities for Faith; *and* Grace in Freedom. *His most recent book, hailed as a kind of synthesis of all his work, is* Foundations of Christian Faith.

From the time of that conversation I see the retired but active Professor Rahner as an "old lion" who, though looking very tired, still has fighting power and, far from drowsing, continues to look ahead with challenging eyes. ("Looking ahead is necessary if you don't want to stagnate in a cowardly and comfortable way in the present, waiting passively for the future.")

And I am not astonished at the boldness of the proposals he makes in his The Shape of the Church to Come, *filled with innovative, provocative ideas. Nor am I surprised to read that the retired Rahner has said*

139

that "even papal and episcopal functions in the church have been subjected to profound changes in their historical concretion," and that it seems to him "essential to adapt the church to the modern situation, without losing the essence of Christianity," but that "in Rome there are many reactionaries who want to hamper the effects of the Council" and "the bishops are all too timid." I'm not surprised to know that he has declared that "in principle, as perspective on the future, if I am forced to choose between capitalism and socialism, I take socialism."

Not in vain has this man spent his life hearing the word of God in the world from the point of view of modern humanity, elaborating the "philosophical impregnation of theology," making possible the "anthropological trend," and opening up the best of traditions to the novelty of God, that is revealed in the novelty of historical change. That's why Karl Rahner continues to be—as he always was—a "disturbing theologian," as much for the champions of doctrinal and structural rigidity in the church as for anarchistic iconolasts.

Fog and silence around the Jesuits' writers' hall in Munich, Zuccalistrasse 16. A large garden and wooded area surrounds the bare cement of a modern building whose interior is given a slight warmth by its low wooden ceilings. Upstairs, at the end of a long corridor with many doors, we are warmly greeted by Karl Rahner (brown shirt, dark trousers). His room is a very bright, spacious triangle that overlooks the woods through wide windows. A curtain half hides the bed at the end of the right angle. Two armchairs. Beyond, two typewriters. And in the background, near the window, the professor's desk with fresh violets in a vase near his mother's picture. To left and right, two enormous bookcases. And in the air, above our heads, a mobile with little paper fish hangs from the ceiling. The professor is in a hurry. I have caught him between two trips and he is in a hurry. (Since he retired from his professorship at Münster in an aura of great prestige, he is in great demand for meetings, lectures, presentations.) "Only a few minutes," he says as soon as I explain why I am seeking him out. (From a life of so much knowledge and such vast theological experience, "only a few minutes." Painfully, we must cut down to what is essential.)

A New Interpretation of Christianity

Professor Rahner, in your judgment what are the greatest problems that the current situation of the world and of the church pose for faith?

To such a broad question I shall respond in a very general way. And I believe that Christian faith, with its content, can really be accepted only from within the specific situation in which humankind lives; if not, faith is reduced to a dead ideology that has nothing to do with life. And since the situation of humankind in the world is subjected to rapid and incessant change, it follows that the task of preaching and theology is enormous and difficult. The problem is simply this: how can I proclaim Christianity and its message to modern people, children of reason, to people who look out on a horizon of world dimensions, the technicians, the people of the great urban sprawls, the people of the pluralist society, etc., so that they can grasp it in their concrete situations? How can we manage to pass from a traditionalist Christianity, tied to a specific period and a specific form of society, from a Christianity of almost folkloric character, to a Christianity that can really relate to the present situation? This is a task proper to the church and its mission to proclaim the gospels, but which also touches theology very closely. It is obvious that such a task carries with it great dangers, among others that of misinterpreting the Christianity that needs a new interpretation, the danger that this interpretation will be carried out with a great loss of substance.

How shall we make that "new interpretation," avoiding the dangers of falsification?

Of course, we can't go out to face this danger while clinging to a lazy and motionless conservatism. We must expose ourselves with great caution to such a danger. There is no alternative to making experiments in theology also, at least within certain limits. It's not possible simply to formulate in theology new *theologumena* so clear and univocal that they represent no peril for faith. All the problems raised by modern historico-critical exegesis, all the problems raised by so-called (and in part justified) "demythologization" are authentic problems. Such problems must be raised in all their radicalness. What do we understand when we say the word "God" and why has this word become a "cipher" that no longer says anything to our contemporaries? What truth is there in the criticism of religions as formulated by Feuerbach, Marx, psychoanalysis, modern sociology, and the sociology of religion? The answers to these questions are not easy, but neither are they impossible.

Aren't these answers being sought now and, at least in part, found by some of you theologians, Professor Rahner?

It's possible, of course, that a given theologian or a group of theologians have already found answers, satisfactory up to a point, to some current problems, but that does not mean that these answers have come to form part of the consciousness of the universal church, of the contemporary preacher and Christian. It's therefore possible that these obstacles to belief *nowadays* may continue to be present for an indeterminate period of time. In this case we must also have the necessary patience and seek to see how it is possible to translate and make intelligible such solutions, which perhaps now already exist at a high theological level, so that they can be understood and assimilated by the average preacher and clergyman, and by believers who cannot devote themselves to theology.

To Take God Seriously Is to Take Human Beings Seriously

Professor Rahner, in your opinion, what would be the most important functions of Christian faith in today's world?

I believe that the functions of faith remain basically the same, even in today's world. Faith and its functions cannot be reduced to an absolute horizontalism, to a simple commitment of Christians in the field of social justice. The living God still exists, whom we must adore and love; there still exists, even in Marxist countries, the real problem of the ultimate meaning of the human being, which can't be solved with a simple improvement of social structures in the world. There still exists, in other words, the first commandment, to love the Lord your God with all your heart, to adore him and to find in him eternal destiny. And there also exists, of course, the other commandment, to love your fellow human beings.

But what does it mean today "to love your fellow human beings"?

Yes, of course, love of one's fellows doesn't have now, as it did in the past, a purely private character. It also means nowadays, in an age when people have to be socialized in a totally different way, a real commitment by Christians—political, critical, social—with a view to achieving greater freedom, greater justice, and greater human dignity.

Do we have the right to choose between the two commandments or to establish an alternative by separating them?

No. For Christians those commandments are not two separated regions, two parallel sectors of their existence; one conditions the other. Christians must find in their commitment to God—if one may use the expression—the ultimate force for their social commitment; and vice versa, Christians establish a relation with God only when and where they truly love their fellow human beings and draw the ultimate consequences from this love, as they are required to do today in the new social situation.

But today, in theory and in practice, the alternative between "horizontalism" and "verticalism" is used as a refuge to defend preestablished unilateral positions.

Quite right. That's why we mustn't limit ourselves to stating that in Christian existence, in the exercise of faith, there is a vertical dimension and a horizontal dimension; we must say clearly that these two dimensions have to be mutually "harmonized." That is, we have to show that these two things, without being identical, condition each other. We know who God is only if we really love our fellow human beings; and we know how far the radicalism of Christian love of one's fellows goes, the radicalism of the commitment to freedom and justice, if we know who God is. Otherwise, there would be a basic reduction in the social and political commitment of humanity to a bare struggle for life (to a bare biological struggle for existence). The ultimate dignity of human beings, to which we, as Christians, have to commit ourselves to the roots, is founded on the dignity and orientation of people to the absolute mystery, which we call God. Only when human beings are taken seriously—to the utmost—is it possible to know something of God, and only when we know something of God is it possible to take human beings seriously—to the utmost. (This does not mean that God and humans are reduced to identity. It is not that God, for human beings, is mythicized and currently a "word" on its way to disappearance, as Feuerbach and the whole Marxist philosophy of religion claim.) In this way there is a mutual influence between love of God and love of our fellow human beings without reaching the point of identification. And that's why it's not possible, in my opinion, to separate this double and unique task of humankind. And today people live in a new situation, within which we must interpret in a new and radical way this double and unique surrender of people to God and people.

A Church for Freedom

If that is the double and unique function of faith, what are probably the most urgent tasks of the church today with respect to faith?

The mission of the church is of course to proclaim the gospel of Jesus in all its integrity and in its permanent newness and grandeur, in exactly the way, as I said before, that human beings and God come to meet each other in their differences and in their unity. The church will be credible in fulfilling its mission only if all its members—the hierarchical church, different groups of Christians, and each Christian in particular—really take seriously their duty to humanity and society in the field of freedom and justice. They must not regard the church as an institution to preserve a given social situation. The church cannot afford to nurture the suspicion that fell on it with the French Revolution, in part right and in part wrong, of being basically only the defender of ancient social structures. The church must show that this suspicion is now without any foundation, that it now has no basis in reality.

In today's culture, to support freedom and justice implies recognizing the legitimacy of a certain plurality of options among the members of the church. What role must the hierarchy play in this?

Naturally, in choosing the concrete sociopolitical changes that they intend to address, and in determining the means that would perhaps be unwise, because they would harm people and their freedom, there can be very different opinions among individual Christians, groups of Christians, and the churches of the different nations, as is stated expressly in *Gaudium et spes*. In these specific problems there can be a great diversity of opinions and, for that very reason, of options.

As for the hierarchy, I think that it also, as hierarchy of the church, would have to try to remove the suspicion that it is only a reactionary force. Moreover, it is not fair to demand too much of the hierarchy in the various social and political currents. The hierarchy has to maintain, under certain circumstances, in the case of diversity of opinions among Christians or groups of Christians, a certain neutrality, as *Gaudium et spes* also states. And if we demand today in all fields a clear and comprehensive declericalization of the church, we cannot at the same time demand of the hierarchy that it march in front waving the banner of social criticism before other Christians. This is not necessary. Independently of the hierarchy, Christians have their tasks and rights of a social, political, and sociocritical order, from which the hierarchy cannot and must not exempt them, and therefore they do not have to be under the orientation and mandate of the hierarchy in these political and social questions.

Between Charism and Anachronism

More and more Christians feel deceived by the institutional church and, more or less distant from the hierarchy, they form "base groups." Is this a "faith without a church" or is it that faith is seeking a church more faithful to the gospel?

I believe that the "base groups" where people lead an authentically Christian life guided by a charismatic initiative are in themselves fundamentally legitimate, Christian, and ecclesial. I've already said that Christians and groups of Christians do not have to wait for an initiative from the hierarchy for all social problems. This would be to demand too much from the hierarchy, and would connote an attenuation of the authentic mission of lay persons, who are not simply receivers and fulfillers of the orders of the hierarchy. But there's no reason for this to lead these legitimate base groups into an anticlerical attitude. I would consider it anachronistic for these groups to draw apart from the total church or from the church of any nation. This would be more or less like a communist group that didn't want to have anything to do with the national party or with organized world Communism. This is, in my opinion, basically anachronistic. Today more than ever religion also needs the institution, and if Christian love and truth break away totally from the institution, we fall into an outmoded individualism and subjectivism that we should have left behind.

Nevertheless, it exists, Professor Rahner. There are not only tensions but distancings and ruptures—more silent than turbulent, it is true, for many have passed from resistance to indifference. And some end up by practically deserting the base groups. Do you see any ways to a solution?

These base groups would have to seek a fundamental link with the hierarchical church, demanded by the very essence of the church, even supposing as legitimate some remoteness from certain representatives of the hierarchy. These base groups must not become introverted and claim to live for themselves. We could also say that it would be desirable for them to bravely walk the long road through the institutions of the church in order to achieve, little by little, a living church in faith and love for all, even though this task is difficult and painful. If the base groups encapsulate themselves individually, we shall never have the church that we desire and the groups will be suffocated by their own narrowness and their individual goals. If, on the one hand, we agree that it is absolutely necessary to have a "great" institution and, on the other hand, we don't find this institution the way we want it, we must have courage, confidence, and Christian hope against all hope to revitalize such an institution. And precisely for that reason, we must perhaps begin, with ecclesial obedience, humility, and self-criticism, the long road through the institutions to improve them and change them, instead of remaining passively hidden in a little corner of a simple base group.

Faith and Revolution: More Questions than Answers

Today we see social, political, and even revolutionary commitment as an important dimension of faith. Some go so far as to think that "revolution is a privileged place of faith." What's you opinion about this, Professor Rahner?

I have already answered this question with some basic principles and perhaps I should now limit myself to the problem of revolution. Well, now, when we speak of revolution we apparently understand something different from social evolution. What do we understand by revolution? This is a very hard question to answer, for revolution, at least in my opinion, is not necessarily synonymous with physically violent revolution. So what do we understand by revolution? What specific possibilities exist for revolutionary change in society, if revolution is to be declared legitimate and different from social evolution, which is also possible? What forms of revolution are acceptable? Is every revolution necessarily a violent revolution in the physical sense, even with bloodshed, or is revolution without violence possible? Can such a revolution without violence be effective or is it only a utopia that, for example, Hélder Câmara proposes, but is not feasible? Can there be revolution today in a highly organized and highly industralized state?

All these questions are very difficult and very obscure. I would say that revolution must be, in any case, the last resort for Christians—when physical violence and even bloodshed are present. But I would also say, with Pius XI, that there can be situations of such injustice, situations in which the fundamental rights of people are in danger, that in fact they legitimize bloody violence as a way of changing the social situation. When such a situation arises, what degree of moderation is morally necessary and what are really the probabilities of creating a more just society? All these questions are very hard to answer, but they are there to be faced.

The clock tells us that we have used up seventy minutes. Too many for Professor Rahner ("only a few minutes"). I shall never forget that Rahner first listens with great concentration, with no reaction, as if impassive, and then bursts into speech with astonishing energy, without faltering and without intonation, as if dictating long paragraphs without a break, and he gesticulates freely, even moving his feet as he sits back in his swivel chair. Nor shall I easily forget the fresh violets next to the picture of his mother, whose smile reflects an immense kindness.

A Conversation with Joseph Ratzinger

Joseph Ratzinger was born in Marktl/Inn, Bavaria (Germany). He studied at the Theologische Hochschule of Freising (also in Bavaria) and at the University of Munich. He was ordained on June 20, 1951. He served as professor of fundamental theology at the University of Bonn, and in 1963 became professor of dogmatics and history of dogma at the University of Münster. Subsequently he was professor and dean of the Faculty of Theology at the University of Ratisbon. In 1977 he was appointed archbishop of Munich and was made a cardinal in the same year. His writings are concentrated in the historical field (church doctrine in St. Augustine, history and theology in St. Bonaventure) and in some theological themes, exemplified by his books Introduction to Christianity; Faith and the Future; *and* Theology of History according to St. Bonaventure.

They say that Joseph Ratzinger's reputation as a theologian has risen a great deal in this postconciliar period because of his moderation. For that very reason, they say, Ratzinger is one of the theologians trusted by even the most centrist bishops in CELAM (Episcopal Council of Latin America). They also say that his "balance" earned him his rapid rise to the archbishopric of Munich and to the cardinalate—very significant promotions at the end of the papacy of Paul VI.

I know that his name has become well known in the last few years. I know about the spreading influence of his writings and the expansion of his teaching. But I don't know whether, in all the talk about his moderation, the truth has been clearly spoken or evil tongues were hard at work. I know only that his answers in our conversation, without being exactly outspoken, seemed to me of a tone that I would not dare to describe as "moderate," because of its realism and openness. Alert in mind and word, this man shows a great mastery of current philosophy and of history, and he knows today's problems well.

I did notice an extreme moderation in his voice, in his gestures, in his face, and in his whole manner, so much so that I could not avoid the contrasting image of Rahner. Certainly Ratzinger did not seem to me to be German, because even the harsh German language was soft on his lips.

Professor Ratzinger is going to answer my questions after voicing his regrets about an oversight that very nearly ruined the stay in Ratisbon. Some days before, we had agreed by telephone to meet at his house "at any hour of the morning." I arrived by train and I simply had to leave by mid-afternoon. The quiet city of Ratisbon seemed to me a desert while hour after hour went by without Ratzinger's giving any sign of life. He had left home very early and nobody could say where he was. With the guidance of a young student we began an exploration of the professor's haunts and, after much searching, we found him, silent, unknowing and unknown, in a corner of the great library of the School of Theology. "Forgive me. I completely forgot." So now we are talking in his office in the school, a large room with a shining inlaid floor, very clean, with yellow curtains in the window and four handsome plants as decoration. A fine frame for the slender figure of Professor Ratzinger, hair prematurely white, fine carriage, elegantly dressed, amiable and gentle, without any affectation.

A Corrective against Arbitrariness and Despotism

In the present situation of the world and the church, what seem to you, Professor Ratzinger, the greatest problems and dangers for the faith?

I see two problems and two main risks, which are opposed to each other, but which are also interrelated. First, the danger that faith will retreat before the world to feel secure in itself, that believers will somehow retreat into the inner world of faith and piety, and only there, in the inner circle of the pious, will they exercise their faith, so that it cannot be impugned by anyone. In this case faith loses its evangelical dynamism, loses its universal and historical exigency, and degenerates into the ideology of a sect.

The other danger is just the opposite: one sees that mere piety uprooted from the world is useless; one sees that faith lived only in the church, in the ambit of the liturgy, does not correspond to the broad dynamic of the gospel. And so for that reason faith changes into pure political action; it identifies the hope of faith with the hope that Marxism offers to humankind, and it thus transforms faith into a mere political ideology. In this case it returns, so to speak, to the faith of the Old Testament. Faith becomes secularized and it empties out without being able to offer anything of its own; it loses its own face, its own activity, and becomes mere appearance.

It seems to me that faith today is facing these two dangers: the danger of a pure introversion into the interior of the church and the danger of an extroversion into pure political action. Both tendencies mean a loss. The great task of our time consists, therefore, in finding a faith that will remain true to the authentic heritage of the gospel, however difficult that seems at this time, and that will be able at the same time to bring to reality this heritage as a living task in this world and at this hour.

So, in your judgment, which would be the essential functions of faith in the church and in today's world?

It's not possible to answer in detail. As for the function of faith for the church, I would point out that within the church faith is a corrective against all human arbitrariness. The pope is bound to the authentic faith of the gospel exactly the same as the bishops or any simple believer. Faith protects people against their arbitrariness and their despotism and gives them a common task, with which common liberation is also achieved. And this also lets us see the function of faith for the world. Thanks to faith we know that every person is a "somebody," a person beloved by God. For the same reason, no persons, whoever they are, can be degraded to a mere "average in a system." Faith gives to each person in the first place an absolute inviolability, and it is radically opposed to any totalitarian system, of whatever origin. And this, I believe, constitutes the first important function of faith: it represents the most energetic protest against any totalitarian system.

The second important function is that faith gives people a hope and a sensitivity that go beyond the merely day-to-day. Faith gives people norms and orientations that help them to orientate their lives and to understand themselves: it keeps them from being absorbed by the world of machines and assures them the scope of what is properly human.

Finally, faith should have a third important function: to assure for people a human community, the community of the family of God, and in this way to guarantee at the same time a model for the formation of the community.

Christians Must Fight the Political Battle of the Gospel

You were talking of the danger today of reducing faith to political action. But today it seems commonplace to admit the political dimension of faith. And some go so far as to say that political commitment and even revolution are a "privileged place" of faith, while there are others who still maintain that faith has nothing to do with politics (and nevertheless have their political option already formed and from it they speak and for it they try to enlist the resources of faith). What relationship do you see between faith and political action?

That faith includes a human commitment, and therefore also a political commitment, is one of the most ancient convictions of Christianity. This brings two things with it: the temptation to retire from the world and, on the contrary, the temptation to completely mix faith and politics. This occurred to a high degree in the Roman church during the flourishing period of the papacy in the thirteenth and fourteenth centuries. In this period we can study perfectly the dangers as well as the tasks of faith. It is well to remember also that in the sixteenth and seventeenth centuries, the golden age of Spanish history, Christianity was perfectly conscious of the political implications of faith. The Dominicans, and also a great number of Franciscans, fought bravely for humane laws of colonization, and in the face of the excesses of colonialism they nobly began the battle for the defense of human rights, starting from the responsibility of Christian conscience and faith. There was therefore at that time a struggle of true believers against the powerful, a struggle for the dignity of humanity that is guaranteed by faith.

I would say that today, as a consequence of great political and social changes, we find ourselves put to the test, as we did then. Today, as then, for Christianity there awaits the great task of validating the rights of conscience in the face of power and the arbitrary acts of power; it must strive through faith itself to limit, control, and organize that power. But I must add that this cannot be the immediate mission of the ecclesiastical hierarchy; its mission lies in proclaiming the central nucleus of the gospel, the essential content of faith as such, and in this way awakening the conscience of Christians. They are the ones who, starting from the gospel, because they are Christians, but with a free and personal responsibility, must fight the battle and for that reason they must find the most suitable form of association. But such an association, in which Christians enroll under the demands of the faith, is not the church but a consequence of the faith and responsibility that the church imposes on us. It seems to me very important to emphasize both things: in the first place, the obligation that faith imposes in the face of power and which is a real duty and, in the second place, not to identify the church with any political program, political parties, or political associations. The church cannot become a party. Faith must not degenerate into pure politics; what it must do is create the sphere of freedom in which people can then fulfill their political obligations. With this I think I'm answering the question about the "privileged place" of faith in politics. On the one hand, it must be proclaimed at all costs that faith and church are above all politics, and therefore freedom for various political solutions must also be respected. On the other hand, it is true that the universal message of faith should call Christians to a political responsibility and to political action.

The Future of the Church Is in the Communities

Which, in your opinion, are the most urgent tasks of the church in the face of the current situation of faith?

It may not be possible to give a general answer to this question, since the situation in the different countries is very different and therefore the tasks have to be differentiated. On the other hand, as the universal church exists only in the diverse individual churches, the task of the church can be carried out only if the individual communities and churches are committed to the tasks of purification and renewal of faith itself. That is to say: the task of renewal and purification of the faith cannot be accomplished by an ecclesiastical center, by one church that would be, so to speak, above all of us; it can take place only in the common effort of the various organs and the various living cells of the church. Assuming this, I would say that what is important is to struggle for the vital core of the gospel and the faith, and at the same time learn to recognize what is secondary. The great danger that still threatens us nowadays is that of putting many things of secondary order too close to, and on the same level with, what is of primary importance, so that there will not be a clear distinction. This unfortunately occurred frequently in past centuries. To return to the struggle and effort to recover what is permanent, what is the essential nucleus, and to separate from it what is the form of expression conditioned by time—I think *that* is the most urgent task that the church has today. And this can't be achieved with theoretical distinctions only; it demands thought, faith, and the daily Christian experience of the faithful throughout the church; it requires the interchange of experiences, dialogue shared by the faithful, by theologians, and by the ecclesiastical authorities.

The church is the mediator of the faith. And it is even, in a certain way, an integral part of the content of faith. But in this time of revision and self-criticism the relation of the baptized with the whole of the official and institutional church cannot be limited to saying "Amen." Today there are objections to and frequently criticism of the visible, official church and its hierarchy, and many Christians live somewhat on the edge of the institution, in groups and communities that in their way are trying to live the gospel. How do you view this phenomenon? Do you see in it a threat for the church or, rather, something promising?

This question can't be answered with a simple yes or no. On the one hand, I see behind this movement something positive and promising, but there is also a considerable danger that this movement will go astray, and this danger is not merely theoretical. I'll try to explain: in the first place, in the evolution of the church in past centuries, there was undoubtedly the danger of considering as the church only the hierarchy and almost solely its supreme representatives, who were above the simple faithful and who lived apart from them. They had forgotten that the church comes alive where Christians gather because of the gospel and are united in the celebration of the Eucharist. They had forgotten what was self-evident to the primitive church: that the church is composed of a multitude of individual churches, of living communities. "Church" no longer meant the living community that *hic et nunc* lets the Lord speak to it, listens to and receives the Lord. At bottom, "church" meant a great bureaucratic organization. Vatican II helped to bring about a change here and made us conscious again that together with the unity of the church there must also be the plurality of the churches, that is, the living communities, which are themselves the church and which bring the church into the present.

I think it's from that situation that we must face today's dilemma. On the one hand, broad sectors of the faithful and also official representatives have preserved the bureaucratic concept of the church: now, as formerly, it is believed that the "church" is the pope and the Roman congregations and, perhaps, also the bishops. This church holds little interest for many believers. It's very far from them. They even see it as estranged from the gospel. In this sense they want a Christianity without a church, without "that" church; they want simple and more spontaneous communities. This is something positive to the extent that they are trying to experience Christian life in concrete communities. I'm convinced that the future of the church will depend largely on whether they succeed in forming concrete, visible communities that can be the bearers of Christian experience and can offer humanity a concrete, vital context. In this sense, I see in this movement something entirely positive, even necessary. Next to this positive aspect I see a danger—because these communities lose their ecclesial character as soon as they isolate themselves and live for themselves alone. If the small, concrete communities don't stay within the greater context of the universal church, they degenerate into sects and cease to be a church.

Consequently, both things are quite necessary: on the one hand, there must be concrete and living communities that recognize themselves as a church; on the other hand, these communities must avoid isolationism, must not assume autonomy, total self-rule; they must in full awareness insert themselves into what is catholic, into the universal community of Jesus Christ that is present throughout the world. The mission of the clergy in such cases should be precisely to represent totality in the particular community and to favor communication between the universal and the particular. Here there is much to be learned not only by the community but by the clergy. It seems to me especially important that the union of clergy and living communities be made in a very concrete way and not up in the clouds, in a bureaucratic sphere. To sum up: what matters is, on the one hand, not to lose catholicity, that is, universal communion with the whole church, and with tradition, with the church of all the centuries; on the other hand, to be able to incarnate and make into a living reality here and now, at each time and place, this catholic dimension.

To Find God in the Man Jesus

Inside the church and also outside it, particularly in the younger generations, there is a strong movement toward Jesus. Will he be a Jesus rediscovered in full, or will he be disfigured if seen, above all, as a perfect man and leader? Does christology win or lose by this?

I would distinguish some three movements, and a consideration of the three will allow us to give an exact judgment. The first movement would be the following: there is no doubt that in Christian piety the truth of the true humanity of Christ got left more and more in the shade in the course of the centuries, and in practice Jesus was seen only as God. So there occurred something like a concealment or a clear Monophysitism in Christian piety that did not adhere to the complete Chalcedonian dogma, which proclaimed Jesus true God and true man, but took seriously only that Jesus was divine. Opposed to this tendency there arose some time ago a contrary movement, attributable above all to the renewal in biblical studies and to the greater attention being given to the word of the gospel. This movement has recalled emphatically, from the gospel and from dogma, the true and perfect humanity of Jesus. Persons in this movement see Jesus not only as the God who must be adored but as our brother who advances in life with us, who sets us an example, and who is, for us, the way. We should add that Christian consciousness has not yet been sufficiently activated in all its amplitude by this doctrine.

A second movement exists, as we are seeing, for example, in the "Jesus movement" in the United States, in which, starting from a secular existence, people again seek a meaning for life, and in their groping they discover the figure of Jesus. I believe that this movement, in spite of all its problematics, is a positive awakening that shows people, in a completely new way, the importance of the figure of Jesus. This movement will surely be inadequate as long as it remains a mere romanticism, a romantic humanism, as long as it does not also touch and find the divine mystery of Jesus. But the fact that it puts all its stress first on the man Jesus and only after this finds God—this is in keeping with the gospel and is also a reminder to those who live in the church and in the faith.

The third movement is made up of those who seek only the political thrust of Christianity, those to whom the theological seems quite useless. That's why they exchange the Christian for the political and therefore see Jesus more as a political hero and an earthly teacher than as God. To the extent that this trend is united with the first two movements, I would not condemn it out of hand; but there is certainly a considerable danger here, the danger that we might ultimately exchange Jesus for Barabbas and thus end in a romantic politics that no longer sees in Jesus precisely what Jesus can most properly give us.

I think that what is important is that we in effect find Jesus as a man with his complete humanity and in him find God, and in turn we must be conscious that we can find God only in the concrete man who is Jesus. He is a man who bears a superior mystery, with which he opens to the human being his great plenitude; and, in turn, this superior mystery does not suppress the human side but, rather, carries it on to its perfect fulfillment.

No Triumphal March of Faith

Considering the growth of "secularization," and with the hope that the process of "hominization" will advance, diagnoses are divided. While Johannes Metz states that "the future of Christianity begins now" and some, like him, call our times "pre-Christian," others assert that we are already living in the "post-Christian" era. What do you think, Professor Ratzinger?

It is always disagreeable to have to prophesy! Behind those statements is hidden a certain philosophy of history. At the roots of the diagnosis that sees our time as the "post-Christian" era is the philosophy of Comte, which holds that, after the age of metaphysics, positivism has definitively imposed itself, and faith as faith has disappeared. And behind the Metz diagnosis is Hegel's history of philosophy, which postulates an ever greater consciousness of the absolute spirit and, for that reason, allows for an ever broader progress of what Christ really attempted. But both philosophies of history are very generic constructions, which do not sufficiently do justice to either the differences among people or the specifics of Christian faith.

On the one hand, we must state, contrary to Comte, that man will never be able to live in mere positivism. Precisely those societies where positivism has been most successful, the United States and Western Europe, are reexperiencing now the strongest metaphysical explosions, for the great Marxist movement, as well as the drug-related movement and the religious movements for liberation, all three are an attempt to break with positivism; they are the cry of an idea. This means that there can never be a merely positivist society, which can now be affirmed on the basis of experience. In this context it also seems to me interesting that the classic theologian of secularization, who once insistently defended the godless city, now has gone on to celebrate and emphasize worship and festival, that is, nonpositivist elements. We can therefore say that there will always be something like worship, faith, something like the call to the idea, to the absolute.

Moreover, the Hegelian concept that the consciousness of liberty and the history of liberty are always moving ahead is also contrary to reality. We can observe how each moment of liberty demands, on the other hand, a renunciation of liberty, centralization, surrender of liberty to major unity, and how all this brings with it new possibilities and new forms of slavery and of enslavement that we couldn't even conceive of earlier. So there occur new lapses of liberty, which bring reactions in search of liberty. From this vision of reality we can understand in a new way the gospel message. This does not in any way announce to Christianity an always increasing and uninterrupted triumph. It always foretells new crosses and new difficulties. This means that there will not be any post-Christian era, but that neither will it happen that the church will now begin its triumphal march. Faith will always suffer persecution, human existence will always be in danger. The struggle to save the areas of humanity and liberty will never be superfluous, but it will be more and more difficult and necessary. In such a sense, it can be said simply that the dilemma of humanity, and also of the Christian, remains, but at the same time we must state that new possibilities for one and for the other always arise.

To Evangelize Is to Interpret and Transform

We are very conscious of the clumsiness of our language in speaking of God. We see that our traditional religious language is out of date and that it falsifies the image of God. And we think that the language of testimony and of works is a more faithful language. Should faith go on talking today or should it act? Or is it wrong to subject faith to this choice of alternatives?

There has certainly been quackery about faith and piety that turns out to be dangerous and discredits faith itself. The danger that we will let slip pious words that turn out to be empty and invite contempt is very great. That's why it's better to live the life of Christ than to discourse about it, and being a Christian should show itself in love and works more than in words. This is according to the gospel. But to take refuge in silence, to limit oneself to commitment without any confession of faith, doesn't help anything. I'd just like to point out what Marx said: that we mustn't just interpret the world, we must transform it. To thought and words he opposed praxis.

But today we are aware that an important Marxist—Kolakowski, if I'm not mistaken—has said that we must interpret the world in a new way, a world transformed so swiftly and unreflectively. Mere change is good for nothing if we can't interpret it. I believe that the joining of these two statements, by Marx and by a great Marxist, gives a good answer to our question: mere words without reality are good for nothing; but people are spiritual and intellectual beings, beings who think and talk, so that we can also say that mere praxis without thought, without words, without intelligence, is also good for nothing. In the long run, people cannot achieve a praxis that they cannot interpret, to which they can't give meaning, whose importance they can't express in words. In this sense, it's necessary, on the one hand, that faith not be lavish with words, that it aim always at reality, but, on the other hand, it must always tend to express itself. A living experience of faith necessarily tends to translate itself into words and, on the contrary, it must really live from the words that have been given to us—because it's not only a word but a force that engenders life, where it is received with faith, and where it can express itself in praxis.

What do you think more urgent for today's pastoral ministry, to evangelize non-Christians or to reevangelize Christians?

I do not like to see an alternative between reevangelization of Christians and evangelization of nonbelievers. Because in the very act of evangelizing nonbelievers we find ourselves always obliged to evangelize ourselves, and then we ourselves learn what faith really is. As we evangelize nonbelievers we see to what extent we ourselves are not believers and we learn to believe once again. For this reason the two tasks are intimately interrelated.

What the decisive content of this reevangelization must be depends on the cultural atmosphere of each place and group of people. Speaking in general it could be said that it should be oriented toward the essential and central content of human existence and the gospel; that is, we must learn again what humankind is at the same time that we learn who God is. We must begin with humankind and ask ourselves why humanity is a divided and problematical thing; what is the meaning of human life. Then humankind could be invested with moral obligation and made to understand the function of truth and conscience. With these presuppositions it would be possible to show humankind an image of a God who is reasonable, Christian, and original. We could then show, together with this image of God, the figure of Jesus Christ and the message of his gospel: present Jesus as the revelation of God and at the same time as the way for us. Together with this, thirdly, goes the essential content of Christian hope and Christian duties. It seems to me that what is decisive and important must be to start with humanity's problems, the situation of today, and, in any case, to concentrate on the fundamental points of faith in order not to get lost in the multitude of details that, rather than helping us to discover the central message, will hide it from us.

"About these themes whole books could be written," Ratzinger said, *trying to excuse the many loose ends that were left in the conversation by these swift verbal syntheses. Theologians accustomed to reworking and polishing their expositions and writings are frustrated when they have to limit themselves to a quick synthesis, inevitably incomplete. That's why I turn now to a passage from one of Ratzinger's many publications. It was first a radio talk, but was then polished and I cite it here as a final word from the amiable professor from Ratisbon, now a high-ranking church official. He is talking about the church of the future:*

"It will no longer be able to fill many of the buildings constructed at a more propitious time. As the number of faithful diminishes, it will lose many of its privileges in society. It will have to present itself, in a much more extreme way than up to now, as a voluntary community that can be joined only through a free decision. As a small community, it will need, in a much more intense way, the initiative of its individual members. It will come to know new ministerial forms and it will consecrate as priests proven Christians who will remain in their professions; in many small communities, for example in homogeneous social groups, the pastoral ministry will take precisely this form. Also, priests engaged fulltime in the priesthood will continue to be indispensable. But in all the changes that can be conjectured, the church must find again and most decisively what is its essence, what has always been its center: faith in the God of the Trinity, in Jesus Christ, the son of God made man, the presence of the Spirit which endures until the end of time. The church will again find its authentic nucleus in faith and prayer and it will again experience the sacraments as divine worship, not as a problem of liturgical structuring. It will be an inward-looking church, not proclaiming a political mandate, not flirting with either the left or the right. It will be a difficult situation. . . . The process will have to be long and painful. . . . So it seems certain to me that the church will face very difficult times. Its real crisis hasn't yet begun. We must expect grave shocks. But I'm also absolutely sure that it will last until the end: not the church of political worship, which failed with Gobel, but the church of faith. It will never again be the dominant power in society to the extent that it has been until recently. But it will flourish again and it will become visible to people as a homeland that gives them life and hope beyond death" (Fe y futuro, *Salamanca, 1972, pp. 76–77; Eng.:* Faith and the Future [*Chicago: Franciscan Herald Press, 1971*]).

A Conversation with
Edward Schillebeeckx, O.P.

*Edward Schillebeeckx was born on November 12, 1914, in Ambères,
Belgium. He studied at the School of Theology of Le Saulchoir, France, at
the School of Advanced Studies and at the Sorbonne, Paris. He was ordained in 1941. He is a doctor (1951) and master (1959) of theology. Since
1958 he has been professor of dogmatic theology at the University of
Nijmegen, Holland. He has been visiting professor at Harvard University.
He is director of the review* Tijdschrift voor Theologie *and he is one of the
founders and directors of the international review* Concilium. *Among his
works, almost all of them translated into the principal Western languages,
we may cite* Christ: The Sacrament of the Encounter with God;
Eucharist; The Church and Mankind; Marriage; Definition of the
Christian Layman; The Mission of the Church; Mary, Mother of Re-
demption; The Understanding of Faith: Interpretation and Criticism;
Jesus: An Experiment in Christology.

*He was the theologian that I perhaps most wanted to meet. For many
years I have had great admiration for Schillebeeckx, renewed with each
new writing of his and after each new accusation or insult aimed at him by
self-appointed "inquisitors," the Roman centers of clerical power, or heart-
less slanderers who think themselves so "Catholic."*

*Admiration can crown people with a halo and make them practically
inaccessible. But when we telephoned Schillebeeckx from Brussels, he made
it very easy. We had only to get to Nijmegen (125 miles) and look for the
Albertinum, the university school·and residence of the Dutch Dominicans.*

158

Jean-Pierre's companionship, Richard with his car, and the springtime made the trip an unforgettable delight. The sun, absolute master of the sky and of the fields of Holland, warmed the earth, provoking the first bursts of color in the tulips. In the bicycles that went safely in their own lanes and in the modern elegance of a functional architecture briefly glimpsed in chalets, churches, and country houses, we sensed a practical, developed, and cultivated people.

That afternoon of our conversation with Schillebeeckx was for me, as for Jean-Pierre and Richard, an afternoon of lucidity and friendship, of the most spontaneous mental exactness and pure simplicity, of discernment, cordiality, and faith.

Nijmegen is a small city, modern, calm, friendly, happy, at its height on a day of budding flowers and the light of the warm sun of an early spring, and at an hour when, between pedestrians and cars, there is a bustling rush of bicycles bearing waves of children. It's now two-thirty. At the far end of a great tree-filled square rises the classic harmony of the dark stones of the Albertinum. The spacious study of Professor Schillebeeckx overflows with books; the ceiling is high and books almost reach it; lots of new books, just off the presses, pile up on the table (gray metal, with a big filing cabinet on one side) and on the floor near the wall. Schillebeeckx (medium height, silvery hair, blue eyes brimming with serenity) as he talks radiates a respectful friendship, sober and at the same time warm. We sit in a pleasant corner, with small, low armchairs around a tiny table on a red rug, facing the window that looks out on a courtyard shaded by fir trees. Our host serves us coffee, which we sip as the conversation flows on spontaneously and cordially about the current state of theology and the church.

Accept the Risks of Change

We live in a changing situation in the world and in the church. The consequences for the faith are deep and demanding, but we don't all fit them together in the same way. What is good for some is bad for others. And we don't know how to live in pluralism either. We polarize, we're edgy, we split apart. What can we do?

To begin with, I'd say it's necessary to clarify for the faithful the why and the how of pluralism in faith, to explain why social expressions are changing and why we are changing the very expressions of faith. Many of the faithful have the impression that we're preaching a different faith. It's urgent, therefore, to clarify current changes in relation to the older expressions of faith that we have had. To theologians I'd say we are dealing with a hermeneutic problem: the relation of faith as such with "today," with contemporary human situations, is something essential for faith. We've never had a totally "uniform" and meta-historical expression of faith; we've never had an expression that wasn't historical. Faith has to be rethought always in contemporary circumstances, just like the suppositions of faith, for we embody our faith in current expressions. But now, more than before, our vision of the world and of humanity, of anthropology, and so on, has changed—so much so that there are different anthropologies, different visions of humanity. It's impossible to express faith now in a uniform way: the philosophical and anthropological suppositions are not the same, nor are they uniform. It seems to me that if we manage to make this clear to the faithful, they will see that there's no cause for alarm, that it's a normal thing for faith, that the revising of exterior expressions has always been a prerequisite for faith. It happens that the rhythm of life is faster today than before. Up to now change was unconscious, imperceptible; it took centuries for changes with regard to faith to be noticed. But now everything is shaking, even our own lives, at this historical moment. In our personal lives we have seen enormous changes because of the acceleration of change in cultural and social life, so that we now have to go through a kind of identity crisis.

Some fear the risks of changes in respect to faith and the forms of expressing it and living it, as if they were assaults upon faith itself.

When we try to give new expression to faith in the cultural and social situation of our time we clearly run risks. We mustn't fear the risks, because it's also a risk for faith to rely on traditional and outmoded expressions. On the other hand, to believe is a risky adventure. So we must accept risks without being alarmists. It's clear that today we're not only making efforts to give new expressions to faith, but there is also a tendency of Christians to commit themselves in the world; seeking social solutions to injustices, seeking strictly human solutions, without any attention to or concern about the specifically Christian contribution of Christian faith, hope, and love. It seems to me there are real threats, but instead of fighting those threats directly we must inquire about their causes, we must ask why our Christians, formerly attentive to the church, now go that way. I think that many react against a kind of religious life that wasn't really religious but "supernaturalistic," a "religious" life based on cultural life, a kind of superstructure. It seems to me that it's young people, above all, who feel that a life inspired by faith can't be a "supernaturalistic" life.

Look to the Future More Than to the Past

"We have passed from a faith turned toward the past to a faith facing the future," you wrote in your book God, the Future of Man. *And you state that long ago in the relations of people with nature, insecurity was a "locus" of faith and that today and in the future we shall see new insecurities that will be new "loci" of faith. But today we criticize the past "loci"*

of faith that were based on the insecurity and the cultural ignorance of primitive people. I ask you: don't you think that when we point to the insecurity of the human present and future as a religious locus we are returning to religious ambiguity? If in the insecurity of the past, people invented false relations with God and false images of God, in the insecurity of the future we can also invent new false images and relations with God.

I would say first of all that the transposition of faith (looking to the future instead of looking to the past) is essential for coping with *all* the changes—in faith, and in political and social life. And I would say that the notion of God (always interwoven into our cultural life) used to be presented to us as eternal, unchangeable, like a massive block, but now, when our whole life is directed toward the future, it is presented to us in another way and we speak of God as "the one who is coming" in history. I'd say that it's a new vision that has many similarities with the biblical notion of God, especially with the Old Testament vision for which God was always the God who was coming, "the one who is coming." Clearly we must recognize that this leads us to new risks and to new ambiguities.

Moreover, in all the reactions of neosacralism in America (which has also reached Europe), we see that they begin with a protest, a critique of our society based exclusively on science and technology; technocracy becomes the only way of making and programming the future, and they answer and protest against the fact of leaving blocked and frustrated certain essential possibilities and capacities of people, such as the contemplative, the aesthetic, the re-creational. We of the West, buried by the positive sciences and by technology, have become incapable of activating all those human capacities. It seems to me that in all the neosacral movements there is a protest of the human psyche that is suffering from this technocratic domination.

People protest being reduced to one-dimensional beings.

One-dimensionality, exactly. It seems to me (and some American psychologists have viewed it the same way) that when those human capacities aren't realized and remain frustrated, people become neurotic. And all those neosacral movements are, perhaps, neurotic movements without a substantially religious content. But, on the other hand, they are a warning for us of the one-dimensionality of our technocratic society.

Is that a sign that there is a place for God, for faith, in the new cultural and technical society?

Yes, but not in the sense that we can give free rein to a new religious certainty by saying: "It's clear that the person of today is religious." Be careful. The human psyche needs to exercise its contemplative, aesthetic, etc., dimension, and this can happen by living an authentic religion. But it's not the need for religion that makes religion real and authentic.

That's the ambiguity that I was trying to point out. And tell me, how do you judge those neosacral movements?

I see in them several dimensions. On the one hand, I see a certain religious significance from its dimension as a response to our society, a warning for the churches, because we also have neglected the mystical dimension of religion. On the other hand, without the background of ecclesial tradition, the content of all those movements can get to be childish. And besides, their critique is a serious warning for all of us from the psychological point of view: they tell us that we are all neurotic.

Renovation of the Summit Will Come from the Base

If there is a crisis of the religious (and Christian) models of the past, and we don't yet have the models of the future, we have to admit that we find ourselves at a very critical moment of evolution. We do not have today any valid "model" to live the faith, to think of God, to talk to God, and to talk about God. Christian life, prayer, and preaching are in crisis.

That's true. But we can already see certain models, in secular and social life as well as in the religious field. For example, the experiments of the small communities, the communes, etc., all those new experiments that are beginning to be made. And counterculture. Attempts have been made to incorporate counterculture into a model for a church-communion. I see possibilities of diverse models for the church. We can see the institution of the church evolving in the direction of a church-communion model—not directly toward world communion, since for the moment it's impossible. It's beginning with the communion of Christian life that tries to be more evangelical in a "base group." This is being done with all the ambiguities and risks that we know, but the idea that people want to lead a more communitarian and more evangelical life seems to me very valid from the religious point of view and from the sociopolitical point of view.

There is a danger that these "base groups" will separate themselves from the hierarchy of the church, from the official institution. In fact, it has already happened, in some cases. Is this inevitable? Is it necessary? Is it completely negative or does it have positive aspects for the church?

It is clear that the base communities, the really new and experimental communities, are a little separated from the official church. Just as there is today reaction against society, there is also reaction against the official church which, from the psychological point of view, is one of the components of that society. I believe we have to take this path to reach a real renewal of the church as institution, for renewal of the institution downward from the top is no longer possible; in my opinion. I did once think it possible and I hoped it would come about. But now it seems to me that the renewal of the summit has to come from the base—and friction is inevitable. All that seems to me necessary and I believe it can be beneficial.

That kind of tension—"productive criticism"—can be desirable, but we see that usually the institution and its summit reject it and those who are critical get tired and quit. Would you say that we are passing from criticism to indifference? There are people and groups who are turning their backs on the official church, in principle, with the intention of living the gospel with greater freedom and authenticity, although subsequent evolution is unpredictable. Will we have to say that they have abandoned the church? Or will we have, rather, to think that they are the leavening of a more evangelical church, with a new visage?

Yes, you're right. In fact, now, in our post-Vatican Council period, people at first got so hopeful about institutional renewal that now, in a kind of disillusion, they have even given up criticizing and have become indifferent. Some haven't kept even a partial identification with the institution. But we have to admit that they have kept an identification, a very serious one, with the gospel. From the theological point of view, I criticize this; I do not accept the possibility of having a Christianity or a Christian community that is not ecclesial. But on the other hand, we not only have to be indulgent with those people, we have to get to understand what is happening: in fact, they identify themselves with the church nucleus that is the gospel; they criticize the current institutionalism and want to be Christians on the basis of the gospel. I repeat that theologically I can't accept this, but I understand these people; I understand them. It's the reaction of disillusionment with an institutional church that is a deception. A somewhat unilateral reaction but in substance—it must be said—a reaction to the experience of disillusionment. There remains a partial or almost no identification with the church-institution, but a total identification with the religious substance of the church, which is the gospel. I believe that it is a way, even though indirect, toward the most authentic, most evangelical reinstitutionalization of the church.

It Is Rome That Is Isolated

Given that the experience of faith occurs now in life (not simply in criticism of church officials or even in indifference) and that, moreover, theological reflection is gradually accepting life as a "theological locus," what possibilities remain for the magisterium, the teaching authority of the church?

I would say, first of all, that the magisterium as such has never been

a *theological locus*. It is the *ultimate judge* of our theological interpretation of faith and revelation. The magisterium is not a theological locus
but the final judge of all the theological loci, sources. There is clearly
also another scientific, theological magisterium, on a different level
from that of the juridical, charismatic magisterium of the church
(because I believe in the charism of the magisterium). Moreover, it can
be said that the magisterium has become "substantialized" as though
it were a source of revelation in itself, whereas, in the whole Catholic
and Christian tradition, the magisterium has had a function of communication with the faithful and the theologians. The magisterium
has to find its substance, its doctrine, in the gospel, in tradition, in the
lives of Christians. We mustn't therefore make a kind of "substance"
out of the magisterium. There has to be collaboration between the
hierarchical teaching of the church and scientific teaching. That collaboration demands dialogue because theologians have to be at the
advanced stages of investigations about matters that must be approved by the church. There is always a tension, a friction, which I
believe is healthy when there is mutual comprehension. But now that
friction is severe. Theologians belong to the church but today they
have a critical attitude toward the institution, and so that friction is
more intense. But the worst thing is the fact that the magisterium, in
judging the new theology, always uses the classic theology of the
theologians of Rome. In my opinion, that is a breakdown in communication, because theologians are judged not by the criteria of the gospel
and the authentic tradition of the church but by the criteria of Roman
theology, and it seems to me that the *legitimate* pluralism of theology is
neither represented nor respected. There are some other legitimate
schools of theology today. But all the other theological positions are
judged by the one that rules in Rome. Nevertheless, I now see new
shadings in the theology that is called Roman.

Are we perhaps moving toward the era of the isolation of Rome?
    It seems to me that that is the great theological and even ecclesiolog-
ical danger today. I think, moreover, that perhaps that will be the only
road that will take us to an evangelical reevaluation of the center, of
Rome. But I see that it is a Rome that isolates itself more and more. I
hope that in the long run this will bring Rome to consider seriously a
decentralization that, in principle, began with Vatican II, but in the
post-Council period has gone back to pre-Council positions of uni-
formism.

To Renew the Great Religious Orders Seems to Me Impossible

*You have also reflected and written on the religious life and its renewal.
How do you view that renewal at present?*

I don't know what the situation may be in Spain. Here, among us, there are more signs of renewal in religious life than in the life of the secular clergy. In Holland the renewal of religious communities has a fairly steady rhythm. There are many new communities, centers of religious "base groups," that are trying to renew religious life. Some experimental houses have been closed because their protagonists gradually lost interest. But there are experimental communities that are very well balanced in the dimensions of theology and mysticism as well as in the dimension of social criticism.

The new vision of "eschatology" (which you promote in your writings), which makes us live in the present the "promises" of God like a leavening that quickens and renews current history—must it not open up new perspectives on the religious life, given its essential role of "eschatological sign" in the church and in the world?

Yes, without question. One of the essential dimensions of the religious life is to be an eschatological sign, but I would say not in the traditional sense of "eschatology"; not in the sense proposed by a certain pseudo-mysticism of the religious life, as a sign of an eschatological life too evasive because it is supernaturalistic. No. Eschatology is now being reworked in two directions, in the contemplative, mystical sense of a vision of the future, and also in the direction of commitment to and influence on life in the world. And the new experiments in religious life that are trying to be authentic must go forward in the two directions: in the renewal of the life of prayer and in a very sincere commitment to social and political life.

It has always been considered that "communitarian life" was something very special in the religious life. But today there is a search for a greater ecclesial and social realism in community life, a more realistic contact with the Christian community and with the whole human community of which we're an active part. Do you think this search is correct? Does it answer the demands of the essence of the religious life?

Yes. Perfectly. I'd say it's absolutely necessary that religious communities stop being like little churches within the church, like ghettos, and that they come to be concentrations of evangelical life that are indeed a "sign" (and an eschatological sign, in the sense already mentioned) for the Christian community and for human society.

Would it be better to go on trying to renew the existent religious orders as a whole and all together, or would it be better to create new groups, to look for new forms of the religious life?

I believe it is impossible to renew the great orders. And I wouldn't say we should try to create new orders and congregations. I would say, rather, that certain people, certain religious of the great orders and of the existing congregations, ought to be able to experience their own lives in new circumstances. But to renew the great orders "as such" seems to me impossible.

Then the best solution for renewing religious life must be to create within a present congregation groups that try to create new forms of religious life, instead of going on attempting the renewal of the whole institution at a uniform pace.

If this were to lead to a division between groups that think themselves orthodox and observant in contrast to small experimental communities or groups seen as "suspected" of heresy and of being formed by less observant religious, I am completely against it. We would have to avoid that risk at any cost. But it seems to me, on the other hand, a solution with a great future to have an order or congregation allow in its midst small groups for experimentation and searchings.

This requires great mutual understanding and a great freedom that would demand of superiors that they relinquish any desire to control things too much.

Clearly. It demands that the superiors who allow in their jurisdictions those new experimental communities should not keep looking over their shoulders but should allow freedom of action. Let them see to it that experimentation is done by well-balanced people and let these people really experiment and search. It happens at times that there are not enough well-balanced people in those experimental groups, and then failure results.

Charity Is Also Politics

Today faith makes us look at the future as a challenge made to the faithful by the "promises" of the God who is coming. And this obliges us to embody faith in human advancement and in social and political commitments. But in the church there are hesitations and fear in view of several risks: exhaustion and reduction of faith to an ideology (at times this fear is a reflex conditioned by the other ideology that has exhausted faith in an opposite sense), new opportunisms, new clericalism. . . .

Of course, there are always risks, but they have to be faced—because this is demanded by the very theology of Christian life, of "charity." St. Thomas says that charity is a theological virtue that has two objects: God and the world. But it is one theological virtue: it is *caritas*—love. That means that love that has only the vertical dimension, toward God, without the dimension toward humanity, would be a pseudo-charity, a pseudo-religion. It must have the double dimension: toward God and toward humanity.

Besides, in modern society, charity is not only interpersonal love (which will always keep its own efficacy and always has to endure) but also social and political commitment because, in the structure of our society, charity does not become really effective if it is not embodied in social and political structures. Which means that the mediation of social and political commitment is necessary if we are to have a true, complete, and effective charity in the world of today. Consequently, the combination of the theological, mystical life of the church and the political and social life of Christian commitment constitute a single reality of religious life. You can't love God without loving humankind. And loving humankind in concrete circumstances is not loving an isolated person but the person who always exists within given structures, in a life that is social and political. And those structures and that social and political life are unjust to a very great extent. So not to change the structures is to give up Christian charity. I, consequently, see no split, and even less opposition, between Christian life and political commitment: for believers they implicate each other. The danger is in completely neglecting religious life, the relation of love toward God, and committing ourselves to the social and political struggle exactly like Marxists or others, as if we were not believers.

Critical and Utopian Functions

What would be the specifics of the role of faith in social and political commitment and struggle?

Faith does not allow us to consider humanity as the universal subject of history. The universal subject of history is God, the living God; it's not the proletariat or the wealthy class. There is not a universal subject of history within it; there is not even a meaning of history in the closed interior of history; there does exist a meaning given to history by God. Therefore one can never identify the universal meaning of history with humanity as such, and, *a fortiori*, one cannot identify the universal meaning and the total course of history with a brief moment of that history, our generation, for example, or the next generation, to which our generation must be sacrificed, according to the Marxists. Or is it that the proletariat is the subject of the universal meaning of history? No. For the Christian it is God himself manifested in Christ who is the center of humanity and the subject that gives universal meaning to history. We must never make a premature identification with what has already been achieved. We must always transcend the status quo.

Moreover, all our plans for the future to achieve a different social structure are always in the terrain of the provisional, subject to the eschatological proviso. That is, neither the individual nor humanity can be completely fulfilled in history. Consequently, humanity, history, always develops within a life toward the *eschaton*, toward eschatology, toward an absolute future that transcends all the future that we can achieve in history. That eschatological proviso always exists.

We are always expecting—in every situation and in every change—we are always expecting a fulfillment of history made by God beyond and above our efforts. This search and this hope are specifics of Christian faith.

But the nonbelieving revolutionaries will say to us: if you never get to the end, if you're always waiting for the final fulfillment by God, you're still in alienation.

When we say or think, "Let things run on, let them pass, let them come, the future is in the hands of God," then religion *is* an alienation. But we can commit ourselves fully and to the very end; we must commit ourselves. I would even say that there are exceptional circumstances in which revolution is the only means of defense against oppressive structures and unjust repression. In extreme cases, revolution can be, from the Christian point of view, legitimate.

What function, then, does faith play in social, political, and revolutionary commitment? From what you have now said we can deduce a critical function, of relativization of all the achieved situations, of the changes, of all that has been acquired.

Two functions. A critical function of relativization of everything acquired, yes. But also a "utopian" function. We must never stop, we must never just let things go, saying, "We must give up, we can't change the world." The utopian strength stimulates us, is always calling on us to improve the world.

Not Every Option for Violence Is Anti-Christian

And when violence is all around us?

It's a very delicate question. Violence and the kingdom of God are basically incompatible. Where there is a bloody revolution, the kingdom of God hasn't yet come. But, on the other hand, in the whole Christian tradition there has been acceptance, in certain circumstances, of self-defense in a violent way. It is possible that in certain countries there exists an organized dictatorship, a dictatorship with a clearly unjust structure, and when all the other means have been tried without success, I think that, to defend the people of those countries, to a limited extent a certain ethics of revolution can be justified. I would not say, on the other hand, that a *theology* of revolution is possible. I favor the limited possibility of an ethics of revolution.

Of violent revolution?

Yes. A certain ethics. I insist that a theology of violent revolution is impossible because it is incompatible with the kingdom of God. But we live in the interim in which the kingdom has not yet arrived definitively. We are not yet in the *eschaton*. We have that very complex situation in which certain Christians say, "We've got to make a revolution," while others say, "No, that goes against the evangelical faith," and others add, "Yes, it goes against the fundamental tendency of the gospel, but the situation is such that if we don't make bloody revolution we become collaborators with evil," with established violence, which is also against the gospel.

Do you think the situation you have just described exists in some countries?
In certain countries, yes, I believe it is real.

In them, therefore, anguishing Christian problems must be met.
Undoubtedly.

Would it be valid to present the problem in these terms: we find ourselves in a mostly "pre-Christian" situation because cruelty and injustice prevail and there is no place for brotherly love, and in order to prepare for the time when it will be possible to live according to the demands of the gospel of love, we act in a rather "pre-Christian" way by violently confronting the violence of established injustice in order to remove it?
I wouldn't say that exactly. Because in fact we're talking about Christians who are living in the interim between resurrection and Parousia. They are clearly not in the full realization of the kingdom of God, since together with it there also exists the "old world" filled with injustices. And those injustices can reach a peak, and have reached the peak in certain countries, and there's no way of escaping them. In those specific cases I think that, from the point of view of Christian conscience, one can't condemn an option for violence against established violence that can't be defeated by other means. But here it's a question of making a completely personal judgment. You can't give valid personal judgments for everyone. Because from the Christian point of view you can always say, "It's incompatible with the kingdom of God; I won't join a revolution." But, though a Christian, I can't condemn another Christian who says, "If I don't side with a bloody revolution, I become a collaborator with evil and this I cannot do."

So, in certain cases, to "kill" may be as Christian as to "let oneself be killed"?
A Christian may say, "I let myself be killed for another's sake." But someone else equally Christian, in extreme cases, may say the opposite. For example, in the so-called just war. And if there are cases where war or bloody revolution can be considered "just," it's precisely in those countries where established violence and oppressive regimes don't allow any other solution.

170 EDWARD SCHILLEBEECKX, O.P.

The choice that Jesus made for nonviolence and for becoming a victim, that's not normative for Christians?

Careful! There's a false alternative there when you make an unwarranted application. You say, "A Christian has to sacrifice the self for others." I say, "Yes, that's Christian, for me to sacrifice myself, but I can't sacrifice *the others* to a system." Can we, as Christians, let someone else be killed? Don't we have an obligation to defend the other, even with arms? There are people socially, politically, and sociologically suppressed by the system. Don't we have the right and the duty to defend them? It's not about me; I could say, "Let them kill me," but I can't let others be killed; I have to defend them. That is a Christian choice.

But we sometimes lack the necessary conditions for revolutionary violence to be effective beyond a certain point, because at times violent revolt merely succeeds in increasing the established violence that then counts even more victims.

All the due conditions are required. When it is clear that revolution will achieve only repression or a change of power with the same consequences of unjust oppression, then it's not an effective, justifiable revolution, nor is it legitimate for Christians.

Perhaps that's the basis of the reasoning of those who militate for active nonviolence.

When you say *active* I agree with nonviolence, but in the strong sense of the word "active," with action, boycott, etc.

Which is also a kind of violence, although not bloody.

It's organized violence.

It's Not Good Theology That Sees Jesus Only as a Man

I'll change the subject. Do you believe that from the theology of the death of God we have moved to the theology of Jesus the man?

Yes and no. The theology of the death of God is the theology of Jesus of Nazareth as a perfect model of life. It is, to be sure, not properly a theology of the death of God, just like that: it's a kind of christology. The theology of the death of God has now completely gone, but there is still this connection with Jesus Christ the man. And for me, from the theological point of view, that is a serious problem: what reason do I have to bind myself to a man so absolutely? It is implicitly a christology, a confession of faith in Jesus. I would still say that it's not good theology. It's necessary to explicate why you bind your own life to another person. If you have no reason, you cannot bind yourself so unconditionally to someone else; it goes against all modern humanism. Therefore there is seen implicitly in Jesus Christ a kind of transcendence. But I also believe that the final result of that kind of theology will be to say, "We no longer need Jesus Christ." And that is already pure humanism. You can't maintain a christology that affirms that the man Jesus, just the "man" Jesus, is the end and example of our lives. Why, if he's only a man? When you think more deeply about it, the conclusion will be, "Let's dispense with Jesus." And that's happening now.

Will we have to talk to the people of today and tomorrow about God as human or talk to them about humans as God has revealed them in Jesus Christ?

That is a hermeneutic circle. We must talk about Jesus, about the man Jesus in relation to God. We can't talk about God except in "secular" terms, in terms of the man Jesus. When we do that, we have the modern formula of the hypostatic union or the relation of the man Jesus with God and of God with the man Jesus, and this is a circle, not vicious but hermeneutic.

Schillebeeckx has to return to his classes and we to Brussels. The court-yard of the fir trees, beyond the large window, has filled up with young people. "We have more than six hundred young people who are studying theology here, at the school; they're not studying for the priesthood, but preparing for new ministries in the church." One would say that the faith of these young people, who are waiting for the future by shaping it, does not come from the past but from the future. One would say that in this there is the hand of God coming like the great future of humankind and the church.

A Conversation with
Juan Luis Segundo, S.J.

Juan Luis Segundo was born on October 31, 1925, in Montevideo, Uruguay, and was ordained in 1955. He pursued his ecclesiastical studies in philosophy at San Miguel, Argentina, and in theology at Louvain, Belgium. He earned his doctorate in letters (philosophy and theology) at the University of Paris. He was director from 1965 to 1971 of the Pedro Fabro Center of Social Studies in Montevideo. Among his published works are A Theology for Artisans of a New Humanity *(5 vols.) and* The Liberation of Theology.

I first knew his Theology for Artisans of a New Humanity *when its five volumes were in course of publication and its author was occupied with pastoral duties directing the Pedro Fabro Center in Montevideo. Then I met him in person. So I first learned that Juan Luis Segundo is a serious, realistic, and critical Christian thinker. Later I learned that he is an amiable man.*

He is one of those "spare-time theologians," to borrow Gutiérrez's terminology, who have collaborated on the creation of Latin American theology. And he gave me the most precise definition of the so-called Latin American theologian (why not simply "theologian"?): "theologians involved in commitment, ours and others', who seek light from faith at the same time that we rethink faith from that commitment."

I was impressed by his characteristic way of thinking and by his deliberate speech, slowing his words with the pleasant musical lilt of gaucho talk.

A rustic garden (in the cool morning of a day that will get warm), with one of its rough wooden benches as seat and table, is conducive to a good

172

conversation. Especially when the speaker has the ability to couch his rich and profound thoughts in very graphic words and images, with elegant irony.

We Are Defending a God Who Does Not Exist

What dangers seem to you most serious for faith?

For me the gravest danger for faith continues to be the divorce between faith and life with its commitments (to use a formula of Vatican II). But I would like to carry this to a conclusion that, it seems to me, was not present in the Council and which, at least in our Latin American situation, I find absolutely decisive: I believe the dangers for faith are viewed in ecclesiastical circles as dangers that threaten orthodoxy. And they are viewed thus because it is supposed that faith is something that, on a par with the sacraments, has a kind of *ex opere operato* effectiveness for salvation. That is, that exactitude in the maintenance of dogmas has an *ex opere operato* efficacy, which means that it is, up to a certain point, like a church possession, as if the church *owned* the truth.

I believe that the gospel warns us against this enormous danger. A people that believed it owned the truth was disqualified by Jesus from being his people. The chosen people believed it possessed the truth. The parable of the man who hid his talent is very important in this respect because it is directed at the Jewish adversaries of Jesus: that one who believed that what he had to do was to put away his talent and not make it bear fruit is not only condemned, but they take away from him the talent that he possessed; they take away from him the truth that he thought he possessed, his orthodoxy. I believe that orthodoxy is being lost because it's being kept as a deposit, as something that mustn't be made fruitful. On the basis of believing that to keep faith it's necessary to defend it and protect it against dangers, it is being kept as a possession of the church, which protects it against the perils of dialogue with those who have no faith. And in defending faith like that we are losing faith even in orthodoxy. For example, we're defending a God who doesn't exist. The Council itself says so: Christians are presenting to many who are atheists a God in whom they, through obedience to grace, cannot recognize as the true God and whom they therefore have to reject. That is, those Christians, although using orthodox formulas, are not within orthodoxy.

I believe that this is the greatest danger: to think that faith is a kind of possession of the church that is best preserved when the formulas are repeated in a strictly orthodox way and when the Christian stays far away from dialogue with others who do not keep the faith in the same orthodox way. For me this is a vital concern: we are suffering because of it.

The Most Urgent Task Is Evangelization

What tasks do you consider now most urgent to awaken or revive faith?

As something fundamental and basic, I think the most urgent task is evangelization: getting faith to reach people as "good news." In fact, it doesn't reach them as good news but as something ideologized, that is, as a restrictive condition for salvation. If you ask Latin Americans what good news Christianity brings them, they'll answer (as we have shown): "For me it's not good news. I yield to it because it's a condition for salvation, as I yield to the law to obtain the benefits of society. I can't hope to have the benefits of society without yielding to the law, whether or not I like it." This comparison between faith and law is very interesting because Christianity ought to be freedom from law. (Paul applies this to the law, first in Galatians, and then, using the same terminology, to the church in Corinth. The Corinthians were not Judaists; just as the law was badly interpreted by the Jews when it was conceived of as a restrictive condition reached after the promise, so the Corinthians go wrong when they imagine a church, coming later, as a restrictive condition of a promise of universal salvation.) For that reason the first task for an authentic evangelization is to convince the church that it is not a restrictive condition for salvation, that it does not possess the truth so that people approach it with a minimum of demands, but that it is a function, a service—just as the law had a function to help reach the promises of Abraham and was not a restrictive condition through which one had to pass.

The First Defect of Evangelization: Its Absence

What defects and falsifications do you see in evangelization?

The first and gravest defect that I see in evangelization is that it doesn't exist. It's confused with wanting Christianity to be accepted, but authentic evangelization doesn't take place. After establishing that it doesn't take place in Latin America, it would be interesting to ask why.

One thing that shows that there's no evangelizing is that nobody identifies the gospel, the faith, and belonging to the church with good news, with great joy. And if Christianity isn't joy, it isn't Christianity, it isn't gospel. I could give you other interesting data in which we can see something serious: that because they haven't been evangelized, Christians don't see the relationship that there is between the evangelical message and the historical process that is going on.

I believe that if evangelization doesn't exist, it's not for lack of good will in our pastors; but they don't take into account some elements that are essential to evangelization. First of all, in my way of thinking, to give the evangelical message with authenticity you have to give the essence of the gospel. The church has been accustomed to have time to give the gospel—long formative years. Thanks to social pressure entire generations gradually became Christian simply by living where they did. Now, on the other hand, dealing with more open-minded people who have other ideas and other possible options, we know that we have at our disposal only the time those people give us, perhaps half-hour's conversation. If in that time something interesting has been said, something that really turns out to be good news, the person will become more interested, but if in that time nothing interesting has been said, the person will say goodbye and depart. So what must the church do when it has to evangelize in the course of a normal conversation? It has to find the gospel message and reduce it to the essentials so that it can be told in the course of a half-hour. To recover the essentials implies going back twenty centuries, for from then on the essentials have been gradually coated by things that were, to be sure, true and respectable, but accidental, secondary additions to what is essential.

In the second place, evangelization has to give the essential as a piece of good news. Which means that evangelization must begin by listening to the expectations of humankind. It must begin not by talking but by listening, a task that the church does not perform. The church thinks it already knows what evangelization is, independent of the expectations of humankind, without listening to humankind. Worse: the church distrusts this listening, because it thinks that this humanizes and horizontalizes faith and creates the danger of giving answers that are merely human instead of answers of faith. And the church *prefers* to give answers without regard to expectations. Thus the good news aspect of evangelization completely disappears.

In the third place, another essential facet of evangelization seems to me to "keep the rhythm" in such a way that the essence stays as essence. Here human freedom comes into play. Freedom needs time to assimilate a truth; it needs to be able to experiment, and maybe it's going to go wrong ten times before applying the truth correctly, but it needs to go wrong ten times to make the truth its own; if not, all it will do is repeat it like a parrot without digesting it. Lercaro said very wisely, commenting on Pius XII's concept of tolerance, that it is truth itself that demands tolerance because truth demands freedom to err. But we in the church want to avoid errors before they occur and we therefore submerge what is essential into the prevention of possible errors. For example: for a person upset by the loss of a love, the essence of the Christian message could perhaps be translated as good news in these words: "No love is ever lost." This might be good news for that person, but we don't dare to leave a person just with the idea that no love is ever lost and that the death and resurrection of Christ mean that no love is ever lost on earth. Why not? Because a person with just that idea can become a Buddhist, a Communist, a Protestant. So we quickly add: "But be careful; you have to follow the teachings of the church." Thereby we are coating the essential with something else, true but accidental, distracting that person's attention. Instead of thinking profoundly how no love is ever lost, they are going to learn the latest lesson from the ecclesiastical magisterium. So once again evangelization is lost. Well, then, to avoid this, evangelization must have a rhythm that respects freedom—not simply as a value in itself, and much less to enter into any subjectivism, but because freedom is a conditioning of truth. Let's admit that the church doesn't have this respect but that it gives its doctrine with such a rhythm that the essence of Christianity as good news is inevitably lost and becomes a warning not to fall into error, practical warnings, necessary or helpful, good things but secondary, that can reach the point of smothering the essentials.

To Exorcise the Demons as They Appear

You have pointed out, as the most serious problem for faith, its separation from life and vital commitments. In the commitments of faith to political and social change in Latin America, do you see falsifications of faith, diminution or ideologization, or could there just be ghosts invented for good or other intentions?

We know that we're not going to find a new formulation and new attitudes and commitments that will sever faith and ideology. We know that we are always going to be exposed to ideological elements, old or new, that will no doubt interfere with and threaten faith in various ways, without our being able now to foresee it all. And for the moment this doesn't worry us to the extent of making us retreat before the task. That's why I want to express my agreement with your statement of the question: ghosts of demons can be created before the demons appear. I believe we have decided to exorcise the demons when they appear and, for that very reason, to enter the struggle facing the demon that exists today and wait until tomorrow for tomorrow's demon. In this we believe we're being faithful to the gospel.

I'll confirm this to you with an example: some people are alarmed when salvation is translated as liberation. But the gospel already does this. Christ says he comes to free people from all slavery and he announces freedom for captives and the oppressed. Therefore, there's no cause for alarm if we understand that salvation is liberation from all captivity and slavery and not just from the first one that appears. But people bristle when we try to go beyond that and say, for example, that salvation and socialism have a relationship for us. I believe they are seeing ghosts of the past. And I say this with the support of the gospel, because the word "salvation" is used in the Bible to designate limited acts of salvation subject to unlimited perils later.

For example, we often use "salvation" to designate cures that are the most provisional that can be imagined, and do not free the "saved" (cured) person from future and new illnesses. "Daughter, your faith has saved you; go in peace." Some would be inclined to say, "What imprudence! Can this person be saved because she has been freed from an illness, when she can be involved in an unending series of other subjugations? How imprudent to use the word 'salvation' to refer to a specific liberation subject to all the threats, ambiguities, and uncertainties of the future!" Well, then, if I see, in the world that it is my lot to live in, that my Latin American brothers are starving to death and if I see a regime, for example, Cuba, where nobody is starving to death; if I know that fifty percent of my Latin American brothers are illiterate and I see a regime that is at least trying to teach reading and writing to over ninety percent of its population, can't I say that we need that regime as an instance of salvation in principle, as a salvation of something that is basically preventing liberation today, even knowing that afterward I'm going to have to struggle and perhaps die so that that regime will free itself of other slaveries that it still has? Can it be so risky to use the same word to designate a new platform of liberative struggle that, on the other hand, nobody takes as liberation from all subjugations but that offers the real possibility that for the whole population of Latin America and not half of it—because the other half is dying of hunger, of slavery, or of illiteracy—we can see where we have to go to achieve freedom from all subjugations?

I believe, then, that there is a kind of initial shock that is paralyzing. And we try to free ourselves from it by relying on the gospel that, with enormous audacity, called things "salvation" which were so only inchoatively. We want to have the same freedom to call "salvation" what really is salvation even though only inchoatively.

To Practice Theology Facing the Questions
That Arise in Latin America

Tell me about the Latin American theology. How was it born?

The beginning of this type of Latin American theological and pastoral reflection is closely tied to the restrictions on theological work in Latin America. There is practically no possibility of being a professional theologian there. In Latin America professional theologians feel frustrated because in Europe they have seen what a professional theologian is, and in Latin America there are no means—no scientific means, no libraries, or anything else—to live one's profession and to succeed in it. The most one can achieve is the following of a group of students, which is to achieve very little in our world. This has disqualified every theoretical theology that there could have been in Latin America. It has disallowed it on all sides: the theologian feels disallowed and the others feel disallowed.

On the other hand, the urgency that we feel to join our Christians in their commitment to theological and pastoral reflection has led us to practice theology well or badly: that is, to practice the theology that we can practice with the means that in fact we have. This can't be put off. If we don't have the resources of European theology, we'll practice it with the resources we have. This decision is expressed in what Gustavo Gutiérrez rightly says, that perhaps in Latin America we theologians have to be "spare-time theologians." We are theologians involved in commitments, ours and others', who seek light from faith at the same time that we rethink faith from that commitment.

What relation do you see between your theology and that of Europe? Continuity or rupture, complementarity or confrontation?

First of all, I don't believe our theology presupposes a rupture with European theology or with what European theology can give us. I believe that in Europe something has developed that is also essential for us, and that many of us have taken from Europe itself: not a "theology" with a problematic and a predetermined treatment that is very European and is a grave danger for us (what I call "the theology of the latest European book"), but the theology that consists in a good handling of the sources in the most critical and realistic way possible. As a Latin American theologian I have a duty to answer the questions that come up in Latin America and I have a duty to answer them without consulting the latest European book (because the questions are different), but by referring to God's own word, which is in the Scriptures. If I have brought from Europe a theological problematic and not a handling of Scripture that is relatively autonomous and critical, I'm never going to be able to answer those Latin American questions.

By what I have said I am describing the Latin American theologian as somewhat handicapped, as someone who has to practice theology with extremely poor means but who tries to elaborate a theology that can answer the new questions, going again to the sources in all their richness. In this the Latin American theologian is the debtor of the European theologian, and we can't think of a Latin American theology that is not indebted to European theology. What I believe tragic is the transplanting of problems rooted in a knowledge of the sources, if the sources are reached through a European problematic. I am not, therefore, so simplistic as to imagine a total break between Latin American and European theologies. They are both ecclesial theologies. But I am not so naive as to think that a Latin American theologian is going to practice Latin American theology based on the latest European book.

I wish to add that our theology, to the extent that it corresponds with an important and valid problematic throughout the world, can have echoes outside Latin America—because that problematic comes from a place that is very much alive today in the church. And if they reach the point of pardoning the errors (let's call them "scientific") of our questions and reach the point of perceiving the problematic, I think this could be a boon for the rest of the church.

Neither Shouts nor Slogans: Reality and the Word of God

What is your method? What kind of reflection do you pursue? We know that today in the church there are two theologies in opposition: one that draws on present historical realities and wants to relate God's revelation to human history to bring light to new situations and one that does not want to draw on present historical realities but, from the principles and categories with which revelation is interpreted, considering them fixed and eternal (since they have their precise cultural origin in other centuries), wants to draw conclusions that are always the same and never get to throw light on new situations, given that in advance it has not been willing to draw on new realities. What kind of theological reflection do you Latin Americans pursue?

You pointed out one of the extreme dangers of the methodology of theological reflection: that those who condition the methodology condition the problematic. I would point out the opposite danger, which we constantly find and which makes us humble before any result of our theology: to call reality what is not reality but a misconceptualization of it, and so to bring to our theology cries of enthusiasm or despair rather than authentic questions that can be answered theologically. This we are seeing confirmed in gospel readings in some communities of committed Christians. Another tendency, common among those who are currently studying theology, is to study in their own country because it seems alienating to study theology abroad. But what does it come down to when some of them come to practice theology in their own country? Their knowledge of the reality of the country is reduced to what I would call a journalistic knowledge: the contact of that theologian with reality is limited to reading the newspaper.

I believe that our reflecting has to be done between two dangerous reefs and that it is very difficult to escape from both of them at the same time. I have no great confidence that our results are going to be wholly valid, but I want to show you where, it seems to me, a method can go that tries to escape those two reefs. I believe that a good method demands a certain preliminary hermeneutics of reality, and here enters the "mediation" that, together with commitment—because without it it's extremely conceptualistic and ideal—contains hermeneutic principles of reality. That is, that the question is how to interpret reality: how to go from the newspaper to what lies beneath the reality that seems ephemeral, contingent; what is at stake beneath the events that are taking place?

If we don't interpret reality profoundly, if even committed Christians don't see beneath the surface, they are never going to question authentically or to accept a questioning of the Scriptures and the sources. In many Christian communities the renewal of life has become impoverished to the point of using evangelical slogans instead of reading the word of God in all its profundity. They never read the whole word of God, even in itself: texts are chosen that can support their own position and commitment, but there is no base for questions in depth and so they can't endure a response in depth.

This man talks as he writes, taking apart with wide-ranging and sharp analysis the accretions piled up by the doctrine and practices of Catholicism that have become custom and convention. His is a boldly critical theology.

A Conversation with
Jean-Marie Tillard, O.P.

Jean-Marie Tillard was born September 2, 1927, on Saint-Pierre et Miquelon, off Newfoundland. He entered the Dominicans in 1950. He studied philosophy at the Angelicum, Rome, and theology at Le Saulchoir, France. A doctor of philosophy and a master of theology, he is professor of dogmatic theology in the Dominican Scholasticate in Ottawa, and he is also professor in the Lumen Vitae Institute in Brussels. In the two fields on which his theological interest has centered, ecumenism and the religious life, he has become internationally known and active as a member of commissions and councils, and as writer, teacher, and lecturer. Among his works is The Gospel Path: Religious Life.

"Je suis français et ne suis pas canadien." He said this to me with a certain energy and with a vague gesture, which I took to mean that almost everyone thought him to be Canadian and he feels "très fier" of being French. "Les îles Saint-Pierre et Miquelon furent le premier territoire français libéré par Charles de Gaulle." That explained everything.

Jean-Marie Roger Tillard is another theologian whom I had admired from afar, supposing him inaccessible, and later on I met him frequently, at first with surprise, then with friendship, and always on the run. Canada is far away, but he is often elsewhere, giving courses and conferences. For several years he has regularly visited Spain. After three successive meetings, our conversation took shape.

Tall, strong, dark-skinned (perhaps from having been born on those French islands off Newfoundland, where almost all the natives are fisher-

181

men), he is friendly, open, lively and critical, as fond of joking in friendly conversation as he is serious in his work. "I agree to do only one written work a year." One thus understands better the quality of his writing. And he's the same way in talking. You ask him about any religious matter and you hear theological rigor joined with human sensitivity.

Between a Closed Mind and Abdication

Are we living through a crisis of faith?

No doubt of it. Christians are more and more giving the impression of walking in the dark, in view of the advances, positive and irreversible, of the conquests of the human sciences, which are forcing them to reinterpret in a rather radical way some of their most traditional ideas. Even the biblical texts are being interpreted along a new line, which is disconcerting to unprepared believers. Psychology modifies certain judgments that for a long time have been tied to the notion of guilt, sin, conscience, responsibility and, consequently, salvation. The endless discussions about secularization have bit by bit undermined, even in Christian minds, the ancient idea of religion, and, given its involvement with the latter, the very notion of prayer and of recourse to the omnipotence of God in the most ordinary situations of life.

It is much to be feared that the churches—at all levels—will not know how to face the challenge of the human sciences. The churches would then fall into one of these attitudes, one being as serious as the other for the future of the faith: (1) the pure and simple repetition of the past, with no attempt to listen to the human sciences or the discoveries of contemporary exegesis, which would be a closing of the mind and an opening of the way to two great temptations: fundamentalism and isolationism; (2) a pure and simple acceptance of the conclusions of the human sciences without critical judgment, accepting ingenuously the extraction of the most central points of the content of faith. It would be abdication, based on an unwillingness to reread the gospel today to draw from it the essentials. These two attitudes are taking shape in some places, and they carry with them an influence on the quality of the Christian commitment in the very heart of the world.

Evangelical Experience in Human Tasks

What are the urgent tasks facing that crisis?

One of the most urgent tasks of the church in this respect is to devote itself to a new reading of the gospel in the light of what we now know about humanity. It is impossible for the church to refuse to accept the questions raised by the sciences and the consciousness that people are going to have from now on about themselves and their destiny. The church has to discover what faith in Jesus Christ can represent for twentieth-century people, sure of themselves and their possibilities, confident of their techniques and convinced that science has not yet disclosed to them all that it can teach them. For this work theologians aren't the only competent ones: the whole people of God has to take an active part.

But, however important this effort is, it's not enough. We have rediscovered the privileged role of action and of practice. It's not enough to proclaim a collection of truths, however beautiful they are and however harmonious they are with the mentality of the people of today. It's also needed, required above all, to live these truths and, in a certain way, to create them by way of life itself. The churches must be able to proclaim not only what they believe but, first of all, what they live. *Confessed* faith must be the translation and the expression of *lived* faith. Evangelical experience thus occupies the first place. A word can't be made *credible* unless it is translating an *experience*. And in today's world, this experience can't remain limited to the single perspective of the search for eternal life, as if Christians were men and women who travel to a world apart, just parallel to the real world in which we find ourselves and which we all try to build. Faith takes root in a life in common and in a communion of destiny with the whole of humankind. It's this world, the ordinary world, that we must lead to its true end. Since human tasks represent what we would call the material of the kingdom, these are the tasks that first of all become the terrain of this lived faith I've been talking about. It's a matter of living those tasks and those human values, referring them to Jesus Christ and to his lordship over the world.

Nevertheless, faith knows well that God's plan for the world, though it goes across human projects, making them his material in a way, is not limited simply to those projects. The kingdom of God is not only the end of those projects. The world desired by the God of Jesus Christ is not located "over there," at the end of the exertions and the efforts of people, believing or unbelieving. The resurrection of Jesus shows that God wants to lead this world from here to a completion that has as its point of departure the power of his own divine love. God has intervened freely in history. That's why the design of the world and its implementation remain constantly open to a criticism that, while emphasizing its positive value, also shows its limits. Human efforts for a better world are already the announcement and the promise of the kingdom of God, and for that very reason Christians also take part in that task, seeing in it a translation of their own life of faith. But God's design is not limited to those efforts; they cannot be absolutized: they are waiting for a completion. Humankind's plans will not be fully completed except in the communion of life with God, of which the resurrection of Christ is the prophetic sign. Living faith for Christians has to proclaim, in its commitment, this certainty.

What specific necessities must we cover with greater urgency?

Among the most urgent necessities, I see one above all: that there be Christians who live profoundly the evangelical demands, in an open and joyous way, signaling the goals at the same time that they penetrate fully into human tasks. God's people must make it clear, with their own way of living, that the great affirmations of the gospel about the priority and the transcendence of God and the involvement in human plans to build the world, far from being contradictory, call out to each other. It seems to me that in this, certain kinds of lives, such as the life of secular institutions and that of the communities of religious life, have a privileged role to play—with the proviso, of course, that those Christian groups be able to renew themselves profoundly.

One of the Gravest Crises in Their History

You say that the communities of religious life must "be able to renew themselves profoundly." In that connection, in your writing you show yourself to be an "optimist." The way you talk about the subject of the theology of religious life reveals a "theological optimism." But if we are speaking sociologically, let's speak realistically: tell me if you see the organization and the lives of religious in crisis.

You're suspicious of my "theological optimism." But to understand my position clearly, you must keep in mind that I am always talking about the *plan* of religious life. The *plan* traces an ideal, a goal that you try to reach even when you know that the ideal will never be fully realized. Idealism? No. People, in their great efforts, carry out a noble work only when a goal shines before them, a goal that is greater than they but one that, at the same time, stimulates them, propels them. If that ideal is reduced to the simple dimension of "the possible," strictly reduced to a "half-way" vision, then it's like going around in circles to drop into a trivial, unrelieved mediocrity. To seek what is beyond the possible is to create spirit, excellence. The more fully I get into the history of the religious life, the better I understand how this religious *plan* has always exceeded the possibilities of the majority of those who were seeking the Lord with generosity and love in that kind of life. And that even in the most difficult moments. Our ancestors were not spiritual "Tarzans." They were "poor" people, eager to overcome their weaknesses, knowing that they were often conquered by their weaknesses. From that came their compassion.

We must admit, nevertheless, that in our time the "religious life," viewed globally, is going through one of the gravest crises in its history. In every way—with the possible exception of some very rare privileged enclaves—religious congregations are showing a decrease in their membership and an increase in the number of defections and internal divisions. But, above all, an erosion in the very sense of their own existence. They end by wondering if their "profession" is a valid response to that call that sleeps in every person and in every Christian. Moreover, it frequently happens that the generous efforts of the most spirited, trying to adapt themselves, to open new ways, are meeting with failure. This gives rise to a crisis of hope. Now, as the psychologist Viktor Frankl has shown in his many books, if the tension of hope is relaxed, life itself is imperiled. I would add, especially the Christian life and, *a fortiori*, the religious life. The Christian is sustained, maintained, by hope. And our communities are suffering a crisis of hope.

Swimming Upstream in the Midst of Change

Which do you consider the most serious causes of the present crisis in the religious life?

Turning to the French nuns, I have tried to discern the main causes of this crisis. They are numerous. I'll give you only a few. In the first place is the crisis of the whole church, of all the Christian communities, Protestant, Anglican, Catholic. This doesn't seem to be understood by certain spirits who judge the "religious" crisis in a shortsighted way. The crisis that is being felt in the communities is the expression—at times exacerbated—of the crisis that is being felt at all levels of the people of God. There is a crisis of the clergy, a crisis of the laity, a pastoral crisis, a matrimonial crisis. As the religious life is at the heart of the church, it's natural for the crisis to show itself there with greater intensity. Let's add that the crisis of the church is very closely tied to a crisis of humanity. A new kind of person is in gestation: a people confident of their own responsibility, secularized, who seek the full development of their freedom and autonomy. The progress of technology and science offers them the means to cure by themselves many ills without having to appeal, as in other times, to the churches. The churches are trying, with many difficulties, to make contact with this new humanity that caught them unawares, perhaps because they were too self-confident. And the religious communities—guided by an apostolic ideal—are experiencing at their corresponding level this search, so filled with consequences, and so frequently doomed to failure. This is heightened if we bear in mind that the crisis of the churches frequently places a ban on essential points of faith. The "suspect" sciences raise for Christians clear but difficult questions. The answers that have frequently been given to these questions have been too superficial to be acceptable. Now, as soon as one begins to touch on certain aspects that are at the very heart of the gospel—and I'm not talking of secondary matters that have been given exaggerated importance in the past—one attacks the very core around which the religious plan is formed. Why tamper with life for the sake of the gospel if the gospel message "isn't as clear as had been believed?"

But the crisis also has other causes, some of which depend on the face given in the past to religious life, which has remained with it and become stereotyped. I'm going to point out some of those causes. First, a certain way of looking at the world, of fleeing from it as if it were only evil and the inevitable source of corruption. How to reconcile this attitude with the discovery of the real place of the world in God's design? In addition, communities have frequently been established with an excessively "spiritualized" vision of humankind. They have insisted only on the spirit, the soul, forgetting that the body also belonged to the profundity of the person and that the grandeur of the person and of personal life were equally dependent on the body. That's the cause of the current upsets and the inevitable uneasiness in an epoch that is rehabilitating the place of the body. Certain religions have the impression that their "religious spirituality" is swimming upstream . . . .

Let us also notice—although this isn't equally valid for all institutes—a certain style of authority and a way of conceiving life in common in a very detailed and minute dependency that prevent the fulfilling of certain personal values, and that have been in force until now. All contemporary education and the deepest aspirations of current society now go in the opposite direction. A certain theology of obedience that confuses obedience with a numbing of personal responsibility has shown in some communities features that run the risk of becoming stereotyped in the eyes of our contemporaries: the features of a person in whom we do not recognize the new humanity that is being born before our eyes. And younger religious are noting with great grief this disparity.

Moreover, most of the communities that have been started in recent centuries have been concentrated in "institutions" (schools, hospitals, etc.). The social situation and service to people demanded this at an earlier time. What to do now? On the one hand, the decrease in membership makes it necessary, if one is to maintain those projects, either to exhaust the religious with inhuman hours of work or to seek patrons (which runs the risk of putting the communities on the side of the powerful). On the other hand, society as a whole is becoming more and more aware of these areas. A century ago, in order to go to help the Africans in social work it was almost necessary to become a member of a missionary community. Not today.

These causes, which I'm sketching for you without much detail, must be placed against the background of what is really a serious cause of concern: the way of serving humanity that Christians will follow from now on. *Christian* commitment is seen more and more on the "sociopolitical" level (in the broadest sense of the word). In the light of this vision—extremely demanding—*religious* commitment seems, in the eyes of many, to be too "abstract" and seems to place too many barriers in the way of a real involvement in the questions that the world is pondering today. How then are we to understand—in a theology of "advice" as opposed to one of "precepts"—that the religious vocation is a vocation to the "perfection" of evangelical life, or is there a charism of the "most perfect" peculiar to religious?

Does the crisis affect men and women religious equally? Which are more disposed to renewal?

We must admit that the feminine communities have embarked upon renewal with great fervor. Their generosity and their sense of obedience to the directives of the church have had a chance to show themselves. It's nevertheless true that in a number of feminine institutes the need for renewal was more urgent than in the great number of male institutions. An overaccented eagerness for thoroughness, an exaggerated clinging to details, a fear of risk, submission to rules often made by men not conversant with feminine ways had obscured at times what was essential. And male religious had "mitigated" the law for themselves. Besides, masculine clerical communities are faced with other problems: the crisis in the priestly ministry. For the nuns the situation was simpler. Whereas many men became religious in order to become priests, for nuns the basic option had always been unidimensional. I add that "virginity," attentiveness to God, the innate necessity of disinterested surrender seem more in keeping with the feminine temperament. This alleviates, for women religious, part of the current crisis. Nevertheless—and without wishing to play the part of a prophet of doom—it seems to me that the current evolution of "women's liberation" is going to pose in feminine communities new problems, which will demand rather radical answers that will call into question many current practices that are quite traditional. The evolution of feminine communities will have to be in unison with the evolution of the overall situation of women. Will all the communities be ready?

Fear of Risk May Kill Us

Frankly, what real possibilities of renewal and survival do you see in the current institutes and congregations of religious life? What is the cost of authentic renewal?

First of all, I want to repeat to you my sincere conviction: religious life, contemplated in its *plan*, is closely allied with the vitality of the church and cannot disappear. I speak not of its forms, which are relative, but of the profound intuition at its core. Evangelical radicalism always tries to penetrate into the life of the people of God.

The reappearance of fervent religious communities in Protestant churches is a sign of it. And I'm not thinking simply of Taizé. I'm thinking especially of the Anglican and Lutheran communities, less well known but equally significant. Moreover, the great shocks in religious life have usually come with the renewals, experiencing crises that in many ways seem like the current ones. The contemporary communitarian movement, though at first sight seeming to go against the religious life, is in its way a search and a true renewal of certain fundamental values of religious life. But certainly the survival of groups that embody the religious *plan* cannot occur without a profound change of current forms. Moreover, change in the world is today too great for us to be content with regilding the old. (This holds for religious life and for other levels of church life.) This is a question of life or death.

You ask me if I see real possibilities in the present situation; that is, if I see roots that can support this change. I say yes. But on condition that there be no fear of clarity, a clarity that has two special points. In the first place, it is clear that in the future the members of religious congregations will be fewer in number. There's no reason to be surprised or saddened. We perhaps suffer at present from an "inflation" in the number of religious professions in comparison with true vocations: the consequence of a situation in the church that is soon to disappear. Second, it's clear that only ardent believers, with a strong Christian personality, really impelled by the gospel, will think of this kind of life.

Well, now these two facts—a reduced number, but strong Christian personalities—imply a kind of progressive metamorphosis in the lifestyle of our communities. And this cannot occur without suffering. If we try not to discourage the vital forces that come (rare but strong personalities), we'll have to leave to them all the room for creativity that they need. Without this, we either stymie them (what a waste!) or we disillusion them and they finally go away. Nevertheless, we have no right to abandon older men or women who, to keep their faith, still feel the need of older forms, more adapted to their experience, to their mentalities, to the environment in which they made their commitment. That's why there's a need for a certain pluralism. We might think of some groupings between congregations (we would have to make their standing precise) in order to permit, in a viable form, the creation of serious cells for search. In the period of rapid transition in which we find ourselves, I believe that will be necessary. And we must agree to it. In many institutes there are spirited members, really evangelical, anxious to commit themselves fully to the religious plan for the church of today. They are in tune with our time. But they are not the majority (and this is normal); other people, also committed, but shaped in a different mentality, form the main body. "We extinguish the Spirit" if we don't allow the small minority to carry out their religious *plan* as a function of the Christian perceptions of today. By killing the life that is growing, we would kill what we believe must be maintained at any cost; we would condemn it to be merely a witness to something else. The fear of risk would kill us.

What specific signs of hope do you see?

I see some, still very shaky, but capable of making the religious life endure if it doesn't smother them: a new style of authority and of fraternal relations (not to be confused with the laxity of a structureless existence), an effort toward the conciliation of communitarian demands and personal aspirations, the distinction between "community of life" and "work team," the appearance of small groups in which the members of different congregations are united for a common mission or a common "spirituality," and above all, the need for *true* prayer and *true* discovery of Christ, beyond all the commitments.

Neither Stagnation nor Rupture: Creative Evolution

Would it be better to work on the structural renewal of the present institutes and congregations or to work on the search for new forms of religious life? Or will both be necessary?

To see mutually exclusive alternatives here is wrong. If new forms of religious life are to come, they should be born with the spontaneity proper to works of the Spirit. Perhaps we could steer in their direction—if there were more flexibility than current legislation allows—certain religious who are uncomfortable in the institutions to which they belong. But it's equally essential for present congregations to incorporate little by little a new dimension. One of the principal functions of today's major superiors in those institutions seems to me that of having a gentle, intelligent outlook that will allow real *evolution*. The word "evolution" says much more than the word "adaptation," which I have never liked. Evolution demands that we follow the same vein—in dealing with charisms and their link with the gospel— and that we accept the appearance of new forms, necessarily different from the primitive forms, although derived from them. Our communities must *evolve*, that is, reject two easy solutions: shortsighted clinging to past forms, which would transform them into "vestiges" of a bygone period, and a pure and simple break with the past, which would carry them blindly toward something that would be religious only in name. Neither stagnation nor rupture, but a bold forward march. But it's clear that evolution moves along pathways where much is unknown. We must let life, daily experience, become the chief guide, together with the Spirit of God. It's therefore impossible to trace beforehand all-inclusive plans, or decide what must be definitive. "Poverty of spirit" today takes on, for the whole community, this kind of insecurity. And we must accept it serenely.

In the Midst of the Human Community

Up to now religious life has been organized, in general, within its own forms and far from the real world of people, even apart from the Christian community. The life of each religious community, its prayer, its sacramental life, everything functioned in places proper to each institution, province, and local house, in very special places, closed off and separated from those of the Christian community. Don't you think that every authentic community of religious life must insist, as an essential dimension of its existence and its ecclesial mission, that it be integrated into the Christian community, preserving of course its identity and its own inner life, but also entering into real and historical communion with everyone and being a ferment in the local Christian community and therefore in the human community? And doesn't this require "relocating" all the elements of the life of each religious community?

I agree. Religious life will have to be embodied in the new forms of human existence: that's one of the principal laws of its evolution. Among the causes of the present crisis I have stressed the appearance of a new type of person and the disparity that it provokes. We must add that religious life has often isolated itself voluntarily from the Christian community, even from the church community, through its way of life: religious have wanted to be "separate," even though they have always worked in the service of human society (schools, hospitals, scientific research). The evolution that I was talking about has application here. Of course, we mustn't be naive. To be able to have its own quality, the religious community has to give itself its own form and it has to find itself as a community. It must really experience, within itself, the *cor unum et anima una*, embodied in a kind of existence of its own, which requires a certain margin of intimacy. Otherwise, we are talking nonsense. But this "community" must likewise, in a concrete and real way, maintain "communion" with the whole Christian community. In other words, it must not agree to be converted into an "enclave." Neither above the Christian community, nor on its periphery, nor like a foreign body, but in the very heart of the evangelical *koinonia:* that is its place.

This demands, especially today, specific attitudes. I'm going to give some examples. Why not, especially on Sundays and feast days, participate in the parish Eucharist, instead of having a mass "for themselves"? Why not (even for nuns) be part of the study groups that are being created almost everywhere? Why not take part in certain important happenings in civic life? More radically: why don't religious, men and women, commit themselves to really civil institutions like other

Christian citizens? Belonging to a religious community is no reason for cutting the ties that bind the religious to the problems and concerns of their human community. On the contrary, they, who by profession are community "specialists," ought to have as an ideal to bring to others the experience that is at the center of their life.

There's a lot of talk about the "prophetic function" of religious life. It seems to me that it's in this field of the human "community" that the "prophesying" has to be done today. In fact, everywhere we hear the call to the experience of "brotherhood." And that call is made not only to the churches but to broad sectors of society. Religious should know intuitively that it is a sign from the Lord. Not that they should try to use that movement for their own advantage (which would be odious) but, on the contrary, to try to encourage it and serve it. But—and I return to my starting point—this requires that in the community itself there be an effort to experience, in an authentic way, evangelical brotherhood, infusing it with that restlessness of the human community and of "co-participation" that I spoke of before. And that can't happen without a calm examination of many of our ways of behaving. I want especially to insist on the need of a true pluralism that accepts, within an authentic "communion" of charity, different points of view about human problems and, at times, different commitments. "Communion" isn't to be confused with uniformity or with the fact of everyone thinking alike. Personal freedom has to be respected. How could strong personalities consent not to be themselves? To be able to spread its influence, the religious "community" has to learn to embody in its daily life a "reconciliation" that is not to be confused with a denial of fundamental human freedoms.

The Vow of Poverty Demands Adherence to the Cause of the Poor

We would have to study calmly, with evangelical authenticity and human realism, what part religious life should play in the social, political, and revolutionary commitment. Since this commitment is an essential dimension of Christian faith, devoting oneself to living the faith in a "religious life" within our human world must have something to do with it. What do you think?

That's a very delicate question. And at a moment when this problem is so much discussed in the church, it would be rash to try to draw immediate conclusions for the religious life. In more than one meeting where these questions have been discussed under all aspects, we have ended by making clear that we would have to begin by first coming to an agreement on the very notions of "revolution" and "political commitment." Because everyone understands these terms their own way. Nonetheless, there is one thing that seems to me certain and clear and that I discussed in an article on religious poverty published in the

Nouvelle Revue Théologique (Louvain). The vow of religious poverty, understood in all its evangelical dimension and in the perspective of the announcement of the kingdom, obliges religious to adopt as their own the cause of the poor, the weak, the oppressed. The signs of the coming of the kingdom are, for the Gospels and the Acts of the Apostles, that Jesus feeds the hungry, cures the sick, drives out misery. Moreover, many communities have been established for *free* service to the poor. But what is happening today? Alas, at the present time, at least in most western countries, alms, aid for the poor, has to take other directions. It's not a matter of distributing surplus goods. Nor can we be content with caring for and curing the wounds inflicted on humankind by society or the maldistribution of wealth. We have to go to the very root of those evils. Here is the place for social and political commitment (in the sense that theology gives this term today). As for the participation of religious in this commitment, at least one thing seems sure to me: religious must avoid becoming accomplices in anything that is opposing efforts to uproot social ills. They must, on the other hand, undertake vigorously everything that seems to them to be required by justice and love. How is it possible for them, who have freely embraced poverty, not to feel impelled to become advocates and champions of the *real* poor? And here we have to take the word "poverty" in all its amplitude. When they have to work beside the "powerful," the "rich," they would have to work at awakening in them their serious responsibilities for justice and the sense of a *realistic* love for their fellow human beings. That is a very good way to concretize evangelical charity for them. In addition, it seems to me that communities ought to think about dedicating, in a serious and total way, some of their members to disinterested service to the very poor, to works of social development in the name of the gospel.

It's obvious that it's not a question of urging religious to wave all the red banners or to support indiscriminately all criticism and all claims, and still less to become propagandists for all calumnies and unfounded opinions. Their opinions should be sound. But where injustice is clear, where the poor are oppressed, or where other people stand up to defend human rights, religious would betray their vocation if they crossed their arms and were silent. They would no longer be "prophetic signs" of the gospel of the kingdom.

The Crisis of Faith: A Tragedy for Religious

But fidelity to the obligation to social and political commitment is based on faith. Faith is the root and the center. And it's precisely that center and that root that is today in crisis throughout the church. Can it also be that in religious the crisis of their faith is the deepest and gravest cause of the crisis of religious life?

In a way I have already answered that question. But it's worthwhile to go deeper into it. I believe so, that the crisis of faith explains in very many cases the deepest and gravest part of the current crisis in religious life. If this had no other basis than celibacy or the community or service to humankind—as some think—as a last resort we could think that even with "some" faith we might still find meaning and means to keep going. You don't necesarily have to be a disciple of Christ to seek community, to want to serve people and, because of this, to consent to celibacy. But the basis of the religious life is the will to "follow Christ" in a radical, zealous way, which necessarily implies faith, and a total faith.

I'm going to explain this "radicalism" and for that I'm going to use the brilliant distinction that Max Weber makes between what he calls the "ethics of conviction" and the "ethics of responsibility." An example will make it clear. You cannot help admiring and praising the Christian who (like Father Maximilian Kolbe) freely offers his life to save another life or the one who, taking literally the Sermon on the Mount, offers a thousand pesetas to the one who demands only, and unjustly, a hundred, or the Christian who offers no resistance to false accusations. These are evangelical deeds. They obey the call of the absolute that is found in the heart of Christian life. But what happens if that man is the father of a family and if those deeds are hurting the security, the honor, the welfare of his family? In this case, doesn't faithfulness to the gospel insist, on the contrary, that it be applied first of all to the duty to one's family? So we see that the gospel opens into two complementary roads of faithfulness, of *sanctity*, of which one is not necessarily closer than the other to perfection. Because can we say that to give all your possessions for a good cause, and by so doing to ruin your family, is an act of perfection? So there exists the way of "conviction": that is, the one that puts Christians in a situation in which they can experience, with strength and "conviction," the dimension of the absolute, of the radicalism that is present in every Christian life, but can't always be carried out fully because of other demands of the kingdom.

There also exists the road of "responsibility," that is, the one that puts the Christian face to face with those other demands imposed by the specific situation of the world. Among those demands that require "responsibility" and the dimension of radicalness, some compromises must be made. Neither of those roads is *a priori* more perfect, more challenging. The church is held in a kind of tension between those two vocations: one that stresses (like a "prophetic sign") the deep stratum of the evangelical calling; the other that stresses the need of a specific and realistic bridge between that calling and the human terrain. And we have to admit that the incarnation of the kingdom demands the second vocation as much as (and even more than) the first. Nevertheless, the first is rooted more unilaterally in the deepest essence of the faith. For even if we suppress faith it's possible to find meaning in a life centered on "responsibility" (in Max Weber's sense): you can devote yourself body and soul to the good of humanity, to the service of the earthly city, to the joy of a home. But if, on the contrary, faith is removed from the first vocation, this vocation of "conviction" becomes absurd and loses all meaning (unless we accept the canonization of schizophrenia). Indeed, how can one continue to center one's whole life on stressing values whose truth one no longer accepts?

Forgive me the hastiness with which I have expressed all this, but I think it's enough to understand why the present crisis of faith is becoming a tragedy for religious. It calls into question their loyalty to what they have chosen as the very basis of their existence.

Faith without Critical Clarity Is Absurd

Logically, then, to renew religious life we would have to consider that what is most urgent and decisive is the renewal of the faith of religious men and women. But it is equivocal and dangerous to say that "what is most important is the conversion of people and their life in the faith," because this is "used" at times by superiors and "spiritualists" to leave structures the way they are, in order not to approach radically the problem of the reform of the structures. And true conversion to faith is at the same time personal and structural. If it's not understood that way, if it's not carried out that way, it's illusory, it's deceptive. Am I mistaken?

No. It seems to me clear that attention to the faith has to occupy the first place in the renewal of religious life. But the danger that you speak of is real and very grave. One thinks that personal conversion, fervor, renewed generosity are enough. And one forgets the great questions raised by the structures, collective behavior patterns, the excessively narrow ways of viewing the communitarian apostolate. When I speak of "reconversion to faith and its dynamism," I do not speak of a kind of leap into a vacuum, into the absurd. I speak, on the contrary, of a lucid adherence to the gospel and to Jesus Christ. This adherence, far from leading to the unconditional acceptance of anything, demands instead a critical judgment on what is placed at the service of faith.

This lack of critical examination in the past was precisely one of the great tragedies in religious communities—especially the feminine ones. There was a tendency to put everything on the same plane of equality, the essential as well as the secondary, faith and devotion, the authentic and the doubtful. Nothing is more interesting in this regard than having a look at community libraries: they are filled with the worst books of piety and pseudo-theological treatises. With such doctrinal nourishment, how can one judge structures and methods critically? And how can one accept calmly the discoveries of exegesis and theology? One ends by being the reed that bows before all the winds, going from one extreme to another, without knowing why.

The renewal of faith, which is radically needed today in religious, implies a training for clarity of faith and discernment. Only at this price can one acquire the serenity that will allow one to advance along the path of progress without thereby giving up what is essential. Otherwise the "evangelical radicalism" that I speak of would run a great risk of being confused with that ecclesiastical calamity that is integralism. It would be very serious—and it would be their death warrant—for religious communities to change today into forces in opposition to the efforts of the people of God to make the gospel readable and viable in the world that is under construction. They would become museum parchments and would no longer be visible signs of the good news.

Neither a Funeral Community nor a Playboy Community

Finally, let's talk about what the religious life can contribute to contemporary endeavors to renew the faith, since this is an urgent necessity for the whole church.

This is a matter that has concerned me a good deal and I have already written several articles on it. I'll say briefly that I believe that religious—who will be more and more involved with other people in their daily work and the concerns of the Christian community—must appear above all as the *existential* signs of the relation of faith with humankind's achievement. They will have to show that the rooting of life in evangelical radicalism, far from overclouding human joy and plenitude, is in harmony with them. In the current situation of the church this seems to me very important: a life that tries to place itself in the heart of faith has to reveal how faith "carries out" humanity's deep desire by orienting people at the same time toward God and toward the service of humanity, heaping upon them the full measure of happiness that this life can confer—but a realistic happiness, marked, like all true human happiness, with the scars of suffering and struggle. It's not the pink, childish dream of an operetta happiness, an adult happiness, of man or woman, that will not be shipwrecked in the naive search for an existence without upsets, deceptions, or tears. Only a happiness of this kind makes sense. Only that happiness can proclaim the lordship of Christ and its impact on humankind. It is the need of God, of which Father Régamey has written very well.

Do we have to add that this will demand that our religious communities offer their members what they need in their life to allow them really to find that quality of happiness? We should observe here that we must avoid two kinds of caricatures. On the one hand, the caricature of the funeral community that still exists; everything in it is somber, sad, as if it had come from a world apart and it looks like an anteroom of purgatory. Just entering it puts an end to smiles and joy. On the other hand, there is the caricature of the playboy community, which is appearing here and there. A community of easy living, of "beggars for the kingdom" who have everything they want (!), of men or women with no worries, who forget that they have *freely* chosen to "follow Christ" on an arduous path. In a word, a "lying" community where impulse and generosity are lacking and out of which only a contemptible kind of person can come, those who shirk the greatest of all responsibilities, that of being sincere with themselves. God's absolute, the "only thing necessary," the awe of his love, have to appear as the very home of the religious life. Above all else, service to God.

I see another level of influence by religious in the faith of the people of God. This lends much importance, especially in the last ten years, to the place of the church in the world and its role in the service of people. We must rejoice in this. The people of God are rediscovering how they have to walk with all people in a common effort for progress, justice, freedom. But the danger is in forgetting or ignoring the relationship to God, which is what gives meaning to this commitment. If religious are in full communion with their fellow Christians—committed also to certain humanitarian tasks—then they recall to these Christians that reference to God, thus pointing out to them the meaning of their efforts.

Our conversation has wandered along the roads of the religious life and its current problems in relation to faith. Tillard is a leading figure among the theologians of the religious life and its renewal. But I notice that he's not like the specialists who can move only in their own field. Tillard is basically a good theologian. Talking with him, one soon gets the same impression as when reading his books: that he is a man of mental rigor, of great theological power, and of enormous human sensitivity.

Bibliography

Principal Works Available in English Translation

Ladislaus Boros

Angels and Men. New York: Seabury Press, 1976.
Being a Christian Today. New York: Seabury Press, 1979.
The Book of Jesus. Cleveland: Collins-World, 1977.
Christian Prayer. New York: Seabury Press, 1976.
The Closeness of God. New York: Seabury Press, 1978.
The Hidden God. New York: Seabury Press, 1973.
Living in Hope. Garden City, N.Y.: Doubleday, 1973.
Meeting God in Man. Garden City, N.Y.: Doubleday, 1971.
The Mystery of Death. New York: Seabury Press, 1973.
Open Spirit. New York: Paulist Press, 1975.
Pain and Providence. New York: Seabury Press, 1975.
You Can Always Begin Again. New York: Paulist Press, 1977.
We Are Future. Garden City, N.Y.: Doubleday, 1973.

Georges Casalis

Correct Ideas Don't Fall from the Skies. Maryknoll, N.Y.: Orbis Books, forthcoming.

Joseph (José) Comblin

Jesus of Nazareth: Meditations on His Humanity. Maryknoll, N.Y.: Orbis Books, 1976.
The Meaning of Mission. Maryknoll, N.Y.: Orbis Books, 1977.
Sent from the Father: Meditations on the Fourth Gospel. Maryknoll, N.Y.: Orbis Books, 1979.
"What Sort of Service Might Theology Render?" In Rosino Gibellini, ed. *Frontiers of Theology in Latin America*. Maryknoll, N.Y.: Orbis Books, 1979, pp. 58–78.

Enrique D. Dussel

Ethics and the Theology of Liberation. Maryknoll, N.Y.: Orbis Books, 1978.
"Historical and Philosophical Presuppositions for Latin American Theology." In Rosino Gibellini, ed. *Frontiers of Theology in Latin America*. Maryknoll, N.Y.: Orbis Books, 1979, pp. 184–212.
History and the Theology of Liberation. Maryknoll, N.Y.: Orbis Books, 1976.

Segundo Galilea

Following Christ. Maryknoll, N.Y.: Orbis Books, forthcoming.
"Liberation Theology and New Tasks Facing Christians." In Rosino Gibellini,
    ed. *Frontiers of Theology in Latin America.* Maryknoll, N.Y.: Orbis Books,
    1979, pp. 163–183.

Giulio Girardi

Marxism and Christianity. New York: Macmillan, 1968.

José María González Ruiz

Atheistic Humanism and the Biblical God. Encino, Calif.: Glencoe Publishing
    Co., 1969.
The New Creation: Marxist and Christian? Maryknoll, N.Y.: Orbis Books, 1976.

Gustavo Gutiérrez

Liberation and Change (with Richard Shaull). Atlanta: John Knox Press, 1977.
"Liberation Praxis and Christian Faith." In Rosino Gibellini, ed. *Frontiers of
    Theology in Latin America.* Maryknoll, N.Y.: Orbis Books, 1979, pp. 1–33.
A Theology of Liberation. Maryknoll, N.Y.: Orbis Books, 1973.

Hans Küng

The Christian Challenge. Garden City, N.Y.: Doubleday, 1979.
The Church. Garden City, N.Y.: Doubleday, 1976.
The Church Maintained in Truth. New York: Seabury Press, 1980.
Infallible? An Inquiry. Garden City, N.Y.: Doubleday, 1972.
On Being a Christian. Garden City, N.Y.: Doubleday, 1976.
Signposts for the Future. Garden City, N.Y.: Doubleday, 1978.

Jürgen Moltmann

The Church in the Power of the Spirit. New York: Harper & Row, 1977.
The Crucified God. New York: Harper & Row, 1974.
The Experiment Hope. Philadelphia: Fortress Press, 1975.
The Future of Creation: Collected Essays. Philadelphia: Fortress Press, 1979.
Gospel of Liberation. Waco, Tex.: Word, Inc., 1973.
Man: Christian Anthropology in the Conflicts of the Present. Philadelphia: For-
    tress Press, 1974.
The Passion of Life: A Messianic Lifestyle. Philadelphia: Fortress Press, 1977.
Theology of Hope. New York: Harper & Row, 1967.

Karl Rahner

Christian at the Crossroads. New York: Seabury Press, 1976.
Do You Believe in God? New York: Paulist Press, 1971.
Encounters with Silence. New York: Paulist Press, 1960.
Foundations of Christian Faith. New York: Seabury Press, 1978.
Grace in Freedom. New York: Seabury Press, 1969.
Happiness Through Prayer. New York: Seabury Press, 1978.
Hearers of the Word. New York: Seabury Press, 1969.
Meditations on Freedom and the Spirit. New York: Seabury Press, 1978.

Meditations on Hope and Love. New York: Seabury Press, 1977.
Meditations on the Sacraments. New York: Seabury Press, 1977.
On Prayer. New York: Paulist Press, 1968.
On the Theology of Death. New York: Seabury Press, n.d.
Opportunities for Faith. New York: Seabury Press, 1975.
The Priesthood. New York: Seabury Press, 1970.
The Religious Life Today. New York: Seabury Press, 1976.
The Shape of the Church to Come. New York: Seabury Press, 1974.
The Spirit in the Church. New York: Seabury Press, 1979.
The Spirit in the World. New York: Seabury Press, 1968.
Theological Investigations (14 vols.). New York: Seabury Press, n.d.
Trinity. New York: Seabury Press, 1970.
Watch and Pray with Me: The Seven Last Words. New York: Seabury Press, 1977.

Joseph Ratzinger

Faith and the Future. Chicago: Franciscan Herald Press, 1971.
The God of Jesus Christ. Chicago: Franciscan Herald Press, 1978.
Introduction to Christianity. New York: Seabury Press, 1970.
The Open Circle. Westminster, Md.: Christian Classics, 1966.
Theology of History according to St. Bonaventure. Chicago: Franciscan Herald Press, n.d.

Edward Schillebeeckx

Christ: The Christian Experience and the Modern World. New York: Seabury Press, 1980.
Christ: The Sacrament of the Encounter with God. Mission, Kan.: Sheed Andrews & McMeel, 1963.
Definition of the Christian Layman. Chicago: Franciscan Herald Press, 1970.
The Eucharist. Mission, Kan.: Sheed Andrews & McMeel, 1968.
God, the Future of Man. Westminster, Md.: Christian Classics, 1977.
Jesus: An Experiment in Christology. New York: Seabury Press, 1977.
Layman in the Church. Staten Island, N.Y.: Alba House, 1963.
Marriage. Westminster, Md.: Christian Classics, 1976.
The Mission of the Church. New York: Seabury Press, 1973.
The Understanding of Faith. New York: Seabury Press, 1974.
Unifying Role of the Bishop. New York: Seabury Press, 1972.

Juan Luis Segundo

The Hidden Motives of Pastoral Action. Maryknoll, N.Y.: Orbis Books, 1978.
The Liberation of Theology. Maryknoll, N.Y.: Orbis Books, 1976.
A Theology for Artisans of a New Humanity (5 vols.). Maryknoll, N.Y.: Orbis Books, 1973–74 (1. *The Community Called Church*; 2. *Grace and the Human Condition*; 3. *Our Idea of God*; 4. *The Sacraments Today*; 5. *Evolution and Guilt*).

Jean-Marie Tillard

The Gospel Path: Religious Life. Westminster, Md.: Christian Classics, n.d.
There Are Charisms and Charisms. Westminster, Md.: Christian Classics, 1977.

Index

Compiled by William E. Jerman, ASI